Women's Fiction

ALSO AVAILABLE FROM BLOOMSBURY

Ali Smith: Contemporary Critical Perspectives Edited by Monica Germana and Emily Horton

Sarah Waters: Contemporary Critical Perspectives Edited by Kaye Mitchell

Women's Fiction

From 1945 to Today

Deborah Philips

B L O O M S B U R Y
LONDON • NEW DELHI • NEW YORK • SYDNEY

Bloomsbury Academic
An imprint of Bloomsbury Publishing Plc

50 Bedford Square
London
WC1B 3DP
UK

1385 Broadway
New York
NY 10018
USA

www.bloomsbury.com

Bloomsbury is a registered trade mark of Bloomsbury Publishing Plc

First published 2006

British Library Cataloguing-in-Publication Data
A catalogue record for this book is available from the British Library.

ISBN: PB: 9781441104267
ePub: 9781441150226
ePDF: 9781441109040

Library of Congress Cataloging-in-Publication Data
A catalog record for this book is available from the Library of Congress

Typeset by Fakenham Prepress Solutions, Fakenham, Norfolk NR21 8NN
Printed and bound in India

For Claudia, who read many of these novels,
and for Ursula, who only read the good ones.

CONTENTS

ACKNOWLEDGEMENTS

Every book is the result of discussions, but because this is a book about what women read, it owes more than many to the sharing of titles and to talk about those titles. Thank you to everyone who talked to me about their reading and who provided copies and recommendations of novels, Claudia, Karen and Garry especially. Ian Haywood got me started on writing about post-war fiction. Nickianne Moody and Julia Hallam of the Association for Research in Popular Fictions gave me the first opportunity to air ideas at the Association's conferences. Jenny Hartley and Simon Edwards invited me to rethink the 1950s at a conference at Roehampton University. Helen Carr, Alison Mark and Barbara Rosenbaum of *Women: A Cultural Review* gave me the chance to first put some of these ideas into print, and all of them, with Alison Light and Judith Williamson, gave me a sense that this work mattered. Colleagues at Brunel University allowed me the time to write the book, and for that, thanks are owed to Stephen Benson, Maureen Moran and William Watkin. Ben Carrington gave me great gossip, Robert Gurney gave me the most terrible pun, and Pete Frame was the source of a stack of copies of *Mirabelle* comic and a fount of arcane knowledge of the 1950s and 1960s. Susan Goodman was adept at unearthing the details of obscure American novelists and helped me to track down novels in New York; Nigel and Lindsay gave me a lovely garden to read them in. The staff of the British Library were an invaluable and unfailingly polite resource, and the staff of the St Johns Hospice were extraordinary. Thanks are due to Anna Sandeman, Sophie Cox and Rebecca Simmonds for their calm efficiency and David Atival at Bloomsbury. Thanks too, to Kate Aughterson for taking me back to Susan Faludi, and to Barry King and John Benson for suggesting Lasch. And Garry Whannel was unstinting in copyediting and moral support, and in helping to trawl second-hand bookshops and charity shops; he knows how much this book owes to him.

Introduction

This is not a book which claims to cover the entire range of women's writing from the post-war period or to comprehensively chart the important women writers of the late twentieth century. Instead, it focuses on those texts which were read by large numbers of women, and is concerned to identify the emergent genre of women's fiction that marked each post-war decade. The novels discussed here were widely read by women readers; they were not all best-sellers (although many were), but they were all written by names which were and are now familiar to women readers, and commanded a loyal following. Many of these novels were to be reprinted over several decades, and many remain in print still. The majority of these texts can be defined as 'popular novels' which enjoyed a wide readership at the time. Although feminist theory and media and cultural studies have challenged literary theory to reassess women's writing and to take more serious account of popular culture, these are authors and texts which remain largely unacknowledged by mainstream literary criticism, and also by much feminist criticism.

The novels discussed here belong to genres of fiction that are rarely reviewed or cited in critical studies, and most are not considered as worthy of entry into the feminist canon. These are, however, the titles that women read in the late twentieth and early twenty-first centuries, as evidenced in their ubiquity in second-hand bookshops, charity shops and public library holdings. These are the novels and authors that are still to be found on the remaindered shelves, testimony to a onetime wide circulation and readership. Some of these texts have been recuperated into a feminist canon, but the majority have not; together they stand as a hidden history of women's reading.

The novels in this study can be classed as belonging to the category of the 'domestic romance', that is: their settings are contemporary rather than historical, they are largely written within a realist tradition, and their focus is on personal relationships. Within these limits, however, there are a great many divergent forms; the 'romance' genre is a complex category. Readers of romance are very sophisticated in their awareness of sub-genres and categories, but these are rarely acknowledged by critics. Literary and cultural theory has a tendency to discuss romance fiction as though it were a homogenous genre, whereas, as publishers, librarians and readers are very aware, it is a genre which breeds sub-genres. Even within the category of the formulaic romances published by Mills and Boon and Silhouette, there is a host of variants. There are fine distinctions to be made between contemporary 'romance' novels, which are of great importance to readers.

Variations of the 'romantic novel' include: medical, rural, tropical, erotic and workplace narratives. And that is not to include the historical saga, which itself has a range of variations. As the position of women has changed over the twentieth century, even within the 'formula fictions' of the popular romance, new genres have emerged which have adapted to and accommodated those changes. The traditionally virginal heroine of the classic Silhouette romance was no longer quite so viable in the 1980s, and so a new sub-genre of eroticized romance emerged in Silhouette's 'Desire' label. By 2000, the sassy heroine of the 'chick-lit' novel represented a challenge to the conventionally quiescent Mills and Boon heroine. Harlequin responded with their own imprint 'Red Dress Ink', publishing novels which featured the young, single woman in the city. The publishing companies associated with the popular romance have had to respond to initiatives from writers and publishers and to the changing experience of women.

If the narratives of the domestic romance do conform to many of the conventions of the formula romance novel, the novels under discussion here do not necessarily end with the consummation of a love affair or with marriage, as the classic Mills and Boon, Harlequin or Silhouette romance requires. These novels do not strictly belong to the formulaic romance genre, although they may share many of the same desires and fantasies. The object of romance for the woman protagonist may not necessarily be a male erotic partner; it may be another woman, it may be a child, it can be the heroine herself, and need not be a person. Among the objects of desire in the novels here are: commercial empires, houses and revitalized families. Whatever the goal of their heroines might be, these novels uniformly articulate some form of desire, and express the wish that things could be different for women.

I would make no claims that these are novels that should be entered into an alternative feminist canon or a women's great tradition, but I would argue that they need to be acknowledged as fictions which commanded a huge readership, and which do articulate the concerns of many women. The popular novel tends to be an aspirational fantasy, and these novels can often represent forms of wish fulfilment. The nature of those aspirations, however, shifts and changes in different historical conditions. To identify the way in which the popular discourses of masculinity and femininity shift in romance fiction is to recognize that the categories of 'man' and 'woman' are not fixed. The idea of what constitutes a 'hero' or a 'heroine' changes dramatically in different historical periods. Even within the output of a single woman writer, the ideal of masculinity and femininity may change. While Rose Franken's perfect husband begins her series of 'Claudia' novels as an unrepentantly dominant male, in the novels after the Second World War, he has to be protected from Claudia's growing self-sufficiency. The troubled husband of the Aga-saga is a very different creature from the existentially challenged man of the immediate post-war period. The powerful women of the 1980s sex and shopping novel are far removed from the anxious housewife heroines of the Aga-saga who were to follow them a decade later. While romances claim to offer eternal partnerships and ideal models, the nature of those models is demonstrably unstable.

The novels discussed in this study can be described as 'women's books', although the literary equivalent for the cinematic term 'the women's picture', a category which is recognized by film critics, audiences and producers alike, is rarely used by literary critics. Nicola Beauman is one who does use it, and who reappropriates the term for fiction in her study of women's writing between the wars:

> there *is* a category of fiction written for women – 'the women's novel' ... They generally have little action and less histrionics – they are about the 'drama of the undramatic', the steadfast dailyness of a life that brings its own rewards, the intensity of the emotions and, above all, the importance of human relationships.
>
> (Beauman, 1983, p. 5)

If the contemporary woman's novel now allows for more histrionics than could be permitted in the stiff-upper-lip era of the interwar years, it remains the case that the 'women's novel' is preoccupied with the domestic and with personal relationships. The Aga-saga as a form is defined by the 'drama of the undramatic', and their narrative trajectories continue to celebrate 'steadfast dailyness'. If the women's novel does take to the world stage, as the sex and shopping novels of the 1980s dared to, the narratives continue to focus on personal relationships and are largely written from the heroine's subjective perspective. Because these novels are largely about personal relationships does not mean to say that they are inconsequential; that the personal is political was a central rallying call of the women's movement. And in their focus on female experience and their concerns with love, family and marriage, these narratives cannot but be concerned with power relations between the genders. Claud Cockburn recognized in 1972 that the popular novel inevitably addresses gender politics and the 'woman question':

> The bestsellers are, of course, rich sources of information regarding what may be called, for very rough convenience, the 'private sector' of life and love, notably love, and spilling over from there to cover the general status of women.
>
> (Cockburn, 1972, p. 14)

The novel may not be a barometer of social history, and is never a simple reflection of its times, but what it can do is to chart the limits and shifts in social discourse, and so offer insights into what can and cannot be fantasized about and publicly acknowledged. John Sutherland has argued that what is significant about best-selling novels is 'what they tell us about the book trade, the market place, the reading public and society generally at the time they have done well' (Sutherland, 1981, p. 5). The distinction between 'best-selling' and 'literary' fiction is less easy to make in women's writing than many critics, both mainstream and feminist, would suggest. It is just as difficult to categorize the readership of these fictions. Women writers and readers would seem to trouble any neat categorizations of the 'literary' and the 'popular' in both texts and readers. Jenny Hartley's study of the reading choices of reading groups (which, as her research shows, are largely made up of women readers) demonstrates that the reading choices of book groups tend not to include the kind of genre fiction that is sold and read by millions of women readers. It appears that women readers are not prepared to publicly admit their private choices of reading material; the espousal of 'literary' titles in surveys and questionnaires is not borne out by the best-seller lists. The best-seller lists of popular titles and the more 'literary' lists from the reading groups do not match up, suggesting that there are large numbers of women who are happily drawing their reading from both ends of the book market. Hartley questions how useful it is to make a distinction between the academic critic and the 'general' reader:

> is this either fair or useful? I think it is fair to say that literary élites and establishments have always defined themselves against the middlebrow ... Reading groups, though, are often reading the same serious literary fiction ... as those literature departments which show so little interest in their activities; and their discussions aren't so different from those in the seminar rooms either – and often better prepared.
>
> (Hartley, 2002, pp. 62–3)

Although many of the novels in this study would not rank as 'serious literary fiction' it would be equally unfair to define them or their readers as middlebrow. Readers of genre fiction have a sophisticated understanding of the conventions and requirements of a genre novel. The critical term 'genre' is, however, a very loose category. In Fredric Jameson's definition: 'Genres are essentially literary *institutions*, or social contracts between a writer and a specific public, whose function is to specify the proper use of a particular artifact' (Jameson, 1981, p. 106). While this is a useful concept, in that it acknowledges the importance of readers, it does not allow for the proliferation of sub-genres that cannot be entirely dictated by writers but which are also constructed by publishers.

The sub-genres of the domestic romance are defined by their historical context, and often themselves contributed to the definition of a decade. With their eye-catching covers, the best-selling novel with 'its vivid colours designed to appeal to mass tastes' (Escarpit, 1964, p. 131) could capture the *Zeitgeist* of a period. This is at its clearest in the sex and shopping novels of the 1980s; the glitzy covers which marked the genre, with their raised gold lettering and their women in bright red lipstick and stiletto shoes, were to become iconic images of the decade. The fashionably acid colours of the covers of the 'chick-lit' genre, with their cartoon stick-thin young women, similarly supplied a contemporary image of end-of-the-century femininity. As publishers define market segments more and more precisely, their categories of fiction become self-defining genres into which the majority of fiction is ordered. Marketing departments identify a popular success, whether this be *Bridget Jones's Diary*, the Aga-saga, or the 'Harry Potter' novels, and seek out authors and texts which can emulate the same marketability. These are then promoted with covers that associate these texts with that category of fiction, and so define a novel as belonging to a genre.

Fictional genres are not only a marketing category, but also a means of bringing together a range of texts and reading them symptomatically for what they share. The texts selected here are chosen because their concerns are clustered around a theme that expresses something significant about gender relations at a particular historical moment. When a number of writers who achieve popular status and a wide readership are preoccupied with a shared narrative structure, as in the picaresque male journey of the 1950s women's novel, or the multi-stranded college novel of the 1970s, then this is a signal that something important is being addressed. Fiction written by women clusters around the dominant discourses of femininity in any given period, either to challenge or embrace that hegemony. Popular fiction is drawn into these clusters as publishers and authors search for a marketable form. 'Literary' novels by women writers are not unaffected by these discourses, and may not be as innovative as they first appear. Writers who regularly appear in contemporary writing and women's writing courses and textbooks can be seen to share a great deal with their populist counterparts. Women writers across the hierarchy of genres are often concerned with precisely the same issues, and can often come to very similar conclusions.

Because this is fiction that is generally not taken seriously by critics, these novels can express commonly experienced doubts and anxieties that cannot be admitted in any other context. And what they share is an articulation of anxieties about what it means to be a woman, the desires of the feminine, that are inadmissible elsewhere. The novel can confront these tensions in a way that cannot be found in other forms of popular culture, even those with a predominantly female readership or audience. Women's magazines present lifestyle fantasies, while soap operas are concerned with stories of communities rather than those of individual women. The novel is a fictional form that can present an entirely subjective point of view.

The narrative voice in these novels is, almost without exception, intensely personal. The narrator, whether first or third person, frequently assumes a tone of intimacy with the reader, often addressing the reader directly. This is a strategy that is employed by women writers as far apart stylistically as Monica Dickens, Alice Walker, Fay Weldon and Helen Fielding. This assumed intimacy constructs an experience that is close to a conversation with a close woman friend (and such conversations frequently figure in the narratives). Dominic Head has described Fielding's *Bridget Jones's Diary* as in 'a new tradition of confessional feminine personal first-person narrative' (Head, 2002, p. 6), but this first-person confessional address is hardly a new convention. It is to be found in the 1940s with Monica Dickens's fiction, Lynne Reid Banks, Margaret Drabble and Andrea Newman all use this voice in the 1960s; it is central to the 1970s college novel, and is also there in the 1980s sex and shopping novel and in the Aga-saga of the 1990s. The first-person confessional voice continues in the 'chick-lit' genre and in the narratives of resentful daughters: the intimate address is a longstanding feature of women's writing.

Nicola Beauman has noted that this assumed intimacy could, in the interwar 'woman's novel', be attributed to the shared class of reader and author:

> The 'woman's novel' between the wars was usually written by middle-class women for middle-class women. Since writers and readers formed a homogenous group it is clear that the woman's novel at this period was permeated through and through with the certainty of like speaking to like.
>
> (Beauman, 1983, p. 3)

It can no longer (if it could ever) be assumed that writers and readers are a 'homogenous group', as publishers and bookshops increasingly target titles at market segments. Nonetheless, the tone of intimacy and the assumption of a shared female experience that Beauman identifies in the interwar novel continue on in contemporary women's fiction. Nicola Humble also asserts that the interwar 'middlebrow novel' 'was widely read by the middle-class public – and particularly by the lower middle-classes' (Humble, 2001, p. 13). However, it cannot be categorically stated that these novels are 'the literature of the middle-classes'. They may have been written by middle-class women, but this is knowable, whereas their readership is not. Public and private libraries and book clubs did not and do not record their members' class. While the heroines of these fictions may be irrevocably middle-class, like those women's magazines that address a class segment above their actual readership, their status may well represent the aspirational rather than the actual.

It is just as difficult in the era of mass-publishing and sophisticated marketing to know who it is precisely who reads which novels. Library borrowings go largely unrecorded, and second-hand and market-stall sales of books do not feature in published sales returns. Steven Connor makes the important point that it is mistaken to make over-easy assumptions about readers and readership, an error that can be made by both publishers and literary critics:

> Mass market publishers and academic commentators on the fiction industry share the assumption that there are distinct groups of people in society known as romance readers, thriller readers, science fiction readers, etc. ... The idea of the homogenous reader thus conditions the assumption that this reader will always read the same way.
>
> (Connor, 1996, p. 19)

It would appear that women particularly are promiscuous readers of fiction who clearly do not always 'read in the same way'. Nor do women readers stick to a single kind of reading but may well share their reading of innovative women writers with the reading of popular genre novels. To be a reader of popular fiction does not, as Jenny Hartley's lists of reading group choices demonstrate, mean a lack of engagement with other kinds of fiction.

The question of the readership of popular fiction is a thorny methodological problem for cultural critics. Janice Radway's anthropological study (Radway, 1984) of a group of readers of popular romance has been invoked by many critics, but there are problems with this methodology. Respondents may not be reliable in their answers to questionnaires (particularly when these deal with the private experience of reading), and they cannot be representative of the entire readership for a fictional title or genre. There are also difficulties in establishing who audiences for a text might be that are particularly associated with the market for fiction. In our research for *Brave New Causes* (Philips and Haywood, 1998), Ian Haywood and I unwittingly emulated the technique that Jackie Stacey outlines in her study of women's cinema attendance in the 1940s and 1950s. Stacey explains that she chose this historical moment because 'this period had been a key focus of feminist work on Hollywood (for example, film noir of the 1940s and melodrama of the 1950s)' (Stacey, 1995, p. 99), and Stacey's research covered much of the same period that we covered in *Brave New Causes*. It seems significant that while this is a period that is much discussed in feminist film theory, as the high point of the film melodrama, there has been relatively little work in cultural or literary studies on the written equivalent. Like Stacey, we wrote to popular women's magazines aimed at a readership of the age that might remember the books we were discussing and asked for readers' memories of those novels. Interestingly, unlike Stacey, we had no replies at all.

The difference between research into cinema and literary fiction raises an important question about the different experiences of viewing and of reading a text. Reading is a very private act, rarely shared except in the context of a student group or a reading group, and these are groups which are largely concerned to read fiction which is confirmed as 'literary'. While cinema going is a public act, women readers cannot be relied upon to be honest about their consumption of fiction. If it is difficult to trace quite who makes up the readership for these novels, it is impossible to assess how they might have been read. While journalists are quick to ascribe published genres to specific generations and groups (as in 'the Bridget

Jones generation'), and publishers target precisely defined market segments, it is clear that readers with similar demographics cannot be assumed to share the same tastes in reading. As one book-group member of Hartley's research puts it: 'Sociologists would probably regard us all as having similar reading habits and preferences!' (Hartley, 2002, p. 80).

While the readership of particular genres and texts cannot be taken for granted, publishing has become increasingly sophisticated in identifying new marketing groups. Steven Connor has argued:

> both the reading and readerships of fiction have become rather more complex, hybrid and mobile in the post-war period than previously. Localised or specialised readerships have arisen alongside the previously established mass readerships for genre fiction. Women's and lesbian and gay fiction have enjoyed marketing successes.
>
> (Connor, 1996, p. 27)

If the readership for fiction has become more fluid, one factor remains constant, and it is not surprising that it is women's fiction that currently enjoys 'marketing success'. Historically, it has always been the case that it is women who are the main consumers of the novel form and who continue to read the majority of fiction: 'almost three-quarters of all fiction is borrowed or bought by women, a mirror image of the purchase of non-fiction by men ... Women readers are vital to the book trade' (Bloom, 2002, p. 51). There is, nonetheless, a hierarchy of fictional genres, and it is the romance, the form most closely associated with women readers and writers, which is the most clearly gendered and which remains the most denigrated form of fiction. As Clive Bloom argues:

> Popular genres do not ... have equal status. Some are considered more serious than others (which often means less 'female' or less 'juvenile'). This becomes obvious when one compares the two leading genres that account for almost all the annual fictional output: detective fiction and women's romance. Detective fiction always had *cachet*.
>
> (*Ibid*., p. 14)

The implication is that romance fiction does not share in this 'cachet', even if a romance title or writer achieves longevity. While those genres most associated with masculinity, the once derided 'pulp fiction' of Westerns and Science Fiction novels, can attain 'classic' or 'vintage' status, the popular romance remains in the lowest position of the league table. If the 'woman's book' is low in the pecking order, it remains high on the packing order, in holiday suitcases and in publishers' warehouses, and sells more than any other kind of fiction. Still, in the post-feminist, post-modern critical age, women's fiction is not accorded the same status as writing by men. The domestic romance is uncomfortably positioned between a traditional literary canon that denigrates the feminine and feminist critics who are looking for explicit innovation and progressive ideas in women's writing.

Even those male critics inflected by the impact of feminist theory tend to include women writers as an afterthought to the male canon, and to contain them in a category of 'feminist writers'. Current studies of the post-war novel written by men continue to marginalize 'women's writing' and tend to collapse the wealth of post-war women's writing into a few key respected women authors. Dominic Head's survey of British fiction from 1950 to 2000 (Head, 2002) includes a section on 'Gender and Sexuality', but his insistent focus on the category of 'serious fiction' limits his discussion to Lynne Reid Banks, Margaret Drabble, Nell Dunn and (oddly, given his undefined frame of the 'serious') Helen Fielding. Bart Moore-Gilbert's survey of the 1960s and 1970s novel (Moore-Gilbert, 1994) includes a strictly limited range of women writers, and does not allow Drabble or Reid Banks into the index. John Sutherland's account of the best-sellers of the 1970s (Sutherland, 1981) includes only two women novelists in twenty-four sections – Erica Jong and Colleen McCullough – although there were many more best-sellers by women writers in this decade.

If male critics have a tendency to sideline women writers, feminist champions of women's writing can fall into an unquestioning celebration of women's fiction, which does not always allow for critical readings. Early second-wave feminist literary criticism, especially Ellen Moers's *Literary Women* (Moers, 1976) and Elaine Showalter's *A Literature of Their Own* (Showalter, 1977) established a school of feminist criticism which offered an alternative to the Leavisite 'Great Tradition', and which was concerned to position women writers within the literary canon. It was an important part of the feminist project to recoup and promote neglected women writers, and Virago and other feminist presses confirmed that alternative canon in publishing, but this celebration and rediscovery of the woman author left little room for criticism.

Virago's reissue of Margaret Kennedy's 1924 novel *The Constant Nymph* in 1983 was published without an introduction or context, and so could make no reference to the casual anti-Semitism that pervades the novel. Current editions of Lynne Reid Banks's *The L-Shaped Room* do not refer to the unquestioningly stereotyped representation of the black character, John, and critical reassessments hardly mention this aspect of the novel. In her introduction to the Virago reissue of Nell Dunn's *Poor Cow*, Margaret Drabble makes no reference at all to the casual racism of the narrative voice (Drabble, 1988). Adrian Henri's introduction to the Virago edition of *Up the Junction* does briefly acknowledge this racism, but evades it as an issue in its praise for Dunn's unflinching reportage (Henri, 1988).

An uncritical recuperation of women's writing can make for confusions in the assessment of these novels as 'literary' or 'popular fictions'. In a call made in 1996 for the reassessment of women's popular writing, Carmen Callil expressed an ambivalence about the category itself, simultaneously asserting a 'venerable literary tradition' of women's genre fiction, and consigning popular fiction to the 'entertainment canon' (Callil, 1996, p. 5). Anne Cranny-Francis argues that the 'feminist generic text' can be distinguished from 'the traditional generic text', her concern is with feminist fictions which do not admit 'compromise' (Cranny-Francis, 1990). This stern admonition and this neat distinction, however, present just the same problems as the attempt to define the readership of the 'highbrow' and the 'middlebrow' in women's writing. The recuperation of neglected women writers into the categories of 'serious literature' or the 'middlebrow' does not allow for the richness and pleasures of women's genre writing, or for the ways in which feminist novelists have drawn upon those pleasures.

The pleasure of the popular text can often derive from the very restrictions of formula fiction and the play that can be made within their limits. Novelists who are acclaimed as literary and feminist writers have themselves frequently made use of popular generic forms. Margaret Atwood, Angela Carter, Fay Weldon and Jeanette Winterson are among the most eminent of the many women writers who have made use of genre fiction; all have worked with the forms of science and fantasy fiction, and have employed variants of the romance, from the bodice ripper to the story of the spurned wife. In the 1980s, self-identified feminist writers such as Zoë Fairbairns and Fay Weldon deliberately chose to write within popular forms and also strategically marketed their work as popular fiction. While women's writing continues to be marginalized in surveys of twentieth- and twenty-first century fiction, and is underrepresented in literary reviews and the academic curriculum, it will inevitably be the case that feminist scholars will tend to celebrate women writers. But contemporary feminist theory has to become more sophisticated than this, and to move beyond an unquestioning championship of women writers, to take account of the historical and social frameworks which can make some women's writing unpalatable.

The novels discussed here uncomfortably straddle Queenie Leavis's neat divisions between the highbrow, the middlebrow and the lowbrow. Nicola Humble's study of interwar women's fiction is one of the few that addresses this categorization, but she does not challenge the terms. The central themes that she identifies in the 'middlebrow' novel between the 1920s and 1950s, 'class, the home, gender and the family' (Humble, 2001, p. 3), continue to be the focus of women's fiction after the Second World War. Humble accepts the 'middlebrow' as a critical category and identifies her task as: 'to rehabilitate both the term and the body of literature to which it was generally applied' (Humble, 2001, p. 1).

However, this rehabilitation of a 'body of literature' had already been achieved by Virago and other feminist presses (including Persephone Press, established by Nicola Beauman) some decades before Humble's own study. The novels that Humble discusses tend to be those that have been republished by these feminist presses, and are therefore by writers who have already been reappropriated into an alternative canon. In a footnote,

Humble notes that many feminist critics are uncomfortable with the term 'middlebrow' (*ibid.*, p. 2), but does not acknowledge that this category may itself be problematic in the discussion of women's writing. Alison Light, one of the critics Humble cites for her reluctance to use the term, has argued that to make a firm distinction between the 'highbrow' and the 'lowbrow' in fiction (as Jenny Hartley has argued of the readership) is not a useful project. Instead, Light suggests that it is more valuable to read across the spectrum of fiction, and argues that this mode of reading makes for a better historical understanding:

> Rather than setting 'highbrow' against 'lowbrow', the serious against the merely escapist or trashy, I am drawn to look for what is shared and common across these forms ... and to see them all as historically meaningful. In any case, not only are such cultural and literary evaluations dialectical judgements – the labels of 'high' and 'low' only make sense in relation to each other – we need to realise that their provenance is always changing: terms such as 'popular' or 'mass' must open up rather than close down historical enquiry.
>
> (Light, 1991, p. x)

The selection of texts here has deliberately involved novels which are construed as 'literary', and includes those writers who do currently appear on academic syllabuses and who are reviewed in the broadsheet press, but situates them alongside those novels and genres which few women are prepared to admit to having read. This study makes use of a number of novelists who are not generally regarded as genre writers, and puts them together with those who tend to be dismissed as writers of 'the escapist or trashy'. In situating all these writers in their historical context and identifying their writing as belonging to a current set of discourses of gender, the pattern of the 'shared and common' becomes evident.

What textual analysis can do, which readership studies cannot, is to draw together structural regularities across fictions. In reading the versions of femininity and masculinity presented in the heroes and heroines of these novels, contemporary discourses about gender and gender relations become very clear. Iris Murdoch has always been acclaimed as among the most intellectual of women novelists, while Barbara Cartland has consistently been derided as a synonym for bad romance writing. In their writings in the 1950s, however, both novelists are preoccupied with the future of masculinity in the post-war reconstruction, and their heroes and heroines exhibit very similar compromises with the brave new world of post-war Britain. Margaret Drabble and Lynne Reid Banks (now both established figures in academic courses and writings on the post-war novel) and Monica Dickens (now largely forgotten by academia, but a writer whose work continues to be in print) write in very comparable terms of the situation of the single mother in the 1960s.

Alice Walker is among the most celebrated of contemporary writers, a

Pulitzer Prize winner who is included on high school and college reading lists, while Rona Jaffe has only recently been rediscovered, but both are dealing with the problems faced by the young woman undergraduate. Andrea Newman is now regarded as a writer of torrid romances, while Marilyn French is a recognized feminist novelist, but both write about the university experience as a moment of liberation for young women. The 'chick-lit' novel has become a journalistic term for 'a gossipy genre of confessional fiction about women' (La Ferla, 2005, p. 1), but the contemporaneous narration of the resentful daughter, which is no less confessional or gossipy, is reviewed admiringly in the broadsheet press. Identifying common patterns and themes in these novels can demonstrate what were clearly preoccupations for women during each decade. The 'best-seller' is a term that tends to be ascribed to those novels that are not considered worthy of serious literary investigation, and this is even more the case for a best-seller by a woman writer. But fiction that commands such a wide level of recognition and readership merits more acknowledgement than merely as popular writing that achieves a broad market. Innovative fiction by feminist writers, Marilyn French, Fay Weldon, Alice Walker, though classed as 'literary', can achieve best-seller status. The best-seller by definition crosses class and cultural boundaries (although, importantly, not always gender boundaries). As Robert Escarpit has stated, novels which achieve that status work at different levels: '[the] crossing of social boundaries constitutes the specific phenomenon of the best-seller. Hence, there may be best-sellers at several levels' (Escarpit, 1964, p. 129).

There is a distinction to be made between the British and American markets for the popular novel; a best-seller in either country was not likely to be defined by publishers as an 'international best-seller' until after the 1960s. The exchange of fiction titles across the Atlantic was limited until arrangements were set up between publishers in the post-war period. These exchanges were to accelerate sharply from the early 1970s; the integration of British and North American publishing companies with a series of takeovers in the 1980s established the basis for the current global market in fiction. The 'paperback revolution' was instrumental in establishing the conditions for a more international circulation of titles, at least for English language fiction. Penguin Books, launched in Britain in 1935, was a key player in the widening dissemination of fiction, in producing affordable paperback versions of novels. By 1945 it was producing at least 100,000 copies of each title. In Britain the success of Penguin was followed by the formation of Pan Books and in America by the paperback company Pocket Books. Corgi books, produced by Transworld, then followed in 1951. By 1997 Transworld were the most successful global publishing corporation, and dominated sales in popular fiction. The paperback marked a shift in methods for the distribution of books (Philips, 1990, p. 146), and brought modern advertising and marketing techniques to the gentlemanly world of publishing.

Publishers in Canada and Britain had begun to exchange manuscripts of popular romance novels since the Second World War, when an arrangement was established between the Canadian publishers, Harlequin, and the British Mills and Boon for the North American rights to Mills and Boon titles (*ibid.*). For much of the 1950s and 1960s, however, British and American publishers tended to stick to their own territories, and there was a limited cross-over of titles. Popular magazines and journals such as *Reader's Digest* (which launched its condensed books list in 1954) were read widely on both sides of the Atlantic. It was through this kind of material that debates surrounding such issues as the Kinsey Report, abortion and contraception could become part of popular discourse in both Britain and America. It was only such hugely popular book titles as Rose Franken's 'Claudia' series or Betty MacDonald's *The Egg and I* which could reach a global English-speaking readership, their popularity confirmed and promoted by film versions of the texts.

George Greenfield explains the circumstances which constrained the exchange of book titles between Britain and America until the 1970s:

> For many years, there had been a gentleman's agreement that for most general trade books, including fiction, the American publisher would concentrate on his home territory and the Philippines, while the British publisher would have the United Kingdom and the Commonwealth.
> (Greenfield, 1989, p. 129)

This 'gentleman's agreement' was finally brought to a halt in 1976, when the United States Justice Department declared that it constituted a cartel. By 1977 it was estimated that about 12 per cent of British publishing was owned by American companies; British publishers also made inroads into American publishing companies. Pearson, who took over Penguin Books, acquired the Viking Press in New York. Steven Connor has written of 'the increasing permeability of British and American markets' (Connor, 1996, p. 27) in post-war writing, but that increasing permeability can be precisely dated, and was strictly limited prior to these British and American acquisitions. It was only in the late 1970s that there was a wide-scale interchange of commercial titles, and an organized global market for book sales. Sheila Rowbotham has argued that 'national boundaries cannot contain the movement of feminist ideas' (Rowbotham, 1989, p. 13); it was the relatively new interchange of books between America and Britain in the early 1970s that did much to facilitate this movement. The women's movement both promoted and benefited from an international traffic in feminist theory and fiction. Widely available in cheap paperback editions, a feminist novel such as *The Women's Room* could now be marketed as 'an international best-seller' (French, 1978, front cover), and become required reading for women's groups on both sides of the Atlantic.

In the 1980s, a series of mergers and takeovers saw publishing in the hands of powerful 'Conglomerates and Aggregates' (Greenfield, 1989, p. 136). The effect was both to ensure much more traffic between British and North American titles, and to promote the international best-selling title. Successful popular novelists such as Danielle Steel could be marketed to enjoy unprecedented sales in a global market. This context also allowed for the marketing of fiction to become much more sophisticated, and to address texts and genres to niche audiences. The 'chick-lit' novel and the resentful daughter narratives of the 1990s could be targeted at very precise generations and market groups.

To achieve a wide readership, however, these must be texts that engage at some level with women's concerns, however romantic or aspirational those fictions might be. The novels discussed here are those which clearly touched a chord with women readers; they express the anxieties of negotiating contemporary modes of femininity. Because they are effectively romance fictions, these texts offer a form of ideal femininity and, to some extent, advice about how to acquire it. The politics of feminism have been such a dominant discourse in the latter half of the twentieth century that the model heroine is inevitably in dialogue with the challenges of the women's movement. Feminism, as a political project, can only allow for contradiction to a limited degree, while fiction can articulate the unacknowledged tensions of the impact of new ideas of gender on women's lives. While all these novels are preoccupied with female experience, they may not necessarily be feminist fictions. Although they may well represent ambitious and proactive heroines, that ambition may not be articulated in terms of a feminist politics. As Clare Hanson has argued:

> there is no necessary relationship between women's novels and feminist novels: in other words, *women's novels* are not necessarily feminist – although they can be so. However, it is wrong to argue that women's novels are not of interest to *the feminist critic*: they are of interest precisely because of the centrality they attribute to women's experience.
> (Hanson, 2000, p. 1)

There is, as the situation for women changes and the focus of these novels shifts, a constant subtext of engagement with the feminist ideas. The Women's Liberation Movement was such an unavoidable undercurrent of women's experience in the latter half of the twentieth century that it is constantly acknowledged in women's writings, whether it is recognized as significant or not. The conflicting expectations of femininity in the late twentieth century presented women with contradictory demands, and the anxieties of how these could be negotiated are articulated very directly in these fictions. Those expectations and the discontents of women change markedly as the twentieth century progresses. The chapters here are roughly divided into a chronology from the 1950s to the present, and are organized around the sub-genre of women's writing that marks each decade. These are not firm divisions; authors and genres are not neatly contained by historical decades.

The immediate period after the Second World War experienced a sharp transition in gender roles in the aftermath of war service for men and women, which necessarily impacted on women's relationships with men. Women writers from across the spectrum of literature, from Barbara Cartland to Iris Murdoch, are preoccupied with what it means to be a man in the post-war context. The 1950s is the decade that is now demarcated as the era of the 'Angry Young Man'; although angry young men are to be found in women's fiction of the period, they are not the Jimmy Porter or Arthur Seaton figures written by contemporary men. Instead, the ideal hero is a good citizen, who is explicitly selected by the heroine for his potential as a loving father and husband. This was the period of the height of the 'Doctor and Nurse' romance novel, the Mills and Boon genre which first established the exchange of popular titles between Britain and North America. The doctor and the nurse are icons of a time in which the preferred masculinity and femininity were models of welfare state citizenship and personal responsibility. The hero is configured in the post-war novel in terms of his consideration and social contribution, and is hardly associated at all with wealth and consumption, as he is so markedly in the fictions of the 1980s and after.

By the 1960s, active female sexuality could be explicitly addressed in women's writing, but a clash of moral discourses is very evident in contemporary writings on young women, in journalism and in fiction. The narrative of the single mother expresses the sexual anxieties of a generation of young women and also provided a site for the negotiation of changes in moral attitudes. The apprehensive pregnant women in these novels offer a sharp contrast to the received notion of the 'swinging sixties' as the era of the pill and sexual liberation. These novels are all directly concerned with issues of contraception, reproductive rights and support for single parents, but these are written about as entirely individualized experiences and not recognized as causes for political action and collective campaigns, as they would later become. These are pre-feminist novels, written before the surge of feminist activism in the late 1960s; nonetheless, the pregnant single woman does provide an image of female independence, if this is an independence that is not so much chosen as necessitated.

A decade later, the single woman has her ambitions focused on college. The growth of higher education in the 1960s and early 1970s saw a rise in women undergraduates in both Britain and America, and an emergent genre, the 'college girl' novel. These narratives initially appear to be about a new-found independence for women, but read as a genre, it is clear that this independence was not entirely unproblematic. The 1970s were declared the 'decade of women' by the United Nations; the impact of feminism had by this time become unavoidable, and rights and opportunities for women had become a part of the popular commonsense. Nonetheless, these novels uniformly express a tension between the pull of liberation for women and a loyalty to their family traditions. Even such avowedly feminist and radical writers as Alice Walker and Rita Mae Brown express a shared nostalgia for the familiarity of home and family.

By the 1980s, the achievements of the women's movement and many feminist ideas that had been radically challenging in the 1960s and 1970s could now be assumed, and to an extent taken for granted. In the entrepreneurial spirit of the decade, working-class and aristocratic heroines alike could succeed as powerful career women; Danielle Steel and Shirley Conran were only two of the many women writers who were promoting the woman's success story. But the emergence of the wealthy and successful heroine in fiction coincided with a right-wing political swing in both Britain and America, and resulted in an uneasy alliance of feminist independence and capitalist celebration in these novels. This was also the decade which saw the defeat of the Equal Rights Amendment in America, and a powerful Conservative woman prime minister in Britain. The 'sex and shopping' novel, with its iconic images of besuited women with padded shoulders, represented strong women negotiating their way through male-dominated worlds of capital and power, who felt they owed nothing to feminism. These novels unapologetically celebrated wealth and consumption, and suggested that skilled consumer knowledge could be the means to make a fortune. These are novels which endorse women's achievements and success, but do so within a frame that does not in any way challenge the structures of power and gender relations.

In the fall-out from the excesses of the 1980s, the 1990s were marked by a nostalgic return to the domesticated and rural romance. The 'Aga-saga' provided a form of post-marriage romance which also articulated a retreat by women from the world of work and naked ambition. That retreat did not, however, involve a repudiation of consumption; these are heroines who may not own the diamonds and commercial empires of the 1980s heroine, but they do appreciate nice houses, good wardrobes and furniture and antiques. Despite their comfortable environments and middle-class lifestyles, the Aga-saga heroines recurrently express some form of dissatisfaction with their lot, and their disappointment in contemporary masculinity is very evident.

The genre that defined the turn of the century for young women was the 'chick-lit' novel, a form of fiction which centred on a single working woman, who was not as financially successful as her 1980s counterpart. These heroines assumed all the gains of the women's movement, but firmly distanced themselves from feminist politics. The chick-lit novel saw a return to the individualized romances of the 1950s and 1960s; their heroines are invariably surrounded by a group of women friends, but, unlike the women's groups of the 1970s college novel, this friendship is based on shopping rather than the sharing of experience. The chick-lit heroine, pioneered by 'Bridget Jones', was expected to be a working woman, but she is notably unambitious, and in search of a male partner who can outstrip her in terms of his salary and sophistication. Like her 1980s predecessors, she revels still in the consumption of fashion and luxury goods and now believes that romance itself can be achieved through a skilled awareness of consumerism.

The turn of the twenty-first century saw the emergence of a new genre of women's fiction, the narrative of the resentful daughters who could not forgive their mothers for their maternal failings and for their ambition. These novels are largely written by women who are the generation born to mothers who were of the same generation as the 1960s and 1970s pioneers of second-wave feminism. While their fictional daughters assume all the benefits of the women's movement, they cannot forgive the mothers who fought for those rights. These novels wilfully refuse to historicize the experience of a very particular generation of mothers and daughters, and deny the impact of feminism on their own lives entirely.

If many of these novels do not see women's experience in political or historical terms, there is a shared perception that the world could be better for women. In each generation of women writers there is a hope that the world will be better for their daughters; there is also a perpetual displacement of the hope for women's equality, but there is also a clear recognition that the next generation should not have to face the same situation. That recognition is one that is shared by both feminist critics and a general readership, and these two categories are not neatly separable.

Writing about these novels has been in part an act of deconstructing my own pleasure in these texts. These are novels which I have read at different stages of my life, and which I initially read uncritically; but that form of reading is not entirely distinct from a feminist critical analysis. It is a comfortable familiarity with genre and forms (and sometimes with the work of a single writer) that enables the identification of structural regularities across genres and texts, and allows for the recognition of why these are texts that call to so many readers.

In 2005 I could write with honesty that I had read and enjoyed all the novels I had written about in the first edition of this book. The same could not be said of the new genres that have since emerged, which have tested my pleasures in popular genres to the limits. One of the striking differences is that the crossover between 'literary fiction' and popular generic novels is much less marked than it was in fiction for many of the decades following the Second World War. While in the 1940s it was possible to identify both Barbara Cartland and Iris Murdoch as dealing with the damage done to men in the aftermath of war, and in the 1960s Andrea Newman and Alice Walker as both writing about the possibilities for women in higher education, there would be no equivalent after 2005. Contemporary fiction exists in a post-modern context, in which cultural forms are much more segmented than they once were. Publishers' marketing departments are very attuned to formulas of design and publicity that identify novels as belonging to or associated with a successful genre, and the commercial success of a memoir such as *Eat, Pray, Love* will ensure that other similar texts will be promoted in the same ways. The growth of reading groups is another phenomenon that belongs to the new millennium – publishers now issue novels with discussion notes for book groups and so identify these titles as distinct from popular fiction.

The two genres to have emerged since the first edition grapple with the problems confronting women who have grown up believing that the position of women in society was improving, if not yet equal, only to be confronted with a retrenchment in state support and in working opportunities. The 'yummy mummy' novel (a name I would prefer not to use, but it is such a standard term of reference to this genre that it is difficult to avoid) and the 'spiritual quest' narrative have become formulaic and both are very much a product of an individualistic culture. While individualism was certainly a feature of the sex and shopping novels of the Thatcher and Reagan years and also of the chick-lit narratives that belong to the era of Bush and Blair, this has become more extreme. The chick-lit heroine (exemplified in Bridget Jones) invariably had a strong group of women friends around her (embodied in the 'girl' gang of *Sex and the City*), but such female friendships are very faint in narratives post-2000. If the 1980s was a decade in which fictional women briefly explored the possibilities of 'having it all', this was not within a feminist framework, and the consequences remained to be explored. While children were largely off the pages of the sex and shopping novels – enormous wealth provided a cushion to the problems of childcare – the contradictions of working motherhood forcibly emerged as a genre in the late 1990s and continue to be a bestselling format. These novels, however, wilfully refuse to historicize the experience of a very particular generation of mothers and daughters and deny the impact of feminism on their own lives entirely.

The 'spiritual quest' might sound like a serious endeavour, and these memoirs do articulate a real discontent with women's lives in an anxious and beleaguered neo-liberal context, but again, that discontent is entirely construed as personal. While these texts may engage with the anxieties and tensions of femininity in the twenty-first century, their resolutions refuse to acknowledge that there is any solution other than for the individual, or that those tensions may derive from structural inequalities rather than individual failure. There is in both these genres a blurring of the boundaries between journalism and fiction. It is notable how many of the writers of the motherhood novel and of the spiritual memoir are (or were) themselves journalists; their published books are extensions of the 'women's column' in newspapers (itself a response to the feminism of the 1960s and 1970s).

The first edition of this book was titled *Women's Fiction*, and all the texts discussed, even those which clearly drew on autobiography, presented themselves as fictional. Not all the texts covered in this new edition are strictly fictional, some present themselves directly as autobiography. There is a slippage between memoir and fiction in these new genres. Many of the authors of the 'yummy mummy' genre are journalists who have explicitly drawn on their own experiences as working mothers in their novels, while the writers of memoirs about their spiritual journey are also journalists, and are constructing a persona for publication. All these authors have written magazine articles and blogs, and are skilled in constructing a persona which is not far removed from the first person character found in many women's novels, and also at providing neat narrative resolutions to the messiness of life experiences. While presenting their stories as 'true', these memoirs can be understood as no less invented than many thinly disguised autobiographical novels; in the age of social media the lines between the private self and a public persona are distinctly blurred.

Personal testimony has become the dominant voice of women's genre fiction, a form that Christopher Lasch identified in 1979 as 'narcissistic':

> the increasing interpenetration of fiction, journalism and autobiography undeniably indicates that may writers find it more and more difficult to achieve ... detachment ... Instead of fictionalizing personal material or otherwise reordering it, they have taken to presenting it undigested, leaving the reader to arrive at his own interpretations. Instead of working through their memories, many writers now rely on mere self-disclosure to keep the reader interested.
>
> (Lasch, 1979, p. 17)

These new genres belong to a post-feminist context. The term 'post-feminist' describes a landscape in which feminism is taking for granted, but it is a loose and baggy concept that can be used in a range of different ways (whether or not it includes a hyphen is indicative of its fluidity as a concept). As Stephanie Harzewski has pointed out, the multiple meanings of the term 'post-feminist' are testament to the impact that feminism has had: 'The multiple and contradictory meanings ascribed to postfeminism reflect feminism's growth beyond a unified political agenda and its fracturing into competing, sometimes antagonistic, strands' (Harzewski, 2011, p. 151). At the same time, the term has been employed as a means of suggesting that feminism no longer has any resonance.

'Post-feminism' once characterized an alliance between feminist theory and post-structuralism with the theoretical developments of the new French feminists, particularly Hélène Cixous and Julia Kristeva. This formulation of post-feminism challenged any stable construction of masculinity and femininity and set out to subvert that binary opposition, to argue that gender was not a fixed category. One of the earliest published books with 'Postfeminism' in the title was the 1999 illustrated guide *Introducing Postfeminism*, which began firmly: 'Postfeminism does not mean that feminism is over.' It went on to explain:

> Postfeminism has developed since the late 1960s from the deconstruction of patriarchal discourses. This is a development of feminism informed by the key analytic strategies of contemporary thought – psychoanalysis, poststructuralism, postmodernism and postcolonialism.
>
> (Phoca and Wright, 1999, p. 3)

While this may have been how the term was understood and taught in the academy, in much of popular culture 'post-feminism' had become a means of asserting that the struggle for women's equality was now over. Susan Faludi has described how 'post-feminism' was appropriated in a backlash against feminism:

> Feminism is 'so seventies', the pop culture's ironists say, stifling a yawn. We're 'post-feminist' now, they assert, meaning not that women have arrived at equal justice and moved beyond it, but simply that they themselves are beyond even pretending to care.
>
> (Faludi, 1991, p. 95)

The extent to which the new genres employ a knowing and witty narrative voice, a cheeriness that belies the pain and confusions that their narratives chart, but which does articulate this post-feminist ironic mode, is notable. 'Post-feminism' is now regularly employed by journalists (among them the writers of these fictions), in Western culture at least, to suggest that feminism is no longer necessary in a global and neo-liberal world.

A generation of feminists, often termed 'third-wave', challenged second-wave feminist politics as irrelevant to them and, according to Gamble, supported 'an indvidualistic, liberal agenda rather than a collective and political one' (Gamble, 1991, p. 298). Many of the feminist cultural critics cited here understand post-feminism as a cultural phenomenon to be resisted, as one which requires women to adjust to that neo-liberal and consumerist environment. For Suzannne Moore, the character of Bridget Jones was an embodiment of post-feminism: 'vapid, consumerist and self-obsessed ... The fiction is that post-feminism is not in fact anti-feminism. It is'. (Moore, 2013). Angela McRobbie also understands post-feminism in terms of a 'relentless' undermining of feminism. She suggests that:

> through an array of machinations, elements of contemporary popular culture are perniciously effective in regard to this undoing of feminism, while simultaneously appearing to be engaging in a well-informed and even well-intended response to feminism.
>
> (McRobbie, 2009, p. 11)

If it is the case that most of these contemporary popular fictions do not see women's experience in political or historical terms, they cannot be entirely effective in 'undoing' feminism. There is in them all some sense of a shared perception that the world could be a better place for women; in each generation of women writers there is a hope that the world will be better for their daughters. There is a perpetual displacement of the hope for women's equality, but there is also a continued recognition that future generations should not have to face the same struggles. The genres that have emerged in fiction for women in the twenty-first century belong to a post-feminist context, in so far as the impact of feminism is undeniable. Feminism may be refuted or contested, but it has had some effect.

There is a contradiction in the construction of contemporary femininity, a paradox in which there is both an acknowledgement of women's potential and achievements and a renewed undermining of equality. As Gill and Scharff point out: 'a discourse of "girl power", "top girls" and "can-do girls" seemed to co-exist alongside the reinvigoration of inequalities and the emergence of new forms and modalities of power' (Gill and Scharff, 2011, p. 1). These texts explore this contradiction, and if finally they will not challenge the 'reinvigoration of inequalities', they do chart the damaging effects and articulate real anxieties about expectations of women in the neo-liberal and post-modern world of the new millennium.

If it is no longer quite true that I read and enjoyed all these books, it remains the case that they have together taught me a great deal and, whatever their resolutions, they have something important to contribute to an understanding of contemporary feminism and femininity.

1

What Did Women Want? Post-War Masculinity in the Woman's Novel of the 1950s

Romance fiction is inevitably concerned with the relationship between the genders. In their representation of romantic encounters between men and women, popular novels construct forms of ideal masculinity and of femininity, which, while they often claim a universality, are necessarily inflected by social and historical circumstance. The aftermath of the Second World War was a moment in which many of the certainties of a pre-war world were up for reassessment. The election of the British Labour government in 1944 and the establishment of a welfare state reconfigured class relations and expectations. The involvement of women in the war effort, both on the Home Front and in the Services, had confronted them with opportunities and forms of work that previously would have been closed to women. Despite an official post-war rhetoric which expected a return of women to the domestic sphere, the shifts in women's expectations, both of themselves and of men, that had emerged in wartime could not be made to disappear. There were now more women working officially than ever before: 'By 1948 there were actually 350,000 more insured women workers than there had been in 1939' (Rowbotham, 1997, p. 244). The contradictions and tensions of what should now constitute a 'woman's role', and in relationships between men and women, were expressed politically and in contemporary fictions. Women's writing in the post-war period is preoccupied with what now constitutes an ideal romance, and with new variations of the hero figure.

Men were by no means seen as essential to a woman's life either in fiction or in other forms of popular culture for women in the post-war decade of the 1950s. The front cover of Beryl Conway Cross's 1956 volume, *Living Alone*, shows the post-war single woman defiantly alone on a desert island, brandishing both a screwdriver and an apron, capable of wall-papering her own rooms and of wielding a hammer. The introduction breezily enjoins women to relish their single status, and the handbook goes on to discuss men as just one aspect, and a rather insignificant one at that, of the pleasures to be taken in modern life. The chapter entitled 'Hospitality: Men and All That' is the only one to focus on masculinity at all, and its subtitle implies that this may well be more trouble than it is worth: 'Men can be difficult'. After sensible advice on 'anti-wolf precautions' (how to ditch an escort), Conway Cross advocates: 'And if she has to settle for something she doesn't want to do ... then it's better for her to join a Sewing Circle. It'll be less trouble in the long run' (Conway Cross, 1956).

Like the contemporary heroines of the 'feminine middle brow' novel (Humble, 2001) and of romance fiction, Conway Cross's woman living alone is a resolutely independent creature, and she is not prepared to settle for any form of masculinity that she 'doesn't want'. The heroine of the Mills and Boon romance of the period inevitably earns her own living (see Philips and Haywood, 1998, for an account of these novels), and is in search of partnership with a man rather than soppy romance. In the modern world, fictional women are equal citizens and demand a new kind of man, and men are a source of considerable worry to the woman writer.

Barbara Cartland debunks the mythology of the dominant male (a myth that was in part of her own making) in her stern advice to young wives and husbands in the 1955 *Marriage for Moderns*. Cartland worked as a 'moral adviser' (Rowbotham, 1997, p. 340) to the WAAF (Women's Auxiliary Air Force) during the war years, but her post-war advice manual demonstrates a marked concern for male virility. A whole chapter is devoted to 'A Shaft in the Quiver', which offers advice on the problems of male infertility and impotence. In one of the very few references to war in the manual, Cartland advises young women that, far from being strong and silent, the contemporary man is a fragile creature who must be protected and cared for:

> The hard ruthless man who is finally brought to his knees by the pure love of a good woman is the ideal every virgin cherishes in her heart, only to feel bewildered and defrauded when she finds the man she longs to be afraid of inspires instead pity and compassion ... War, world unrest, family insecurity, economic fluctuations, all leave their mark on a developing character, a growing personality. Is it any wonder that the instinct of the male in a changing, difficult and dangerous world is to cling to the only person that has never failed him?
>
> (Cartland, 1955, pp. 56–7)

Rather than respond to this changing, difficult world, Cartland's own romantic fiction of the decade displaces any such anxieties about contemporary gender relations into a safe pre-welfare state past, in which men were hard and ruthless, and heroes always aristocratic: the hero of the 1954 *Desire of the Heart* is the Duke of Roehampton; *The Captive Heart* (1956) is set in Monte Carlo in 1872; *Stars in My Heart* is set in the Court of Austria in 1876 (Cartland, 1957a). One of the very few romance novels with a contemporary setting that Cartland wrote in this period is the 1954 *Wings of My Heart*, published under her married name of Barbara McCorquodale, a signifier that this is rather more serious fiction than her romantic novels published under the name Barbara Cartland. The 'modern' hero of this novel remains, however, an heir to a title, to 'the money, estates, everything', and is first encountered skiing in St Moritz. His inheritance is contingent on his marriage to a fellow aristocrat (rather harder to find in post-war Britain than in the Court of Austria). The narrative is concerned with the need to produce an heir in order to ensure that the family house and fortune continues to be held by the 'right' people. The war and the post-war welfare state have clearly confused what were once neat class and geographical boundaries; the heroine, a professional ice skater, is apparently Swiss, and initially has worryingly foreign associations. It transpires, however, that her father was an aristocratic cousin of Hugo's, who has been killed in the war, and that she is indeed a reassuringly English heroine, appropriate to become mistress of the house. *Wings of My Heart* was written only three years before Richard Hoggart wrote of the 'upper crust': 'How little ... the aristocracy now counts in the folk-lore ... It no longer has much power even to inspire ill-will' (Hoggart, 1976, p. 86). Even Barbara Cartland, for whom the aristocracy had once provided the source for the ideal hero, could no longer entirely celebrate the aristocratic male. The post-war aristocrat hero is not acceptable as simply a member of the idle rich; Hugo's experience in the war has taught him discipline and, it is suggested, has enabled him to become a committed and active citizen:

> He had got used to rising early when he was in the Army ... Those who considered him merely a rake, a man with too much money and far too much time on his hands, would have been astonished if they had seen how many details of his farm, estate and fortune Hugo dealt with himself – and usually while those who criticized him were still asleep.
>
> (McCorquodale, 1954, p. 16)

Hugo, as a wealthy landowner, has his future and responsibilities in the post-war world clearly mapped out; but the majority of male characters in fiction by women are men who are in search of a male identity that is no longer defined by the pre-war class system or by the rigid stratifications and discipline of wartime. There are, it should be remembered, several generations of men in the decade of the 1950s, and their experience of the period is markedly divided by their relative positions in wartime. There is one generation of those who have seen active war service, and another of those who were too young to have experienced the war directly, but who were recruited to National Service in the aftermath. In the words of one of the chapter titles in John Osborne's 1981 autobiography, this was a generation who were: 'Too Young to Fight and Too Old to Forget'.

The post-war decade sees the publication of a number of both popular and 'middlebrow' novels written by women about the generation who were old enough to fight, in which women writers assume a male voice. A male protagonist coping with the repercussions of war service is the central focus of the narrative, or can be the first-person narrator. These novels share a narrative structure in which a man, recently discharged from the Services, undertakes a picaresque journey through an assortment of career situations, potential romantic partners and domestic worlds, in an exploration of the options presented by the post-war world. From Iris Murdoch's Jake, in the 1954 *Under the Net* (Murdoch, 1967), searching London for a way to live his life (the publishers even provide a map to trace his journey), to Monica Dickens's Ben, in the 1958 *Man Overboard* (Dickens, 1962), crossing the country in search of a job and a home, these are male characters who have lost their illusions and bearings and who travel through contemporary England in search of a reconfigured male identity. These novels chart their search for a post-war mode of being and for a woman to love. But the romantic and career choices represented are bound up with the question of how to be a man, and, implicitly, with how a form of masculinity demanded in wartime can be reintegrated into a post-war landscape.

Monica Dickens's novel *The Happy Prisoner* presents a vivid, but nonetheless reassuring, image of the damage done to men by the war. First written in 1946, the narrative had a long life throughout the 1950s in the form of a successful play. *The Happy Prisoner* offers a literal representation of wounded masculinity and an image of emasculation. The hero, Oliver, is recovering from his war wounds in his mother's country house; he has lost a leg and has a heart condition because 'A shell splinter just grazed the outer muscle of the heart' (Dickens, 1946, p. 16). Oliver's response to his injuries typifies the bluff and brisk understatement found in these novels of the damage and pain endured in wartime; despite its potentially bleak subject matter, the 1958 Penguin paperback edition of the novel was marketed as a comedy. The novel's dedication is to Dickens's nephew Christopher, the son of her only brother, who himself had died in the navy. Her own brother's death is described in her autobiography with a prosaic but painful brevity: 'Bunny was bitten by a malarial mosquito ... and died on the cruiser H.M.S. London' (Dickens, 1978, p. 28).

Oliver's account of his wartime experience is similarly self-consciously unheroic, and concerned to establish that his injuries are no worse than those suffered by many other 'chaps': 'I was wounded at Arnhem. The same shell that smashed up my leg left a bit of itself in my chest as well ... Quite a lot of the chaps got hit and I was sure I would soon – I was stiff with fright all the time' (Dickens, 1946, p. 44). Oliver, having lost a leg and confined to bed, is himself unable to travel through the new opportunities of post-war Britain; romantic and career opportunities instead present themselves at his bedside. The novel is written as an interlude, a period of forced passivity that the hero accepts with resignation. The novel charts the healing of his body and the soul, as Oliver is shown to come to terms with loss – not only the loss of his health and his leg – but also the loss of a heroic masculinity. The fearless manliness championed at the beginning of the war is seen in retrospect as a deeply misjudged romanticism:

> those gallant days when Oliver thought it was all going to be like what one had heard of the last war. He was posing about fatalistically and planning a few last riotous days in a London teeming with girls eager to let him drink champagne out of their slippers before going out to mud and blood.
>
> (*Ibid.*, p. 130)

This description of the soldier's dream of glamour, written in 1946 about a man who did go out to 'mud and blood', is close to John Osborne's bitter account of a cheery wartime masculinity, which he sees as having bypassed his generation:

> Wartime dreams of being a Jolly Jack, obligingly serviced by a fleet of randy Wrens, being entertained by concert parties of Hollywood Stage Door stars and flattered and cosseted by a grateful nation, had died with the twang of burning piano strings on 8 May, gone with the matey Churchillian past.
>
> (Osborne, 1981, p. 165)

'The Happy Prisoner' was among those who did live out the experience of being a 'Jolly Jack' but, although he is cosseted by his family, it is clear that the state will not flatter him unduly. Oliver will, once recovered from his physical wartime wounds, have to fend for himself. He is, like so many of these post-war heroes, a 'man overboard' (in Monica Dickens's phrase), adrift in a world which will not allow for any illusions or for heroism.

Oliver may be a 'happy prisoner', but he is contained in a household of women: his sisters, his mother and a private nurse. His enforced incarceration means that Oliver has to be integrated into a domestic world of femininity; he becomes the confidante of the all-female household and the novel is structured through a sequence of their stories of the Home Front experience of war. His sister Violet has been a land girl, and the war has allowed her to enjoy a freedom previously denied to her: 'When the war came and she started to work at the farm, she felt justified in having her hair cut short' (Dickens, 1946, p. 31). As women's wartime experience has given them a form of independence, so Oliver's confinement gives him a new understanding and respect for the world of family and domesticity:

> Being in bed had given him a profound interest in other people's behaviour which he had not felt before. He had never taken much notice of his family, except in relation to himself. He was far more aware of

> them now that he was a spectator rather than a participator in their lives, and liked to think that he understood them better. Certainly he had not made much attempt to understand them before.
>
> (*Ibid.*, p. 24)

Elizabeth, the romantic heroine, who modestly does not immediately declare herself as such, is a participant in family life, as a nurse. She is a post-war new woman, competent, professional and discreet, with an 'inconspicuous efficiency' (*ibid.*, p. 145), and as such the perfect partner for the inconspicuous heroism of the wounded soldier. In an image of an ideal Englishness, which offers a strange conflation of post-war modern advertising and traditional English values, her ability to make a perfect cup of tea declares her appropriateness as a wife:

> A Spode cup in a deep saucer like a bowl, with a grey and white cow and a farmhouse on one side and a woman feeding hens on the other, it stood steaming there like a tempting advertisement for something that could not possibly taste as good as it looked.
>
> (*Ibid.*, p. 127)

The comfort expressed in this image also articulates a deep need for continuity, and it is Elizabeth's modesty and efficient nursing that can provide this for the damaged Oliver and, by extension, for the household and wider community. This ideal of a soothing and restorative femininity was to become a key element of the post-war heroine that had far-reaching implications; as Rowbotham has described, 'a version of womanhood as heroic service and personal denial ... was to live on in the post-war period and become a crucial linchpin of social cohesion' (Rowbotham, 1997, p. 221).

Oliver and Elizabeth are thus poised at the end of the novel as ideals of masculinity and femininity, fit to take over and continue the running of the household and the traditions of English family life. Oliver's family house represents English tradition, but it is also constructed as an organic place which must both be protected from the extremes of modernity and adapt to changing times:

> Hinkley was a small manor farm, four hundred years old in places ... It was not self-consciously period; it had never been restored or preserved or quainted up with spinning wheels and wrought iron lanterns. Since Tudor times, people had lived in it and furnished it according to the fashion of their day, but incongruities, as long as they were comfortable, did not spoil the atmosphere.
>
> (*Ibid.*, p. 36)

The novel's conclusion, with Oliver's decision to become a country gentleman and cattle farmer, argues for a return to the traditions of a rural

England. Characters who visit Oliver from his metropolitan past in London are represented as inauthentic and trivial compared with the demands of the land, of history and family. The rejection of a glamorous London girlfriend (an actress, in a recurrent trope of inauthenticity in novels of this period), in favour of the competent Elizabeth, suggests that the wounds of the war will heal, nurtured by women who have themselves been transformed by the experience of war, and that the future lies in the rural traditions of a family home.

Dickens's 1956 novel *The Angel in the Corner* (Dickens, 1960) presents a less optimistic image of family life and the home. Published in the same year as *Look Back in Anger* (Osborne, 1993), the novel can be read as an inversion of Osborne's version of a miserable cross-class marriage, in that it presents a doomed union from the point of view of a middle-class woman. Conway Cross, writing *Living Alone* in the same year, enjoins her readers to be grateful that they are single rather than in a bad marriage: '... why does not the living-alone woman compare her life with that of [a woman] who has a husband who'd make any woman miserable?' (Conway Cross, 1956, p. 56). Dickens was herself an agony aunt for *Woman* magazine, and in *The Angel in the Corner* she writes the narrative of a woman with a husband who does make her miserable.

The heroine Virginia begins the novel with a 'lively ambition'; she is training to be a journalist, in a narrative that is very close to Monica Dickens's own 1951 account of her experiences as a journalist in *My Turn to Make the Tea* (Dickens, 1951). The heroine, Virginia, is the daughter of a divorced couple, her mother an unmaternal woman. It is the need to escape from her mother that prompts her to marry the handsome Joe, who lives in a grim bed-sitting room in Chelsea. Virginia chooses the bohemian Joe over the respectable doctor Felix (the preferred hero of Mills and Boon romances of the same period). Joe's virile desirability is confirmed by the experience of war, which has effected his transformation from boy to man:

> Joe was better-looking now at thirty than he was as a young man ... [T]he war, and the first disciplined life he had known had filled him out and toughened him. It had taken the softness from his mouth and the smoothness from his skin. It had weighted his immature shoulders with a man's muscles ...
>
> (Dickens, 1960, p. 93)

Although there is little in the novel about Joe's war experiences, the loss of the disciplined life in the forces is seen as disastrous for Joe. He begins the novel as an unemployed barman with vague ambitions to write a book, but lacks the discipline (as a war veteran, he is too old to qualify as an Angry Young Man). Over the course of the novel Joe takes on a series of more and more demeaning jobs, finally flirting with small-time criminality. Joe is constructed as an unsuitable match for the middle-class and rather prim Virginia (as her mother constantly points out), and shares many of the characteristics of a Jimmy Porter. Like Jimmy, he is enraged by his wife's 'pusillanimous' stoicism: '"Why are you so damned long-suffering?", he flung at her' (*ibid.*, p. 206). The class distinction that has rumbled throughout the marriage becomes explicit in a final melodrama of disaster, as the husband attempts to kill Virginia and shoots himself. Class difference, the narrative rationale for Joe's increasingly violent behaviour towards Virginia, erupts in a vehement conviction that she believes herself 'too good for him': 'You belong to me. You're my wife, that's all you'll ever be ... You think you're too good for me, don't you. I could kill you when you look at me like that, you damn ladylike –' (*ibid.*, p. 286).

Virginia's response to this unprovoked attack is very like Alison's weary resignation: 'She was not angry any more. She was disheartened and suddenly very tired' (*ibid.*, p. 228). Like Alison and Jimmy's child in *Look Back in Anger*, Virginia and Joe's baby dies, the death a direct consequence of Joe's parental neglect; an emblem of the fact that this relationship can have no future. Despite the appalling extremes of Joe's behaviour, he is written with some sympathy; Virginia stays loyal to him throughout beatings, the loss of their livelihood and the loss of their child. The novel does, however, end with the conclusion that some forms of masculine behaviour are unacceptable, and kills Joe off, leaving Virginia damaged, but free for a partnership with the middle-class and acceptable doctor.

If class difference rather than wartime experience informs the representation of masculinity in Monica Dickens's version of *Look Back in Anger*, her 1958 novel *Man Overboard* is entirely concerned with the generation who came out of the army or the navy to confront the confusions of civvy street; these men had to recognize that the nation, although grateful, was not in any position to 'cosset' them once out of uniform. Ben is only one 'man overboard' among many, as the back cover to the 1962 edition puts it in a neat plot summary: 'When Ben, the Lieutenant-Commander was retired from the Navy at thirty-six, it was neither Ben's nor England's finest hour. For, like so many of his kind, Ben was not at all well equipped for the rigours of civilian life' (Dickens, 1962, back cover).

The novel charts the re-entry of a naval officer into civilian life, and represents Ben as emblematic of the generation who had achieved rank and a sense of purpose during the war, but who now are uneasily classified in the new civilian post-war Britain. The novel is narrated entirely from Ben's point of view (although not in the first person), and takes pains to promote sympathy for him. He is the single father of a young daughter, a widower whose feckless wife has conveniently died in a car accident. Ben's sense of his masculinity is, as the novel begins, defined by his position as a naval officer, and the status accorded to his senior position and war record in the navy. His girlfriend, television star Rose (in yet another actress image of the inauthentic), is attracted to him because of his uniform and status: 'Rose introduced him ... emphatically as *Commander* Francis'. His daughter proudly introduces him as 'my father, Commander Benjamin Francis, Royal Navy' (*ibid.*, p. 11).

Benjamin is nonetheless depicted in the novel as emphatically unexceptional, 'an average naval officer' (*ibid.*, p. 20); he is not a high achiever, nor a particularly heroic figure. The experience of redundancy from the army and navy is represented as one that is simultaneously happening to large numbers of men recruited for war service. Ben typifies the 'average' naval or army conscript; like Oliver, he is modest, and has shown an unassuming courage in the 'everyday hazards of war'. He has a respectable but not remarkable war record:

> Ben had never been anybody special ... Other people did spectacular things ... the risks he had run were the everyday hazards of the war at sea ... Ben had only the regular campaign medals, and a set of confidential reports that were satisfactory; neither outstanding nor peculiarly bad.
>
> (*Ibid.*, pp. 36–7)

The novel begins at the point of Ben's demobilization, and with the loss of self-esteem in the face of a literal and metaphorical redundancy, which is not ameliorated by the fact that it is shared by a generation of men:

> Ben read a newspaper article in which he and the other ex-officers were referred to as The Lost Men of Britain. Everybody was sorry for him, it seemed, but what use was that? He did not want to be treated like a paraplegic charity case. He wanted a decent job ...
>
> (*Ibid.*, p. 71)

The deflation of masculine pride is shown as compounded by a national and public indifference to the situation of war conscripts. Ben's search for a brilliant career sharply demonstrates that there are few opportunities suitable for ex-Servicemen, and particularly those of the officer class. The 'resettlement officer' has only a limited set of options: 'some nice lines to offer in the way of sanitary inspection, or personnel officer in a cement works on the upper Tyne' (*ibid.*, p. 64).

The narrative charts Ben's experience of a series of unsuitable jobs, and so maps out in brief snapshots the dreariness and lack of promise in the rationed world of post-war England. Each job is in some way shady and unsatisfactory. Ben works briefly (and innocently) for a scam involving insurance and pensions for ex-Servicemen; he then mixes with a marginal population of unskilled workers as a cafeteria worker, and works as secretary to a successful popular novelist and screenwriter. The forms of work that Ben is offered are shown to be lacking in substance and social value: the financial job is run by unscrupulous loan sharks; the novelist is 'lazy and without any artistic conscience'; the cafeteria serves food in 'livid' and unnatural colours. Each job that Ben takes up is seen in some way as part of the 'corrupt brightness' that Richard Hoggart so bewailed in the post-war world (Hoggart, 1976, p. 282).

The blow to male pride experienced with unemployment is also exacerbated by the loss of male camaraderie. Ben, like Oliver, leaves the masculine world of the navy for a world of domesticity and femininity. Barbara Cartland diagnosed contemporary life as pervaded by: 'the terrible enervating atmosphere surrounding modern existence ... stripping the twentieth century male of his virility' (Cartland, 1955, p. 148). Ben is clearly in danger of becoming what Cartland described with horror as the 'over-civilised male of Western Civilisation'. Demobbed from the navy, Ben is confronted (like Oliver) with a life of unalloyed femininity; he lives in a household in which his daughter is brought up by his bohemian mother-in-law. The jobs that Ben is offered are 'un-masculine'; his role is to service others as a waiter, secretary, salesman. The one job that appeals to him, as warden at a reform school for boys, is not offered to him because he lacks a wife. Ben's girlfriend is an actress who is weekly performing different versions of femininity, and she is surrounded by media effeminacy. If Ben and Oliver are represented as feminized to some degree by their post-war experience, they are presented as emphatically not homosexual.

The acquisition of a reconfigured male identity, and the antidote to the inauthenticity and disillusion of civilian life, are found in the novel in a nostalgia for a pre-war world. It is Ben's return to a pre-war fantasy that provides the romantic, career and familial resolution to the novel; he ends the novel in a new relationship with the daughter of the house that he has watched from a train window since childhood. Like Oliver's childhood home, the house represents a continuity with a pre-war past and offers a secure and stable image of middle-class Englishness:

> he had travelled on this line hundreds of times, and knew all its landmarks ... There was one house on the London side of Basingstoke which never changed. The same family had lived in it for as long as Ben could remember, and the house itself remained the same, neither prosperous nor down at heel, unaffected by wars or weather or the growing up of the family ...
>
> (Dickens, 1962, pp. 41–2)

This happy ending is equivocal and promises little more than a form of masculinity that is comfortable but unspectacular and an English family tradition that will continue. Ben finally finds fulfilment in family, the rural and the domestic, but ends the novel bleakly reconciled to an unexceptional life; the novel ends: 'He was not clever at all. Not clever enough to find and keep a job that would offer security, success, any kind of position in the world ... Happier being nobody very special' (*ibid.*, p. 267).

A similarly bleak acceptance of the constraints on post-war masculinity is to be found in the novels of Storm Jameson. Andrew Daubney is the hero of the 1952 *The Green Man*, who begins the novel 'unashamedly happy, whipped along by his energy' (Jameson, 1952, p. 3). The novel is written from the retrospect of 1947, but begins with Andrew's gilded youth as an undergraduate at Oxford in 1930. Andrew is the heir to a landed property:

> Daubney House with a hundred acres of garden and rough fields, three hundred acres of moor, gorse, bracken and a single farm, the home farm, with its orchard, two hundred acres of pasture running downhill into admirable rich fields ...
>
> (*Ibid.*, p. 55)

The estate is represented as already in decline in the pre-war years, but nonetheless signifies a nostalgic glow of English childhood happiness throughout the novel. As for Oliver and Ben, the family house represents a mythical resolution of tradition and modernity; it is constructed as a repository of memories which acts as a bulwark against the threats of the post-war world:

> he was set as his father on keeping the house alive, and with it its memory of childhoods and the future – since past and future grow together inextricably, the one lives only through the other, and a future not pulsing with memory is a poor deathly thing. But the house was worth saving because it had its own meaning. Nowadays, when so much of our lives is dull, repetitive, a copy of copies without energy or salt, *one* such thing is worth saving.
>
> (*Ibid.*, p. 567)

However, unlike the heroes of Dickens's novels, Jameson's hero is unable to 'keep the house alive'. The final section of the novel, set in 1946–7, sees the main house succumbing to the demands of contemporary commerce; it becomes an anonymous business office which has erased any human or family history: 'any living use of the house would have been better than this rigidifying into a business headquarters, where the caretaker was the only tenant' (*ibid.*, p. 734).

Andrew can only keep the pre-war family traditions going in a severely truncated form: he devotes himself to farming the land in the Home Farm that once was a small part of the manor house. The novel ends in an uneasy reconciliation of the future and the past, in a more self-consciously literary version of Dickens's description of Ben's reconciliation to the unexceptional life. Andrew, like Ben and Oliver, denigrates his own heroism as commonplace. Although the novel charts his hospitalization after being shot down, Andrew's own version of his war is that: 'He was lucky, he had a war he enjoyed. Not a dull moment' (*ibid.*, p. 318). While Jameson's Andrew asserts himself as a lucky man, and sees his wartime survival as a cause for thankfulness, there is nonetheless a stubborn contradiction in the novel's final lines, where Andrew's assent to the modern world is given grudgingly:

> The trick is to be alert – to accept ... to be believing, lucid, sceptical, patient, amused, humble. No, no, I'm showing off, he thought lightly, all I mean is that, at all costs, we go on, we try to get through ... My God, how happy I am, he thought, how fortunate, and – he sought for a word – how I have been let off.
>
> (*Ibid.*, pp. 754–5)

Jameson's novel *A Cup of Tea for Mr Thorgill*, explores the loss of certainties for contemporary masculinity in a more explicitly political narrative. Written in 1957, a year after the Soviet invasion of Hungary and the consequent disillusion in Europe with Soviet policy, the novel takes on the effects of a loss of faith in Communist Party politics. It is also preoccupied with the impact of post-war class mobility. The novel traces an Oxford scholarship boy, Rigden, who is the son of a 'casual labourer bringing up his family in a London slum, in two rooms' (Jameson, 1957, p. 4). Rigden is the contemporary scholarship boy, coping with the snobbery of Oxford and with the acquisition of a cultural capital not shared with his family. There is a painful dimension to his disdain for the 'shiny barbarism', in Hoggart's phrase, of the mass production of the post-war reconstruction, which his family has embraced:

> His sister's little house was new, its bricks scarcely grimed yet; the small rooms were light, no boards grey with ancient dust, no suffocating unpleasant smell. Most of the furniture was new and only too believably copied from a bad copy ... They pleased Catherine now, and although she might suspect that he admired them a little less, she could have no notion how much less.
>
> (Jameson, 1957, p. 62)

The working-class Rigden has been a Communist Party supporter since the 1930s, but in the aftermath of 1956, the contemporary party politics of Communism are seen in the novel as murky and damaging. It is Rigden's rigid and unwavering support for the Communist Party that loses him everything gained from the opportunities offered in the post-war democracy; the academic career that the welfare state allowed him, and the upper-class, educated woman that post-war social mobility enabled him to marry.

The Thorgill of the title is the moral centre of the novel; an old academic socialist whose politics cannot be rehabilitated into the new democratic consensus, he typifies what Hoggart describes as 'A middle-class Marxist's view of the working classes ... part-pitying and part-patronizing' (Hoggart, 1976, p. 5). Thorgill is represented as a relic of a bygone era of principle, espousing a form of socialism that cannot adapt to modern times. Political faith is no more certain in this novel than was Andrew's faith in the family home in *The Green Man*, and neither can offer their heroes any consolation.

If Monica Dickens and Storm Jameson write about lost illusions from a male point of view, Iris Murdoch goes further in the 1954 novel *Under the Net* (Murdoch, 1967), and assumes a male voice with a male first-person narrator. Murdoch's anti-hero, Jake, also suffers from a loss of conviction and of virility. The novel begins with Jake returning to a grey and bureaucratic London from France. Jake's 'lazy' talent is more than the product of La Nausée (in Jean-Paul Sartre's title), of post-war existential angst – although he does know the Paris Left Bank well, and drinks at the Brasserie Lipp. Jake's disenchantment is with post-war Britain. The only magic to be found in London is in the world of illusions, the theatre and the cinema, but those illusions are literally paper-thin. The pre-war theatre has been displaced by the dead hand of post-war bureaucracy, the carnivalesque props and scenery discarded by an incoming welfare state office. The film studio can only offer cheap reproductions of civilization and of art; a backdrop of the city of Rome is made of 'plastic and Essex board'.

Jake spends the novel at large in London, over the course of several weeks (rather than the months of Dickens's *Man Overboard*). A vague desire for a woman who is destined for Hollywood and a vague search for an old friend link the narrative episodes, but without much conviction. Work and money are not hard to come by: friends appear and easily lend money, financial windfalls keep coming; opportunities present themselves. Jake travels through a London which offers him a range of different worlds: the Mayfair flat of a British screen star, the pubs of Cheapside, a film studio in South London, philosophy discussion groups in the Goldhawk Road, experimental theatre in Hammersmith. Each seems to promise excitement and intellectual engagement, but like Meursault in Albert Camus's *The Outsider*, Jake remains unengaged and isolated throughout, experiencing only 'a sentimental loneliness' (Murdoch, 1967, p. 188). He shares the resolute ordinariness of other fictional heroes of the period, and describes his wartime injuries with a similar dismissive briskness: 'I have shattered nerves. Never mind how I got them. That's another story, and I'm not telling you the whole story of my life. I have them; and one effect of this is that I can't bear being alone for long' (*ibid.*, p. 21).

Neither Jake's shattered nerves nor how he got them are dwelt on in the novel; they merely become a part of his generalized ennui. Although he is involved in what initially seem to be intellectually stimulating literary and bohemian circles, Jake remains unambitious and unengaged. He is described by one associate as 'a talented man who is too lazy to work'. 'A literary hack', in his own description, Jake Donahue is a writer who finds it easier to translate the work of others than to produce any original work of his own. As Jake returns to London, he and his manuscripts are turfed out of the house he once shared with a woman who is now about to marry a bookmaker, an image of commerce supplanting the intellectual. Jake's writings, however, like Thorgill's politics, belong to a previous age of illusion:

> the time when I had ideals. At that time too it had not yet become clear to me that the present age was not one in which it was possible to write an epic ... [N]othing is more paralysing than a sense of historical perspective, especially in literary matters.
>
> (*Ibid.*, p. 19)

Political engagement is also seen to belong to a pre-war age of innocence. Once in the Young Communist League, Jack is now an uninvolved Labour Party member, but as his friend 'Lefty' points out – trying to recruit him to what seems to be the New Left: 'you hold left-wing opinions but take no active part in politics' (*ibid.*, p. 96).

Redemption for Jake is found in the world of work; he takes an unskilled job as a hospital orderly on a passing whim and, like Ben, takes pleasure in the menial tasks of washing up and mopping down floors in the service of others. There is a pride in 'not only ... having got the job, but also in the efficient way in which I turned out to be able to perform it' (*ibid.*, p. 203). The world of work is, however, a feminized place – the hospital dominated by women, the Ward Matron, the nurses – and Jake is shown as emasculated: 'the nurses ... none of them took me seriously as a male. I exuded an aroma which, although we got on so splendidly, in some way kept them off; perhaps some obscure instinct warned them that I was an intellectual' (*ibid.*, p. 204). To be an intellectual is not seen as masculine in the modern world. Jake's intellectual labours do not play any part in the post-war reconstruction and are not necessary to it; while the hospital, feminized as it is, is an emblem of the welfare state and of a new independence for women.

Like Dickens's Ben, Jake has a need to work, and takes a satisfaction in manual labour, whatever form it might take. Physical work engenders its own sense of satisfaction:

> I could combine a considerable feeling of tiredness with a feeling which was almost entirely new to me, that of having *done* something. Such intellectual work as I have ever accomplished has always left me with a sense of having achieved nothing.
>
> (*Ibid.*, p. 208)

This novel also has an equivocal ending. Jake comes to a renewed sense of his intellectual work, but also comes to recognize his own and the social need for manual labour. In an uneasy reconciliation of physical and intellectual forms of work, the novel attempts a pragmatic response to the demands of post-war democracy, and tentatively suggests that this compromise might provide a bulwark against the threat of ennui:

> It occurred to me that to spend half the day doing manual work might be very calming to the nerves of one who was spending the other half doing intellectual work, and I could not imagine why I had not thought before of this way of living, which would ensure that no day could pass without *something* having been done, and so keep that sense of uselessness which grows in prolonged periods of sterility, away from me for ever.
>
> (*Ibid*., p. 209)

A shared 'sense of uselessness' pervades the representation of masculinity in these British novels, each novelist offering her own version of how these men might adapt to the loss of a sense of purpose. There is a structural regularity in these novels of a male protagonist on a journey through post-war England, in which he is confronted with the possibilities of different worlds and with different modes of being. Each of these women writers has their preferred mode of writing and their own set of priorities: for Barbara Cartland, it is romance; for Monica Dickens, a form of professional realism; Storm Jameson's concerns are with the politics of the left; Iris Murdoch's with philosophical problems. But the consolations of philosophy, of politics, career and romance are seen as no longer adequate to the needs of the British post-war man. In each of these novels, the loss of illusion and of male certainties are answered with a reversion to a nostalgic construction of 'authenticity', an authenticity that is to be found in the traditions of manual labour, family, and heritage, traditions which the impact of war had threatened.

The significance of the 'Home Front' to the British war effort and the bombing of British cities meant that the fact of war was inescapable for all women in England, and not only those who were mobilized to serve in the forces. For American women writers, the war could not be as direct an experience as it was for their British counterparts, although the war effort did involve large numbers of American women workers, and gave them the opportunity to work in previously male-dominated industries. With the entry of America into the war in 1941, a new image of the American woman worker, 'Rosie the Riveter', became prevalent, and by 1944, seven million women who had 'previously been full time homemakers' (Rowbotham, 1997, p. 252) went to work for the first time. American women were not, however, conscripted into the war effort as British women were, and for many of them, the war could remain a remote geographical event. For those not involved in war work and who did not have a husband or partner fighting overseas, the war had little impact on their everyday lives. The two best-selling women writers of the post-war period in America both present narratives of happily married women 'homemakers', which became iconic images of American domesticity. While 80 per cent of these new women workers wanted to remain in work at the end of the war, the prevailing ethos was that they should return to the home. The idyllic domesticity of the 'Claudia' novels fitted this ideology neatly.

The eponymous first novel of Rose Franken's hugely successful 'Claudia' series was published in 1938, billed as: 'The famous story of America's most lovable young wife and her warm and wonderful marriage' (Franken, 1962, front cover). The story of the child-bride Claudia and her romance and marriage to the older and wiser David was to develop into a sequence of eight novels, which went on to appear and reappear in a variety of compilations, compendiums and revised versions throughout the 1950s. Each novel was a best-seller, and they remained in print right up until 1972. The first novel became a Broadway play and was filmed in 1943 (*Claudia*, 1943, dir. William Perlberg), and the second novel followed, with a script by Franken, in 1946 (*Claudia and David*, 1946, dir. William Perlberg). 'Claudia' stories were published in magazines such as *Redbook* and *Good Housekeeping* in the 1950s, and were turned into a radio and then television series. In the words of the archivists of Franken's papers, Claudia and David 'have become part of the contemporary cultural fabric' of America (Rare Book and Manuscript Library, Columbia University. www.library-columbia.edu., accessed 2002).

The war does not register at all on Claudia and David's relationship in the early volumes of the sequence, which were later revised to take more account of historical events. Claudia's focus in these novels remains entirely on the house and family: 'she was only vaguely interested in the life that lay outside the house' (Franken, 1962, p. 39). The house cannot, however, entirely avoid the intrusion of 'life' outside. The family's loyal retainers are German, but it does not cross Claudia or David's minds to question why this German couple might be in America, or occur to them that Fritz and Bertha could be Jewish refugees (although Franken was herself Jewish, and this would have been highly probable in 1938). Claudia merely remarks: 'I'm glad we're not German' (*ibid.*, p. 6). Claudia is vaguely aware of political events in the world, but far too preoccupied with her household to ponder them further. The 'realities' of life for her are her husband and family:

> it was a full-time job to learn to keep house properly and for months she didn't think about anything else. She tried to be concerned about the war in China, and what Hitler was doing in Europe, and Roosevelt in America, but she could not completely down the conviction that the crystallized, essence of life and reality lay in the loving of two people and the building of a home.
>
> (*Ibid.*, p. 5)

David, 'who read a lot', does have some intimation of 'a world going crazy' (*ibid.*, p. 98), but chooses to protect his young wife from difficult knowledge, and Claudia does not enquire further. Claudia's brother and sister-in-law do discuss 'inflation, and would the United States get into the war, which was silly, as of course it wouldn't said Claudia' (*ibid.*, p. 207). Claudia despises a relationship in which 'they didn't have anything to talk about except war and politics' (*ibid.*, p. 208), and reflects contentedly on her happiness with David. In the volumes which chart the early years of her marriage, Claudia is content, if slightly guiltily, to leave world events at a remote distance:

> Personally, Claudia couldn't keep track of all the upset and felt that it was fortunate that David knew enough for both of them. She often thought how dreadful it was to be so pleased with life when there was war and persecution and unemployment going on in the universe, but now that she was pregnant, she felt justified in enjoying each day to the fullest.
>
> (*Ibid.*, p. 98)

By the appearance of *Young Claudia* in 1946, however, 'all the upset' has intruded directly into the family home. As her story extends over several novels, even Claudia's blissfully happy marriage cannot remain entirely immune to the impact of war. In *Young Claudia* (a novel that was to be later inserted into the already existing sequence), David has been called up to serve overseas, in some unspecified 'Islands'. The war remains a remote geographical event for Claudia, experienced largely as the pain of David's absence. Nonetheless, Claudia has had to learn to become self-sufficient without her husband, and to manage their farm holding on her own. The novel begins with a rather ambivalent reassertion of David's masculine authority, although he is absent:

> she could hear David add hedge-cutting to the list of things women shouldn't be allowed to do. True, the war had put quite a dent into that list, but according to her knowledge of David, he was not going to change his mind about the fundamental laws of nature, war or no war. That thoroughly reactionary quality in him was what made him the ideal male ... [A]s far as Claudia was concerned, David was perfect in spite of his pig-headed ideas.
>
> (Franken, 1972, p. 5)

The once unquestioning child-bride has acquired a measure of self-sufficiency. Claudia is indeed cutting the hedge, despite her husband's injunction, and begins to suspect 'Perhaps ... David did not want her to grow up' (*ibid.*, p. 111). Claudia has acquired many of the manual skills that the war has added to the list of things women now have to do: 'she had learned how to handle the tractor and the milking machine' (*ibid.*, p. 5). David's wartime experiences are not dwelt upon, because, as for the British returning soldiers, 'modesty' is the valued quality in a man, a modesty that requires silence. For Claudia the war remains an incomprehensible and distant disruption to normal life: 'War. War was something she must have dreamed, fabricated out of the monstrous legends of history books. Battles lost, battles won, convoys sunk, convoys saved' (*ibid.*, 1972, p. 15).

Like his British comrades in arms, David has returned to his family more fragile than he was. Weakened by malaria, he has to confront his 'inadequacy as a wage earner' and face the prospect of unemployment. Throughout this novel in the 'Claudia' sequence there is a new concern for David's masculine 'pride' that is directly attributed to the war: 'Pride ... had always been David's weakness and the war had aggravated it into a disease' (*ibid.*, p. 27). Claudia learns to negotiate her new independence with great delicacy; she is able to recognize that her situation is not unique, but shared by a generation: 'All over the world, men would be coming home to families who had learned to live without them. "If women don't go back to being women", she thought, "it will turn the whole world topsy-turvy"' (*ibid.*, p. 23).

It is the potential revival of Claudia's career as an actress that presents the most serious threat to David's authoritative masculinity and to the womanhood that was happy to stay in the home. Claudia had apparently cheerfully given up the stage for her marriage in the first novel, but starring opportunities in summer stock, Hollywood and Broadway, remarkably, continue to come her way. Although Franken was herself a very successful playwright, the theatre is here once again structured as an image of the inauthentic, the artifice of 'that tinsel paradise' set against the 'realities' of family life. The novel ends with the conception of Claudia's third child, in a neat device which puts paid to any future theatrical ambitions. Claudia sternly resolves that 'it is the right of soldiers to come home and find the wholeness of a life that they had fought to preserve' (*ibid.*, p. 19). It is Claudia's task to uphold that way of life, and to become, once again, the dutiful wife.

Betty MacDonald's *The Egg and I* was to become another classic American text of post-war domesticity, and to prove as popular a version of contemporary American femininity as that of the 'Claudia' novels. The novel was also repeatedly reprinted and made into a film in 1947 (*The Egg and I*, 1947, dir. Chester Erskine), and the subsidiary characters of Ma and Pa Kettle later went on to star in their own sequence of nine feature films, produced by Universal Studios from 1949 to 1957. Although written in 1945, MacDonald's memoir of rural life on a chicken farm was able to ignore the Second World War entirely; there is a brief reference to 'draft dodgers during World War 1' (MacDonald, 1947, p. 132), but none at all to army recruitment in the Second World War. Ma Kettle describes her sons' evasion of the 'Government men who had come out to get my boys to enlist' (*ibid.*) and leaves it historically vague as to which war it is that the boys are avoiding, in a clear suggestion that either war was of very little significance to the lives of contemporary rural Americans.

MacDonald's caustic account of her husband's venture into chicken farming in the mountains of Washington State established a form for the narrative of a city woman finding her way in rural life (which was later to become a model for the American small-town novel of the 1990s). The Washington setting of the farm is constructed as a timeless world of rural eccentrics, animal husbandry and 'mountain farm tradition' (*ibid.*, p. 76), which evokes the sturdy qualities of the American women pioneers. The first-person narrator, 'Betty', dutifully recounts the domestic and farming duties that are required of her, but if she does not undertake them entirely gracefully, she does accept her husband's authority without question. The first section of the narrative is subtitled 'Such Duty' and prefaced with a Shakespearean quote of a woman's duty to her husband; if there is an ironic tinge to this, it is one of grudging acceptance rather than refutation. Betty's marriage does not have the rosy glow of connubial bliss that Claudia finds with David; her husband is a remote presence in the text. There is an intense loneliness in Betty's account of her rural life and a real sense of distance between herself and her husband Bob: 'Bob and I were poles apart as far as emotions were concerned' (*ibid.*, p. 283). The mutuality of the 'companionate marriage' (Collins, 2003, pp. 168–70) that was such an ideal for the post-war British couple is not evident in either Claudia or Betty's loyal devotion to her man. In post-war America, Claudia and Betty's marriages and their domestic rural lives provided a model that answered to the suburban ideal of family life.

Those ideals of family prosperity and the dutiful wife could not be sustained in the British context of rationing and a soaring divorce rate. In both Britain and America, however, the aftermath of the war meant relations between men and women needed to be reconfigured and masculinity re-evaluated; even Claudia's ideal husband David is less certain of his role. What it meant to be a hero could no longer, as with so many other apparent social certainties, be taken for granted. In his 1981 autobiography, John Osborne quoted an editorial from his school magazine, which was written at the war's end:

> **EXCELSIOR**
> And how time has marched on since our last issue. VE Day, VJ Day, a Socialist Parliament, the Atomic Bomb. What next? ... even the blindest of us must see the utter necessity of holding onto decent ideals and humane principles, each and every one of us, as never before.
>
> (Osborne, 1981, p. 149)

For the generation of men and women who fought in the war, confronted with the knowledge of the Holocaust and of Hiroshima, it was no longer clear what those 'decent ideals and humane principles' might be. The British men in these narratives travel through the options available to them in the brave new world of the post-war welfare state, in search of a way to be a man of principle. The old certainties of politics, philosophy and class can no longer provide the frame for a male identity, and the only source of consolation in these novels is to be found in the past; these are men, who like Murdoch's Jake, are paralysed by 'a sense of historical perspective'. The recurrent ending of these *Bildungsromans* is one of a male acceptance of the need for continuity, and of reconciliation to the commonplace. This is the generation of men who are faced with both their own and a social repression of their experiences in wartime. It is the later generation, the Angry Young Men, who are in a position to refuse to 'endure the contemporary anger'. It is the later figures of Jimmy Porter, Arthur Seaton and Joe Lampton who will not stand for the 'lucid, sceptical, patient, amused and humble' masculinity that Storm Jameson recommended and which is offered in these novels as the proper way to be a man. Women's novels of the period represent a generation of men who are unable to mourn, and who therefore remain stuck in melancholia.

2

'Mothers Without Partners': The Single Mother Novel of the 1960s

If the 1950s novel was preoccupied with the status of the single man, it was the single woman who was to become the object of analysis in the 1960s. The single mother was the focus of official and popular discourse in Britain throughout the decade, an 'issue' for moralists and legislators and for fiction. Barbara Cartland in 1957 was already bemoaning what she saw as the alarming increase in the number of children born 'outside wedlock' (Cartland, 1957). The moral panic in the contemporary media surrounding the 'gymslip mother' was much overstated. Although it was statistically the case that births outside marriage had risen since the 1950s, the numbers were relatively few: 6 per cent of births 'outside marriage in the UK' (Office for National Statistics, 2004). Nevertheless, there was a general consensus that 'moral standards' were in decline; a report from the Committee on Children and Young Persons, published in 1960, asserted: 'there has been a tremendous material, social and moral revolution in addition to the upheaval of two wars ... [W]hat a complete change there has been in social and personal relationships (between classes, between the sexes and between individuals) and also in the basic assumptions which regulate behaviour' (quoted in Marwick, 1982, p. 149).

The single mother was seen as a symptom of the challenge to conventional moral codes, and became a focus for discussions of contemporary social expectations of femininity. In fiction, the position of the single mother was a means of exploring how the generation of young women who grew up with the benefits of the post-war welfare state were to negotiate the contradictory demands of motherhood and independence.

The narrative of the single mother constructs a fictional world in which men are peripheral; the focus is on the choices and experience of a young woman. The early 1960s produced two iconic 'women's' novels which addressed the tensions of femininity through the experience of single motherhood; both were widely disseminated in the period, as films and later as set texts on the school syllabus: *The L-Shaped Room* by Lynne Reid Banks and Margaret Drabble's *The Millstone* (filmed respectively as *The L-Shaped Room* in 1962 and *A Touch of Love* in 1969). Jane, the heroine of *The L-Shaped Room*, and Rosamund, of *The Millstone*, are used to address the situation of 'mothers without partners' (the subtitle of a contemporaneous guidebook written for single mothers). These heroines are emphatically middle class, but they have to learn what it means to be outside what was acceptable in contemporary society. For Jane and Rosamund, single motherhood is a way of exploring what it means to be an independent woman in the early 1960s, but the fact of pregnancy means that this independence is not so much a choice as it is imposed.

While Jane and Rosamund are relatively privileged and financially secure, they are both escaping from conventional morality and distancing themselves from the mores and values of the previous generation. Although highly educated young women, these heroines remain resolutely unaware of the extent to which their situation was under discussion in this period; they deal with their pregnancies as if they were an entirely individual experience, and defiantly choose to go through them alone. The discourse of the condition of the single mother was, however, on the agenda for the Church of England and for sociologists, educationalists and legislators; all were preoccupied with discussions of the 'unmarried mother', the 'fatherless family' and issuing reports on how these could be prevented. As Dr Julia Dawkins, the author of a manual for parents to use with their children, wrote in 1967: 'Arguing and propounding theories about sex and teenagers has become almost a national sport' (Dawkins, 1967, p. 11).

As adult women in the early 1960s, Jane and Rosamund would have been educated before the recognition in Britain of the need for sex education in schools. A 1960 conference of the National Council of Women discussed a motion (put forward by a Salvation Army officer) that proposed sex education for young people, but it was not passed (Brewer, 1962, p. 140). In 1962, the Church of England Board of Education held a conference that did acknowledge a need for sex education in schools, but it remained the policy of Local Education Authorities to leave the decision up to individual head teachers as to whether classes in 'health and hygiene' (a contemporary euphemism for sex education) should be part of the school curriculum. Fay Weldon remembers the extent of sexual ignorance and the perils of sexual encounters in the Britain of the late 1950s and 1960s. As she notes, for many young women, the experience of the early 1960s bore very little relation to the hedonism and sexual exploration now associated with the decade:

> Hard for the new generation to comprehend just how different life was in the late fifties, early sixties, pre-pill, pre-coil, when the man not the woman was in charge of contraception. When the very word was still almost too rude and explicit to be mentioned and body parts were a

> deep mystery to everyone but medical students. There were a few Marie Stopes 'birth control clinics' for women in the major cities, but you had to show a wedding ring to get access to one. Men had condoms, but often preferred not to use them. Abortion was frequent, dangerous and illegal.
>
> (Weldon, 2000, p. 22)

The 1963 handbook *Raising Your Child in a Fatherless Home: A Guidebook for All Mothers without Partners* offers some insight into contemporary attitudes towards illegitimacy and the single mother. Ostensibly sympathetic to its readers' condition, *Raising Your Child in a Fatherless Home* starts off as a breezily positive guide for single mothers, but soon slips into referring to 'illegitimate mothers' and goes on to sternly warn that the relationship between mother and child is fraught with problems in an 'incomplete home' (Jones, 1963, p. 4). While claiming to be liberal and sympathetic, the handbook's author heaps withering blame upon the unmarried mother; she accuses her implied reader of immorality, immaturity and neurosis, indictments which are no less disturbing because they are couched in psychological terminology. This is precisely the kind of book that the middle-class and educated Jane and Rosamund might have read, although there is no reference in the novels to either of them being aware of the range of similar guidebooks dealing with precisely their situation.

Raising Your Child in a Fatherless Home advises that a 'mother without a partner' should construct a narrative to disguise her 'guilty' secret; that she should represent herself as a divorced or widowed woman and should move:

> to a location where your past doesn't play an important role ... After you have moved to a new city, taken a new job, or cut off all friendships with people from your past, you need to present to new people a story about yourself that satisfies their curiosity – lest by creating an air of mystery, you provoke speculation that you are not the widow or divorced mother you present yourself to be. And you also must withstand fear and insecurity about the possibility that some unlucky happening may disclose your real past.
>
> (*Ibid*., p. 34)

Both Jane and Rosamund effectively enact this advice: Jane leaves her father's house and moves to another part of London and Rosamund retreats, 'cutting off all friendships'. She is relieved that her doctorate will mean that her title of 'Dr' disguises her marital status. As Lesley Hall notes, this was a period in which 'The single mother was still a stigmatised figure' (Hall, 2000, p. 171). Once her baby is born, Jane, in the sequel to *The L-Shaped Room*, experiences exactly the 'speculation' Jones describes: 'I was "that sort of girl", irrevocably until I either married or started to tell lies about widowhood' (Reid Banks, 1970, p. 37).

As Stuart Laing has pointed out, while *The L-Shaped Room* offered a new kind of heroine, its scenario was not as original as it first appeared, in that it shared elements of Shelagh Delaney's 1958 play *A Taste of Honey* (Delaney, 1959): '*The L-shaped Room* ... reconstituted the elements of *A Taste of Honey*, pregnant independent girl, a homosexual, a coloured man, a vaguely bohemian ménage, into fiction' (Laing, 1986, p. 79). Written in 1960, on the cusp of the new decade, the novel is in many ways looking back in nostalgia at the 1950s and the Angry Young Man, to whom there are frequent references. The narrative begins with the heroine, Jane, arriving at the dingy bed-sitting room of the title, a scene which evokes Joe Lampton's arrival in Dufton in John Braine's 1957 novel *Room at the Top* (Braine, 1969). The setting has all the grimness of post-war London:

> It was a greyish sort of day, which suited the way I was feeling, and it looked greyer because the window needed cleaning ... My room was five flights up in one of those gone-to-seed houses in Fulham, all dark brown wallpaper inside and peeling paint outside.
>
> (Reid Banks, 1962, p. 7)

The motley collection of characters in this 'gone-to-seed' house also has connotations of the era of kitchen-sink drama. Toby, the Jewish novelist who is to become Jane's romantic interest, is clearly in the mould of an Angry Young Man, while the black and gay jazz musician John is a character who could belong to Colin MacInnes's 1959 novel *Absolute Beginners*. The father of Jane's baby is a publisher of Angry Young Man fiction. Jane begins the novel, like many heroines of 1950s fiction (see Philips and Haywood, 1998), as a career woman. Like Reid Banks herself, she was once an aspiring actress, and now works as a press secretary in a hotel, a job which is more a matter of a good salary and a means of occupying her time than a source of pride and ambition. Jane's choice of the grim house in Fulham, it is strongly suggested, is a manifestation of her guilt and a recognition that her pregnancy has made her a social pariah:

> I'd instinctively chosen an ugly, degraded district in which to find myself a room. There was the practical aspect of cheapness, I'd never been any good at saving money and the need to do so now was acute. But there was something more to it than that. In some obscure way I wanted to punish myself, I wanted to put myself in the setting that seemed proper to my situation.
>
> (Reid Banks, 1962, p. 36)

The household which contains the L-shaped room is a collection of the 'flotsam' rejected by contemporary respectability: a black jazz musician (who is also homosexual), a Jewish writer, the genteelly impoverished, the basement inhabited by prostitutes. Jane belongs in this environment because of her outsider status as a single mother. The move to this alternative household is prompted by Jane's unwanted pregnancy, but it is also a means of escape from the parental home and from a suffocating father. Jane's mother has died giving birth to her, and her father is grudging about his daughter's stabs at independence. The strength of Jane's resentment at her father is indicated by the use of italics in an extended interior monologue, a silent fury which remains uncommunicated to her father: '*The day I took my first secretarial job you told me I'd never stick it, that any girl who could be content to sit behind a typewriter all day must be a cretin ... What do you want of me, Father?* I thought fiercely, *What have you ever wanted?*' (*ibid.*, p. 24).

Jane's feelings on leaving the parental home are a mixture of elation and guilt, a psychological confusion which is sustained throughout the novel. Over the course of the narrative, the household transforms from a threatening and grim environment into a louche and bohemian alternative world. As Jane begins to overcome her prejudices she comes to feel affection for all the house's inhabitants and to form a romantic attachment to the Jewish writer, Toby. The narrative takes care to establish Jane's liberal and modern credentials. Her initial contempt for Toby is not because he is a Jew, but because he has anglicized his name. Confronted by John, the black musician in the next room, she is initially scared but self-aware enough to berate herself for her first reaction. Despite Jane's professed liberalism and her espousal of Judaism, a vestigial racism is tangible through the narrator's professed affection for John. Jane describes him as having a 'powerful negro smell', and Toby, unchallenged by the narrative, compares him to a child and a monkey: 'he's just naturally inquisitive. Like a chimp, you know, he can't help it' (*ibid.*, p. 46). While Jane apparently accepts John's homosexuality, she still sees it as a pitiful condition, perhaps inevitably in a society in which homosexuality was still illegal. While the Wolfenden Report of 1957 had suggested that the state should not intervene in private sexual behaviour, homosexuality was not decriminalized in Britain until the Sexual Offences Act of 1967. As Arthur Marwick has put it: 'The year 1967 was something of an annus mirabilis as far as liberal legislation in the sphere of sexual mores was concerned' (Marwick, 1982, p. 151). The same year saw the Medical Termination of Pregnancy Act, which finally made abortion legal in Britain, as long as it was carried out with the approval of two doctors.

Jane has the income and the knowledge to find a sympathetic doctor who will approve an abortion, even well before the 1967 Act. As Sheila Rowbotham notes: 'a semi-legal practice had developed for women who could pay, making it blatantly obvious that there was one law for the rich and another for the poor' (Rowbotham, 1997, p. 360). Jane does have the income to access this 'semi-legal' practice, and visits a reputable doctor who in coded language indicates his willingness to procure a safe abortion. Jane's motivation in rejecting this option is unclear; her antipathy towards the doctor, it is strongly suggested, is informed by her anger at her father. Writing from the retrospect of 1976, Reid Banks was later to wonder at her refutation of abortion as an option: 'looking back on it fifteen years or so later ... neither Jane nor I knew what we were doing. If I had known what bringing up children ... was actually like, I doubt if I could have ended the book so glibly, nor dismissed the abortionist so indignantly' (Reid Banks, 1976, p. ix). If the novel is finally compromised by the limits of legality and of liberalism in 1960, *The L-Shaped Room* was significant in that it did allow for an unapologetic expression of female desire, and that it was not at all judgemental about Jane's pregnancy. Jane may not experience any pleasure from the conception of her baby, but the scenes with her lover, Toby, are erotic and tender.

Jane and Rosamund are highly educated young women (their intelligence and qualifications repeatedly noted in the narratives); however, both protagonists experience their pregnancy and the early stages of motherhood in splendid and self-inflicted isolation, largely dismissing any state or social support that would have been available to them. *The Millstone*, first published in 1965, was Drabble's third novel. It was to be reprinted every year and, like *The L-Shaped Room*, was to become a school set text. Drabble later wrote an introduction to the school edition in which she claims that the subject of single motherhood was incidental:

> The story of *The Millstone* is very simple. It's about a girl who has a baby. The baby is an illegitimate baby, but to me, as I wrote it, I don't think that was the main point at all ... In a sense the fact that the girl in the book isn't married is almost accidental – it's just one of the circumstances I chose for her, when I started to write. It was far more important to me that she was a lonely, proud and isolated person, and the fact that she wasn't married was simply an aspect of this loneliness.
>
> (Drabble, 1970, p. vii)

This is a disingenuous claim, even if written from the retrospect of 1970. By 1965 the situation of the 'mother without partner' and the illegitimate child was very firmly on the social and educational agenda. Novels and films such as *The L-Shaped Room* had firmly established the single mother as a topical subject. Single motherhood was even the theme of a children's novel published a few months before *The Millstone*, Josephine Kamm's *Young Mother* (Kamm, 1965). Like *The L-Shaped Room*, *The Millstone* is narrated in the first person in an intimate conversational style; there is little difference between Rosamund's spoken confidences to friends and the address of the narrative voice to the reader. Rosamund is still more privileged than Jane, her superior education and cultural capital signalled very loudly. We are told that Rosamund is a Cambridge graduate in the second paragraph of the novel, and throughout the text there is a repeated insistence on her intellectual success. Despite Rosamund's academic abilities, her understanding of her body is limited. The sexual experience which results in her pregnancy is, as it is for Jane, joyless, bleakly described as 'two inept, unsatisfactory performances of the sexual act, which gave so little pleasure' (Drabble, 1965, p. 33). Lorna Sage, a real-life intelligent and ambitious young woman, whose pregnancy threatened to disrupt her university career, reiterates that sexual ignorance was prevalent among even the most intelligent young women of this generation (Sage, 2000). None of these women has any understanding of birth control, a situation that is borne out in Geoffrey Gorer's 1969 study *Sex and Marriage in England Today*, in which he found that the majority of sexually active unmarried couples did not use any form of contraception. As Jane does, Rosamund conceives after a single sexual encounter. The father of Rosamund's child is entirely peripheral; he never knows of his parenthood, the conception referred to repeatedly as 'the act'.

Like Jane's flight to the L-shaped room, Rosamund's response to her pregnant state is one of withdrawal. Throughout the novel she is represented as isolated. Although she has sympathetic family and friends, these remain largely absent from the narrative; Rosamund will not allow them to intrude. This isolation is, like Jane's, both a physical and a psychological removal of the self. Rosamund's own assessment is that it is her cleverness that keeps her apart from other people; she refers to 'my isolation (through superiority of intellect) as a child' (Drabble, 1965, p. 18). While apparently modest about her attainments, the reader is left to deduce that Rosamund is an academic star. Rosamund's intellect is used throughout the novel as a means of distinguishing her from the experience of 'ordinary' women. Rosamund is loath to join the ranks of women who have come to 'the peasant acceptance of physical life' (*ibid.*, p. 57), and she expresses a real distaste for the pregnant bodies of other women. She constantly differentiates herself through her status as an intellectual woman, even her body has a superior recovery rate after giving birth: 'the muscles of my belly snapped back into place without a mark, but some of the women looked as big as they had before' (*ibid.*, p. 109).

Rosamund's intelligence, class and financial situation are all used to disconnect her from the ordinariness of pregnancy and childbirth. As Tess Cosslett has pointed out, Rosamund is a very privileged single mother: '*The Millstone* enacts a repudiation of the other women encountered through the NHS, in terms of class and of maternity ... [S]he easily escapes the physical and social problems that weigh down the other women' (Cosslett, 1994, p. 94). Rosamund's environment is very different from the Fulham bed-sitting room which offers Jane a form of (alternative) community; instead, her experience of pregnancy takes place in a central London mansion flat that belongs to her parents, who are conveniently absent in Africa. Rosamund's position as a postgraduate student allows her to evade a fixed class definition; she is at a point of transition, her status and lifestyle still to be confirmed. She does, however, have an income in her own right, derived from her intellectual capabilities: 'about five hundred a year in various grants and endowments' (Drabble, 1965, p. 9). Rosamund has considerably more than the 'room of one's own' that Virginia Woolf advocated for the woman writer. Rosamund clearly has, as Jane does, the wealth and knowledge to find a doctor to perform an abortion, but although she gets as far as obtaining an address of a sympathetic doctor, she chooses not to proceed (a recurrent trope in these novels). Associating the medical profession with moral disapproval, Rosamund opts for the gin bottle instead, a half-hearted attempt at self-induced abortion that is doomed to fail because of her naiveté about her own body. Rosamund is statistically unusual as a graduate in seeing her pregnancy through; an American survey had found that in a 1959 sample of college educated women, only 2 per cent of such pregnancies ended in birth (Gebhard et al., 1959, p. 62). Rosamund's financial and cultural capital give her a defence against intrusive encounters with state provision for pregnant women; she is entirely dismissive of a doctor's suggestion that she should contact the National Council for Unmarried Mothers. While Rosamund is clearly positioned as a child of the brave new world of the post-1945 Labour government, she constantly expresses scorn for anything that the welfare state could provide. Although a young woman of the 1960s, Rosamund is less bohemian and liberal than her parents; she betrays a class snobbery in her dismissive mistrust of their

> extraordinary blend of socialist principle and middle class scruple ... the way they brought us up, they were quite absurd, the way they stuck to their principles, never asking us where we'd been when we got back at three in the morning, sending us to state schools, having everything done on the National Health, letting us pick up horrible cockney accents, making the charlady sit down and dine with us, introducing her to visitors, all that kind of nonsense. My God, they made themselves suffer. And yet at the same time they were so nice, so kind, so gentle.
> (Drabble, 1965 p. 27)

While dismissing the liberal-left ethos of her parents, Rosamund is equally despising of the middle-class conventional lifestyle represented by her brother and his wife, who provide the only note of social disapproval that she encounters. Rosamund does ally herself with her parents' principles to the extent that she names her baby after Octavia Hill: 'one of those heroines of feminism and socialism' (*ibid.*, p. 170). Feminism, however, remains a politics that belongs to a previous generation, a maternal legacy that represents a burden rather than a liberation: 'My mother, you know, was a great feminist. She brought me up to be equal. She made there be no questions, no difference. I was equal. I am equal ... I have to live up to her, you know' (*ibid.*, p. 29).

Feminism is hardly a part of Rosamund's thinking about her own situation and pregnant state, and intrudes even less into her academic work; she is working on sixteenth-century poetry, an area of study far removed from her personal life. As Clare Hanson has pointed out: 'The novel charts the progress, side by side, of her thesis and her pregnancy, and shows how the pregnancy brings knowledge and experience which cannot be articulated within the terms of academic discourse' (Hanson, 2000, p. 6). There is, however, no sense in the novel that this knowledge could itself become part of Rosamund's academic life. Scholarship is for Rosamund an end in itself; it has no political or feminist edge. This is an era before there is any concept of women's studies as an academic discipline.

The novel structures a clear opposition between femininity and the body and the intellect and academia. Rosamund's pregnancy is initially suffused with negative connotations, derived from popular fiction, magazines and mythology. The implication of the narrative is that motherhood initiates Rosamund into a more authentic world, but she still resolutely refuses to join a communality of femininity, holding fast to her exceptional status as a successful woman academic. A contemporary review of *The Millstone* endorsed the disjunction between woman and scholar that is such an organizing principle of the narrative:

> The form of Margaret Drabble's cool and lucid novels is becoming familiar. She takes a clever, classy, arty but essentially self-contained modern girl and treats us to an exposition of her very reasoned and ordered inward musings. She has captured the essence of a certain kind of intellectual miss: half scholar, half woman and ceaseless cerebrating.
>
> (*Times Literary Supplement*, 1965, p. 820)

For Dominic Head, *The L-Shaped Room* and *The Millstone* represent 'serious fiction' which addresses contemporary shifts in gender relations: 'the certainties of gender relations are beginning to be questioned anew in serious fiction; in such a context the glimmerings of feminist assertion are significant ... a dawning feminist consciousness is dramatised' (Head, 2002, p. 85). It is, however, overstating the case to claim that these novels are indicative of a 'dawning feminist consciousness'. Both Jane and Rosamund firmly elect to deal with their situation on their own; there is no sense in either novel of a sisterhood, or of any willingness to share female experience. These are novels written in the early 1960s, before the upsurge of the Women's Liberation Movement; the first Women's Liberation conference was not to take place in Britain until 1970 at Ruskin College, Oxford. If Drabble and Reid Banks do write about independent heroines who cope, they do not yet have the language or sensibility of a feminist consciousness.

The discourses of gender relations and shifts in the role of women were not only dealt with in fiction that Head would accept as 'serious'; the dominance of the 'single mother' in contemporary discourses of femininity inevitably found its way into women's writing across the range of contemporary women's fiction. Andrea Newman is best known for her torrid melodrama *A Bouquet of Barbed Wire*, published in 1969, but her earlier 1966 novel *The Cage* (Newman, 1978) deals with an unwanted pregnancy and its impact on the ambitions of an intelligent middle-class young woman. Val, unlike Rosamund, has to make a choice between university life and motherhood. Val may be less of an academic high-flyer than Rosamund, but she is nonetheless a credit to the educational system and a model of schoolgirl achievement:

> I did eight 'O' levels, then three 'A' levels and scholarship and entrance to Oxford and Cambridge, who as it turned out didn't want me, and London, who did ... I 'played a full part', as they say, in the life of the school. I was form captain five times. I was captain of tennis, netball and swimming teams. I did a lot of acting and wrote articles for the school magazine. I had it all taped; I was so well organised.
>
> (*Ibid*., 1966 p. 27)

Academic achievement offers an escape route from provincial life and menial work, a possibility that is more available to this generation than it was for earlier generations of women. For Val, the idea of university is imbued with romance and excitement and is clearly seen as a means of achieving financial and personal independence:

> To me it was Mecca because it represented so many ambitions: not just studying a subject I loved but obtaining a degree that would make me independent in a way she (my mother) had never been by giving me an earning capacity that could surmount disaster. Not just obtaining a degree but meeting people with my interests among whom I would find the one who made everyone else vanish.
>
> (*Ibid*., p. 110)

Pregnancy disrupts these aspirations, and reduces the ambitious Val to a sociological phenomenon: 'no longer Valerie Ayden, snob, going to university, but Valerie Ayden, unmarried mother' (*ibid*., p. 47). Literary allusions sustain her throughout the pregnancy, evocations of a different kind of life: Swift's misanthropy resonates with her own sense of the world, eighteenth-century writing offers an 'age of reason' that is not to be found in life. A supportive woman teacher sustains Val's academic endeavours, as was the case for Lorna Sage, but unlike Sage, Val is unable to move on to university. The earnest literary references which recur throughout the text offer Val an escape from domestic drudgery and, as they do for Rosamund, serve as a recurrent reminder that the pregnant Val is more than a body, that she also has an intellect.

Val despises her partner for his lack of intellectual ambition (he reads James Bond novels, while she reads *Tom Jones*), but she is alone in these single mother novels in taking pleasure in the sexual act that brings about the pregnancy. While she does not love the father, there is a sustained relationship with him. He supports her and the baby, but the heroine's disdain for him ensures that she goes through the experience of birth largely alone. Unlike Rosamund, Val is condemned to become a 'captive wife' – a term used in the title of Hannah Gavron's study of the housewife, published in the same year (Gavron, 1966) – her degree deferred indefinitely. Val learns exactly what it is that Betty Friedan had earlier described in *The Feminine Mystique* as 'The Problem That Has No Name' (Friedan, 1965): 'I was alone in the house as I had never been before ... [T]his heavy, unknown young woman in her empty flat, mechanically dusting and washing up' (Newman, 1978, p. 112). The novel ends with Val's sullen resignation to her lot, and the promise that her daughter will not have to face the same fate:

> Experiencing this dependence of woman on man has been a giant lesson to me; I swear Vicky will not have to learn it. I'm going to see that she's independent and that nothing cuts across her life as it has across mine. She's going to have a real marriage and a real career – everything she wants, no less.
>
> (*Ibid.*, p. 205)

Like Jane and Rosamund, Val is unclear as to her motives in continuing the pregnancy. None of these novels' protagonists expresses any ethical objections to abortion, and all refuse to censure it, despite its illegality at the time of writing; yet none is prepared to go through an abortion. For Val, as for Jane and Rosamund, the continuation of her pregnancy is not an active decision so much as a refusal to make a choice: 'I had no ethical objections, certainly ... There was a certain doomed inevitability about the whole thing which seemed appropriate' (*ibid.*, p. 33). The heroines of *The L-Shaped Room*, *The Millstone* and *The Cage* all share this sense of 'doomed inevitability', that sexual experience will result in pregnancy. While these novels might be read as morality tales in which the heroine is punished for a single sexual encounter, their conclusions are more equivocal than that; Val's rhetorical question 'Was it a fair punishment?' (Newman, 1978, p. 196) throws out a challenge to the reader that is shared by all these narratives.

The 1967 *Textbook of Sex Education* advises teachers to instruct their pupils that 'illegitimate pregnancy is a tragedy' and should be handled with 'compassion' (Dawkins, 1967, p. 88). While all these protagonists experience conflict and difficulty, their experience of pregnancy and childbirth is emphatically not tragic, and they have no need for compassion. All come to love their children, and all come to some form of resolution. However, with the exception of Rosamund (who is clearly constructed as unusual) these novels cannot yet envisage the possibility of reconciling motherhood with female ambition. A world in which women can be both scholars and mothers is not seen as generally available to this generation of young women, but it is envisaged for their daughters.

The heroines of these novels are relatively fortunate examples of single motherhood, but the discussion of the issue in women's fiction was not restricted to the narrow world of the middle classes and of higher education. Monica Dickens's 1964 novel *Kate and Emma* (Dickens, 1967) is haunted by just the same issues as Ken Loach's 1966 television film, *Cathy Come Home*. *Kate and Emma* is a self-consciously 'social issue' novel that addresses poverty, homelessness and the fear that the authorities could take children away from the mother. At the time of writing the novel Dickens, by then an author of popular fiction, was an observer with agencies involved with child welfare; as she put it in her autobiography, she had 'started going around with inspectors and case workers from the National Society for the Prevention of Cruelty to Children' (Dickens, 1978, p. 162). The novel is clearly based on this experience: the descriptions in the autobiography of 'that terrible English winter of 1963 ... that ironclad winter' (*ibid.*, p. 162) are very close to those of the novel, and the character of the fictional social worker, Johnny Jordan, is clearly based on Dickens's real-life Mr Bowes, down to the use of the same reported conversation in both novel and autobiography.

Kate and Emma can be read as a contemporary morality tale, the character of Kate and her circumstances reminiscent of the pages of reports from the National Council for Unmarried Mothers, with its conviction that illegitimate births are related to class and education. The novel is structured by the parallel narratives of two young women who both relay their stories (as in all these novels) in the first person, but in very different voices. The novel begins from the point of view of the middle-class Emma, the daughter of a magistrate, who first encounters the impoverished Kate in her father's courtroom. Kate is a deprived child, who has been taken into the 'Care and Protection of the Courts' to remove her from her violent family. The narrative traces their friendship into adulthood over the course of five years, as their paths inexorably move in different directions. Emma moves into a career in retail and then a suitable marriage, while Kate becomes a pregnant teenager, marries the father reluctantly and ends the novel with four neglected children and her husband in jail.

Kate's decline into poverty and despair is shown to begin from her first sexual experience. The conception of her first child is, as for the middle-class heroines of *The L-Shaped Room* and *The Millstone*, a loveless affair, a single sexual encounter with a man who is insignificant to her. Despite the illegality of abortion in 1964 and her poverty, like Jane, Rosamund and Val, Kate is aware of ways in which she could end her pregnancy. She briefly considers undergoing an illegal abortion, but while Jane and Rosamund's class and financial status give them the option of a medically sanctioned termination, it is clear that Kate only has access to a backstreet abortionist. As with Jane and Rosamund, there is an ambivalence about terminating the pregnancy. Kate gets to the point of acquiring the address of an illegal abortionist and of borrowing money from a woman friend: 'Just asked if I wanted an address ... One of the Indians. They'll fix you up if you've got the money' (Dickens, 1967, p. 95). Her decision not to be 'fixed up' is less to do with moral scruple than it is with confusion.

Kate's first pregnancy is a guilty secret that she copes with alone, her information and support coming not from social services (although she is very much in the frame of social service care) but from popular magazines, as Rosamund's response to her pregnancy comes from popular fiction. Neither calls on medical or social support until it is absolutely necessary. Kate's mistrust of welfare services is at the opposite end of the class scale from Rosamund's patrician disdain, but both share a resentment at any state intervention into their personal lives. As independent young women, they both perceive medical and welfare officials as the world of 'Them', as described by Richard Hoggart: 'a composite dramatic figure ... the world of the bosses, as is increasingly the case today, public officials' (Hoggart, 1976, p. 72). Kate is made to marry the father of her child by well-meaning representatives of the social services, and is scathing in her appraisal of middle-class professionals and their attempts to support her: 'these women with folders and little cars, their own lives aren't up and down enough, so they get this craving to go out and live in someone else's' (Dickens, 1967, p. 207). Kate perceives state support not as a right but as an unwanted intrusion; there is a stubborn pride in her rejection of any social benefits available to her:

> Marge Collins who lives downstairs, and has three kids in Care by different fathers and has milked every government agency and charitable institution, says I can get baby clothes just for the asking, but no thanks ... They don't stop at baby clothes. They want to rehabilitate you. My life is mine now. I don't want no case workers ferreting out my business.
> (*Ibid.*, p. 158)

There is a tension throughout the novel in that the narrative, through Emma, supports Kate in her stubborn pride, while simultaneously charting her descent into squalor and irresponsible parenthood. Emma finally betrays her friend by calling on social services to place a 'Safety Order' on the eldest child. Despite all the interventions of middle-class support, Kate is finally unable to cope. Middle-class ethics are themselves shown to be under strain; Emma, while she is the voice of moral certainty for much of the novel, is having an affair with a married man. Her father, the respectable magistrate, leaves his complaining wife to set up home with another woman. Emma is equivocal about her marriage to the comfortable American, Joel, which will require her to give up her burgeoning career in marketing: 'He wants me to give up my job ... Then I shall be an Air

Force wife, planning nothing more challenging than Wives Clubs teas' (*ibid.*, p. 215). For readers of Monica Dickens's fiction, this would have an added edge in that the unhappy marriage of an English GI bride to an American Serviceman is enacted in just these terms in her 1953 novel, *No More Meadows*. The contradictions between ambition, motherhood and marriage expressed in that novel are no more resolved a decade later for the women in *Kate and Emma*.

While there is a strong affirmation of the friendship between Kate and Emma (a solidarity between women that is notably absent from the novels by Drabble, Newman and Reid Banks), and their story is told in both their voices, the novel is firmly framed by a middle-class perspective: it is Emma's account of events which begins, ends and dominates the novel. There is a disturbing eugenicist suggestion at the end of the novel that poverty is endemic to women such as Kate. Kate's class dooms her to a life of deprivation in which, despite the best attempts of Emma and of social services, she is made to repeat the experiences of her mother. The novel charts a spiral of abuse, which culminates in Kate reproducing the damage done to her with her own children. The narrative finally endorses, through Emma, Johnny Jordan's understanding of poverty as a natural state, and adds a troubling edge of racism:

> He said then that poverty was a disease. They keep slipping back, he said, like malaria, and I thought he was wrong, but now I am not so sure ... for this is a neighbourhood where immigrants of all nations have come precariously to roost, bringing with them their less savoury habits from home.
>
> (Dickens, 1967, p. 178)

If Nell Dunn is no less a middle-class woman slumming it with the working-class women in *Up the Junction* than Emma or Dickens herself, she does give their voices a greater energy than doomed Kate is ever allowed. The women of *Up the Junction* (1963) and *Poor Cow* (1967) have a raucous exuberance that is entirely lacking in *Kate and Emma* or in Drabble's representations of 'ordinary' women. Kate's story is not dissimilar from that of Joy in Nell Dunn's *Poor Cow*. Joy, like Kate, is not strictly speaking a single mother: she is married to the feckless Tom who, like Kate's husband, is in jail for most of the narrative. While Kate sinks into a quagmire of despair, Joy's is a story of grim survival.

Dunn's writing shares the traces of the casual and unknowing racism found in *Kate and Emma* and *The L-Shaped Room*; in each of these novels the presence of black characters is used to signify poverty and deprivation. While there is a liberal awareness that racist remarks should not be condoned, Dunn's narration claims reportage of working-class voices and there is a marked reluctance to challenge such attitudes. *Up the Junction* first appeared as a series of short stories in the left-wing magazine *New*

Statesman and was screened as a BBC play directed by Ken Loach. The play came under attack from Mary Whitehouse's National Viewers and Listeners Association and the popular press, largely because of its treatment of abortion. The text was filmed in 1967 (*Up the Junction*, 1967, dir. Peter Collinson), with a poster strap-line that foregrounded pregnancy: 'Don't get caught is what she wasn't taught!'

The title of *Up the Junction* evokes the contemporary slang for pregnancy – 'up the duff' – while *Poor Cow* is an epithet that expresses sympathy for a potentially shared condition. Unlike the women in all the other novels, pregnancy is not experienced in these texts as an isolated state, but as one that occurs among a community of women. The first story in *Up the Junction* is titled 'Out with the Girls', in which 'me, Sylvie and Rube' are out on the town. 'Me', the narrator, is a version of Dunn herself, a married 'Chelsea Heiress', a participant observer of working-class women's lives. The next story in the sequence offers an ironic cautionary note of the possible consequences of such a night out: 'Sunday Morning' is set in a home for single mothers and their babies. Here, grisly tales of seduction and attempted abortions are caustically shared among the women.

These discussions of illegal and backstreet abortion are more graphic and painful than anything found in the novels of Reid Banks, Drabble or Dickens. While Rosamund and Jane have the funds and class status to find a sympathetic medical professional and even the deprived Kate is not concerned with the potential physical danger of an illicit termination, for these women abortion is a messy and dangerous business. *Up the Junction* is packed with the prosaic details of chemists who must be lied to, of gin, quinine, and tablets of unknown provenance. The grim actuality of illegal abortion is confirmed through interviews with real women who were sexually active in the early 1960s. Agnes, interviewed in 1976 for the British feminist magazine *Spare Rib*, remembered the shifty doctors, the syringes and the after-effects of botched abortions with bitter clarity, and in very similar terms to those of *Up the Junction* (Rowe, 1982, p. 360).

The 'Poor Cow' of the title of Dunn's later novel is the ironically named Joy. Motherhood, despite her name, is not any source of pleasure to Joy, but a limitation and an obstruction: 'What did I go and get landed with him for, I used to be a smart girl?' (Dunn, 1967b, p. 10). A split narrative voice that shuttles between Joy's first-person account and the third person allows the reader to be party to Joy's dreams and fantasies, but also to critically observe her, much as Kate's story is framed by Emma's perspective. Joy has aspirations, but no idea of how to fulfil them; a 'career' is an abstract desire that she has little sense of how to achieve: 'I wish I had a career. I need one more than anything' (*ibid.*, p. 29). While she has ambitions to take evening classes in Elocution and Deportment, she never gets as far as finding out where they might be held, and the classes never happen.

Joy's dreams and desires are instead shaped by advertisements and popular songs, with contemporary lyrics and advertising slogans scattered throughout the narrative. Her idea of maternity is also shaped by advertising imagery: 'she'd take ... Johnny out of the pram and lay him down on the floor, and herself down beside him, like she'd seen in the advertisements' (*ibid.*, p. 15). There is a stark contrast between these ideal images of domesticity and the grim drudgery of Joy's home life, but these are dreams that she clings to; her fantasies of an ideal life are structured through women's magazines and brand names: 'Prestige Happymaid; Dish Drainer, a 'Bex "Decorair" and four tea towels; Kitchen Timer and Hand Towel; Gent's Winter Weight Pyjamas, Six Table Mats' (*ibid.*, p. 123).

The novel slides from Joy's initial romanticism about domestic life into a sharp recognition that both marriage and sex are a means of exploiting men financially. The spectre of prostitution as a means of survival (and also as a means of acquiring small luxuries) constantly hovers over the narrative. While Joy draws the line at selling sex 'Up West' (a euphemism for prostitution), she comes very close to selling her body, posing as a nude model for a group of male amateur photographers. She sees no reason not to masturbate the bar manager for extra wages nor why she should not exchange sex for her driving certificate. Other women in the novel have similar defences against acknowledging that what they do is prostitution: Beryl, a prostitute's maid, is happy to take clients, and to go 'Up West' occasionally, but does not see herself as 'on the game'; Aunt Em is a retired prostitute, still dreaming that a man will rescue her. Although Joy exists among a community of women, she does so with resentment, associating femininity with desolation: 'it's being bogged down every blessed moment and all day among women' (*ibid.*, p. 130).

While Dunn does allow her women characters to take pleasure in sex, and she does allow Joy to articulate her dreams, in her 1960s writings she gives her no means of fulfilling them, and offers her no way out of becoming the 'Poor Cow' of the title. The women in these narratives are offered no options beyond menial factory work or financial dependence upon men, whether through marriage or forms of prostitution. It is not until the much later sequel to *Poor Cow*, *My Silver Shoes* (1996), that Joy can finally have her career, working in a state-supported Job Club, and at last achieving the domestic environment of her dreams. The Job Club is seen as a form of welfare support that really does make a difference to people's lives, unlike the resented National Assistance of earlier fiction. By the late 1990s, Joy can have her own source of self-esteem and economic independence and has come to value, rather than despise, her friendships with women. These are possibilities that 1960s fiction could not allow. It is only the exceptional Rosamund who can see no reason to interrupt her career trajectory; for all the other heroines, compromised ambitions and a hope for the future is the best that they can manage.

The sociologist Ronald Fletcher concluded his 1962 study of family and marriage with the recommendation that in the future:

> individual discrimination and responsibility will come to be emphasised as the basis of morality. What people actually do in their own sexual behaviour – whether pre-marital, marital, or extra-marital – must be their own responsibility. Our public duty can only be to make available all relevant knowledge – of sex itself and reproduction, of venereal disease, of contraceptive techniques – so that everyone has an adequate basis of knowledge on which to take their decisions.
>
> (Fletcher, 1962, pp. 245–6)

These contemporary fictions of single motherhood do show women very much taking responsibility for their own sexual behaviour, but they do so in a world that clearly does not 'make available all relevant knowledge' to them; all these women acknowledge their sexual ignorance. The heroines of these novels have intimations of the beginnings of a liberalization in sexual attitudes but they do not see contemporary society as supporting them in any way, and resolve to deal with their situation entirely on their own terms.

3

'She's Leaving Home': The College Novel of the 1970s

While Andrea Newman's 1966 novel *The Cage* had represented a young woman deprived of the opportunity to go to university, and Rosamund's academic life in *The Millstone* is at odds with her emotional life, the next generation of women's fiction was to make the university experience for women central to contemporary novels. The period from the late 1960s and throughout the 1970s saw the burgeoning of a genre of women's writing which dated back to the early 1960s: the narrative of a young woman who leaves home to go to university, and who there encounters a wide world of intellectual and romantic opportunity. The 'college girl narrative' became a publishing phenomenon in both Britain and America, coinciding with a growth in higher education and with an increase in the numbers of women students.

For British women students, the expansion of higher education gave them access to the postwar academic opportunities that had largely benefited the 'scholarship boys' of the 1944 Butler Education Act. In Britain, the decade was marked by the building of new universities committed to modernity and widening access; in America, the number of women undergraduates rose dramatically throughout the 1960s. As Arthur Marwick has argued: 'A crucial aspect of the liberalization of the 1960s is the realm of higher education' (Marwick, 1982, p. 154), and with access to university, more young women were encountering and contributing to that liberalization. The figures for American women students had risen steadily since the 1950s, and the university experience became part of the agenda of popular culture for young women, as Susan J. Douglas explains:

> Magazines like *Glamour* added regular columns and articles about getting into and attending college, and while their back-to-school issue each August featured the 'best-dressed' college girls ... the magazines nonetheless imparted a taken-for-granted quality to college attendance for girls. In 1965, the number of degrees awarded to women was double

> what it had been in 1955; by 1969, the number had tripled, and it kept zooming up.
>
> (Douglas, 1995, p. 142)

College represented a set of opportunities, but this new generation of college-educated women were also to experience class mobility, which did not come without its problems. Just as for the 'scholarship boys' in the post-war generation of the 1950s, women who were the first of their family to attend college could find that the experience caused tensions between generations and led to a distancing from parents and home. In Britain, the egalitarian hopes for the group of new universities set up in the 1960s are expressed in a 1968 account of contemporary education; this describes the political recognition

> that Britain's future depended very largely on the educational opportunities it offered to young people. State and County Grants based on a means test meant that any boy or girl could now afford to go to university, but there were just not enough places for those who were qualified for higher education. Completely new universities were founded in places such as Brighton (1961), York (1963) and Lancaster (1964).
>
> (Peacock, 1968, p. 367)

These State and County Grants were to support British students and give them a measure of financial independence, until the Labour government of 1997 introduced a system of bursaries and student loans that owed much to the American system of educational funding. The question of how to finance a degree was not on the agenda for the British heroines of the college narrative in the 1970s; the issue of financial support, and the consequent obligations to jobs and parents, are, however, central concerns for their American counterparts.

The writers of the college novel had often themselves been at university in the 1960s, and belonged to a generation of women who had vocally asserted their rights. Women's equality in education, however, was to prove relative, despite the establishment of new universities, and the rising numbers of women undergraduates. Even after the Equal Pay Act and the Sex Discrimination Act in Britain, men continued to outnumber women as university entrants and graduates. Writing in 1974, Barry Turner demonstrated that in the late 1960s, the higher the level of education in Britain, the fewer the numbers of young women to be found there. The more élite the academic institution, the more difficult the access for women applicants; medical schools and Oxford and Cambridge Universities operated a quota for women students throughout the 1970s. A 1971 report found that 4.6 per cent of women in England entered university, compared to 7.6 per cent of men, and estimated that women students represented one in three of undergraduates (quoted in Adams and Laurikietis, 1976, p. 53). Turner noted, 'as a general rule, women needed to be better qualified than men to get a university place' (Turner, 1974, p. 196). The fact that women were in the minority in higher education made for a particular kind of heroine in the campus novel: the intelligent, achieving woman. Women undergraduates, well into the 1970s, had some reason to consider themselves, in the title of Alice Adams's 1984 novel, *Superior Women* (Adams, 1985).

The growing numbers of women students provided a newly identifiable market for women's fiction. As John Sutherland points out, the growing numbers of educated young women alerted publishers to the fact that women were the greatest consumers of fiction:

> One of the great realizations by the book trade in the 1970s ... was that the woman reader accounted for much more than a fifth of the market for fiction. In fact surveys – taken to heart by the book trade – revealed that women consumed around 60 percent of all novels sold ... If the 1970s demonstrated anything to the publishing industry, it was that women's fiction was not restricted to genre products, but could have its 'blockbusters'.
>
> (Sutherland, 1981, p. 74)

The college genre did produce a number of best-selling novels in the 1970s, directly marketed at a women readership. The form offers a female version of the *Bildungsroman*, in which the heroine matures as she moves into a wider world. The undergraduate is in the process of moving from family home to university, and so offers a paradigm for the transition from childhood towards adult possibilities and choices. Katherine Payant has argued that: 'the bildungsroman ... seems to have been the dominant form in the 1970s, clearly illustrating various feminist theories by showing the maturation of a young protagonist seeking to find herself in a hostile patriarchal world' (Payant, 1993, p. 8). The college narrative clearly fits neatly into this *Bildungsroman* form, in taking a young woman as a central character, and placing her with a group of similar young women in a strange and new environment. The narratives and heroines may not, however, necessarily be feminist, and the world of university is not always experienced as hostile and patriarchal, but can be a liberating space.

According to Douglas, in the American context, the collectivity of the women's movement represented a challenge to the ideology of individualism and presented a contradiction for many American women: 'In the 1970s, millions of women of all ages struggled with the tensions between embracing sisterhood and clinging to that bulwark of American ideology, democratic individualism' (Douglas, 1995, p. 225). The college narrative structure could neatly resolve that tension between solidarity and individuality, as a form that could follow the development of an individual character, or more often, characters, and simultaneously present these *Bildungsromans* in the context of a collective female experience. The use of multiple narratives or narrators allowed for the story of a group of women, rather than the individual experiences recounted in 1960s novels such as *The L-Shaped Room* or *The Millstone*. A cohort of students is a means of exploring a generation of young women. The university is a site which is occupied by intelligent young women on the brink of adult life, who are confronted by new ideas and a sense of their own potential. These novels repeatedly exhibit an ambivalence about female independence: while university is used as a metonym for ambition, their narratives also express an anxiety at leaving the restrictions and familiarity of the family home.

A 'runaway' best-seller in both Britain and America, Mary McCarthy's *The Group*, first published in 1963 and filmed in 1966 (dir. Sidney Lumet) was to establish the framework for this genre of novels. Randall Jarrell (who was among McCarthy's intellectual set) had already written a comic novel set in a women's college in 1954 (Jarrell, 1954), but his satirical focus is on the faculty of the fictional 'Benton' university, while McCarthy writes about the women students of Vassar. McCarthy had written an earlier 'college' novel in 1952, but the focus of *The Groves of Academe* is on the academic staff at the university rather than its students (McCarthy, 1980). The narrative structure of *The Group*, with its interlocking stories of eight young women, allowed for a great many variations; most later versions were not to be as cynical or as progressive as McCarthy's novel. The 'group' of friends first meet at Vassar (McCarthy's own alma mater) in 1930 and the narrative follows their progress across a decade. The young women in the novel are a generation who are resolved to be self- sufficient, and are determined, as were the young women of the 1960s and 1970s, to distinguish themselves from their parents' way of life:

> They were a different breed ... from the languid buds of the previous decade: there was not one of them who did not propose to work this coming fall ... The worst fate, they utterly agreed, would be to become like Mother and Dad, stuffy and frightened. Not one of them, if she could help it, was going to marry a broker or a banker or a cold-fish corporation lawyer, like so many of Mother's generation.
>
> (McCarthy, 1966, pp. 12–13)

The Group's multi-stranded tales of a beautiful group of friends, the excitement of a room of one's own at a prestigious university and the availability of men established a set of conventions for the women's college novel. The narrative voice of *The Group* was also to be emulated by many other writers, with its slippages between the third and first person and the use of intimate address to the reader. The structure of a set of linked women's stories was taken up as a form by both British and American writers who, in response to the women's movement, were becoming more attuned to the collectivity of women's experience. The college novel became a popular publishers' genre throughout the 1970s, but the tropes which repeatedly appear in these fictions are already established in *The Group*. Many of the covers of later imitators invoke McCarthy's novel, with a series of portraits of young women and cover lines invoking McCarthy as a predecessor. *The Group* introduced a narrative structure and set of elements which were to become standard to the form: the group of friends, and one central young woman who is encountering her first sexual experience. The different women of the group provide narrative strands which address contraception, abortion, domestic violence and lesbian sexuality, all issues which were to become key to the feminist movement. Whenever the college experience is set (and this ranges from the 1940s to the 1970s), variations of these elements recur in both British and American versions of the student experience for young women.

Newman's first novel, *A Share of the World*, originally published in 1964, follows a young woman's experience at the University of London, where Newman herself had been a student. *A Share of the World* is a significant title, expressing the ambition and demands of the woman undergraduate. The first-person narrator, Lois, is fully appreciative of the opportunity that university represents; she recognizes that she is one of a newly privileged generation which has access to student grants and college places for women: 'We were lucky, had been born at the right time and we were having our chance' (Newman, 1979, p. 107).

Newman's London undergraduates may be a continent away from McCarthy's Vassar students, but they inhabit a similar world of Freshman mixers, college dances and the fear of pregnancy. As in *The Group*, the university dormitory presents a range of young women characters taking full advantage of this 'chance', and exploring the emotional and sexual choices available to them. University represents an alternative world away from the constraints of home and family, and requires the heroine to begin to develop her own set of ethical codes. For Lois, this is compounded by her parents writing to inform her of their divorce; home is no longer a secure environment and parents can no longer be seen as moral arbiters. This is a generation caught between value systems. Sheila Rowbotham has commented on the conflicting messages about sexuality that were addressed to young women in the 1960s: 'Between contradictory messages, young women ... were caught between the polarities and forced into uneasy compromises ... [P]opular media sex advice was getting odder and odder' (Rowbotham, 1997, p. 394). Lois and her fellow students offer a range of women negotiating their way through precisely these polarities and compromises: Anne, the engaged and sexually active woman; Jeanne who is determined to hold on to her virginity until marriage; Lois who is exploring the options available once her first love has ditched her. As in *The Group*, one of the college friends is painfully discovering her lesbian identity, her sexuality signified through her reading of Mary Renault and Radclyffe Hall. There is a recognition in the novel that forms of sexuality once considered as strange are literally coming closer to home. Lois is intrigued by her friendship with the lesbian Ruth, and is also coming to acknowledge that her brother is gay. Challenges to the accepted conventions of sexual behaviour are everywhere in the novel: Lois's father has a much younger mistress; a close friend has a string of lovers; Lois herself embarks on an affair with a married man.

Despite the confusions of contemporary sexual mores, there is a new confidence and excitement about their sexuality available to young women of this generation, a confidence that not even the achieving Rosamund of *The Millstone* could have shared in the early 1960s. The women demonstrate an awareness and responsibility about contraception, Lois is advised by a friend to 'get a little gadget' (Newman, 1979, p. 25). The pill was available in Britain from 1961, and intra-uterine devices could now be offered to single women. Abortion was still illegal for Lois's group, but when one of the friends becomes pregnant there is a general recognition of the absurdity and double standards of the current law, and a unanimous acceptance among the women friends that a demand for an abortion should not require justification.

Their emotional and sexual education has much more excitement for Lois and her group than do the intellectual challenges of university life. Academic life is on the periphery, a small price to pay for having a room of one's own, dormitory friendships and regular college dances: 'There was a kind of satisfaction in keeping my translation up to date or turning in a good essay. But I suppose my chief interest at this time was in Anne's wedding' (*ibid.*, p. 162). Although Lois is studying literature, expressions of love and longing in the literary canon apparently have little bearing on Lois's own experience. Feminist theory is not yet a concept for the 1960s woman student; the idea of an academic life that could bear any relation to the concerns of young women is so remote that it is a shared joke among the women students: 'I wish I could do finals in life, love and sex ... A psychological expose of the feminine mind and heart ... It's a far cry from the Development of the Language and Literary Criticism' (*ibid.*, pp. 174–5). Even a romantic involvement with a married male lecturer cannot break down this firm separation between personal and academic experience.

University represents for Newman and for Lois an untrammelled three years in which career and romantic possibilities can be tried out: 'a space ... in which you could experiment' (*ibid.*, p. 189) before the demands of family and working life have a chance to intervene. Lois observes her contemporaries at college:

> all spending three years of their lives poised between school and work or marriage, or both, in the no-man's land of university life. Time to look round, which we might never have again; a breathing space in which to study books, people, life, ourselves – what we will.
>
> (*Ibid.*, p. 104)

The college 'girl' is a young woman caught between versions of herself, in a transition between family expectations and self-definition. The university narrative therefore offers a neat point for the discussion of tensions between generations, and especially between fathers and daughters. All these writers express more affection for father figures than for mothers. The love between fathers and daughters is a recurrent theme in the college novel, but it is made explicitly sexual in Newman's most notorious novel, *A Bouquet of Barbed Wire*, an Oedipal Romance in which a father is in love with his student daughter. The family romance is a central theme throughout Newman's work. In the 1977 novel *An Evil Streak* it is an uncle who is in love with his student niece, and who disastrously plays Pandarus to his set-up of her as Criseyde with his domestic help as Troilus. The heroines of both *An Evil Streak* and *A Bouquet of Barbed Wire* do not have the optimism of Lois's story; both come to tragic ends, their fragile independence doomed by the intervention of the family. In allowing these heroines to die, Newman displaces the anxieties of what is to become of educated young women once they have left the family home. These young women never progress to the point of establishing a new family unit or independent life on their own terms; they are forever preserved, like Lois, as young women on the edge of a new life. What that new life might involve is carefully evaded.

Deborah Moggach's first novel *You Must Be Sisters* also presents a heroine caught between the values of her suburban parental home and the alternatives that university life presents. *You Must Be Sisters* uses a family of three sisters rather than a group of friends to explore educational options for young women. Each of the sisters is at a different point in the educational process: the eldest, Claire is a teacher in a secondary school; the youngest, Holly, at boarding school; while the focus of the narrative is on the undergraduate Laura. Each sister is experiencing her own form of conflict between the demands of family and her own life. Holly is described as having two selves, one for school and one for home, while the sensible Claire experiences tensions between the expectations of her parents and her lover. The conflict is acted out at its most dramatic by the middle sister, Laura, who has to reassess her own and her family's values when she is confronted with the independence of university life.

While the novel is not written in the first person, it shares the immediacy and breathless quality of Newman's prose; it is almost entirely presented from Laura's point of view. As for Lois, university is for Laura a transition into self-definition, but Laura's family represents a stronger tie than Lois's divorced parents. The novel begins with Laura's parents delivering her to university in Bristol, where Moggach was herself a student. Laura begins the novel as a naïve virgin, free from parental restraint and in search of romance and passion, but is disappointed to find only adolescent fumblings and a college full of people like herself. While university represents for Lois a blank page of opportunity, Laura's later experience is shaped by her expectations and a self-consciousness about student life. By 1978 the university experience is no longer so exclusive; Laura is peeved to discover that she is only one among many rebellious students: 'it irked her to be such a typical student' (Moggach, 1978, p. 17). Laura belongs to a generation and a middle-class world where university is an expected rite of passage; her parents' cocktail party is full of the parents of current and aspiring students.

Laura determines to differentiate herself, and rejects the 'college' experience and the relative safety of dormitory life, choosing instead a bed-sitting room (which is unequivocally sordid, with none of the redeeming features of *The L-Shaped Room*). She is drawn to 'something intangible from which all her life she'd been sheltered' (Moggach, 1978, p. 79). This 'something intangible' is an encounter with class difference and poverty, a world from which she has been protected by her middle-class, suburban upbringing. Laura is shown to be politically naïve: 'She didn't know much about politics, but what she did know was that she should admire the Left' (*ibid*., p. 189). She chooses a lover whom she mistakes as having a more 'authentic' working-class masculinity than the pleasant male students she encounters: 'He didn't look like a student ... He didn't have that cultivated scruffiness, he looked as if he'd been born with his' (*ibid*., p. 74). Mac is, however, revealed as no more authentic than Laura's rebellion; he is an art-school dropout, whose parents are proud of his upward mobility.

The excitement of university life in *You Must Be Sisters* is again derived from the opportunity it offers for erotic encounters and independent living rather than from any intellectual challenge. Lectures are for Laura, as they are for Lois, peripheral to the sentimental education that college can provide. One lecture leads to a page of doodled horses; in another, the lecturer's voice is a distant assault: 'The lecturer's final burst of rhetoric was rising to a climax ... Oh, but the sun shone and her room waited!' (*ibid*., p. 57). As Laura disdains lectures in favour of erotic dreams, it is her sexual life that is used to distinguish her from the dull students of campus life and from the dreary housewives of suburban Harrow. Sexual freedom is shown to come at a price, however, and Laura is made to pay it. She accidentally becomes pregnant, despite her sensible appointment with a doctor and the fitting of a Dutch cap; Laura is another young woman confronted with the choice between abortion and single motherhood, but unlike the young women of the 1960s, the decision is made relatively easily. Although the idea of abortion does evoke uncomfortable feelings: 'black wings ... in her head', a quick visit to a clinic ends the pregnancy, with very little regret: 'Most efficient, the whole business' (*ibid*., p. 214).

As in *A Share of the World*, there is a recognition that university life represents only a temporary form of rebellion. Laura disparagingly writes to her sister of 'all those safe little rooms where one could pretend to be rebellious' (Moggach, 1978, p. 94). Laura is finally reclaimed by family and class loyalty, and finds herself once again at home in suburbia: 'Despite everything she was still part of it, this house with its ... tiny routines ... this was her home' (*ibid*., p. 136). There is throughout the novel a tension between a nostalgic affection for family life and the challenge that university makes to those values. University sharpens a generational distance from her parents, and also Laura's awareness of class privilege. The novel confronts her with the dilemma of how to negotiate between the security of home and the potential of independence. When her parents visit the university, they do not fit into her new environment; when her lover arrives in the family home, he does not fit in there either. Laura has to decide where she fits; her life at university has disrupted the family closeness and the shared class and cultural assumptions of her childhood. The sisters talk to one another in a childlike language which persists into adulthood, a shared nostalgia for a safe and uncomplicated world in which loyalty to parents and home remains unchallenged. The novel ends with the youngest sister, Holly, on the brink of negotiating the same split between family and independence and so suggests a lack of resolution for Laura's dilemma and the continuing hold of the nostalgia for the security of home and parents.

Claire, Laura's much loved elder sister, despite her own teacher training, perceives Laura's university experience as generating 'a snobbishness, a withering dismissiveness that created areas of people or things, packaged them and bundled them aside as middle-class and suburban' (*ibid.*, p. 96). Susan J. Douglas has similarly described herself in her own college years as full of a 'deep antipathy and contempt for the status quo and an inflated sense of our mission to reject it' (Douglas, 1995, p. 160). Laura acts out this contempt, but her 'inflated sense of mission' is finally deflated, as she comes to a new respect for her parents and their values by the end of the novel. There is nonetheless a clear recognition that the experiences of the previous generation belong to another time and another social world. If parents can no longer be relied upon to understand the challenges of the next generation, it is Claire who represents the voice of reason throughout the novel. Claire herself is unmistakably middle class and suburban, marrying a conventional man and choosing to live in a suburban house. She is the secure port of call whom Laura comes to rely upon and who makes Laura come to recognize that her future lies with the family values rather than with her own fragile construction of independence. Through Claire, the novel finally endorses conventional respectability; Laura comes to recognize her stabs at an alternative lifestyle as immature: 'they were only playing' (*ibid.*, p. 15). University can again only provide a temporary room of her own for the woman student.

If university represented an independence for British women undergraduates throughout the 1970s, this was in large part because of state support for their education in the form of government grants, a system which gave students a limited financial independence. The British student was not financially obligated to family or required to be an exceptional student. The American student, however, was reliant on scholarships or family help to fund a college education. The issue of financial support and the difference that this can make to a choice of university is on the agenda in the American version of the college narrative, and families have a greater financial and emotional hold over the student. Nonetheless, college represents romance and possibilities for American women throughout the 1960s and 1970s just as it did for British women. A great number of American women writers express in fiction a wistful nostalgia for the freedom of their own college years, and the woman undergraduate became a regular heroine for popular novels. Erich Segal's hugely successful novel of college life and interclass romance, *Love Story* (Segal, 1970), was filmed in 1970 (dir. Arthur Hiller), and established the American college girl as a fashion and romantic icon. The heroine (another doomed young woman, who dies) is a Radcliffe student.

Rona Jaffe's fiction is firmly in the tradition of the multiple narratives of a group of college women established by *The Group*, and she evokes that novel in her regular use of Radcliffe as a setting. Jaffe was herself an undergraduate at Radcliffe in the 1950s, and her first best-selling novel, published in America in 1958, *The Best of Everything* (Jaffe, 1959), already makes use of the multi-stranded narrative in its structure of five 'career girls' setting out in New York. On the republication of the novel in 2005, *The New York Times* referred to *The Best of Everything* as: 'the very prototype of the hot women's novel'. This belated reassessment of Jaffe identified her as a foremother of the sexually explicit confessional narrative, and framed her 1950s novel in terms of the current most popular women's genre: 'Notorious in its time for its candor about sex, it is today widely regarded as a cultural marker, providing the template for the gossipy genre of confessional fiction about women popularly known as chick lit' (La Ferla, 2005, p. 1). Caroline, the central heroine of *The Best of Everything*, is a Radcliffe graduate, but this novel is set after her graduation, and the college life becomes much more important to Jaffe's later novels. Jaffe uses the form of the multi-stranded narrative to explore the shifts in life choices available to young women; as her heroines confront the 1960s and 1970s, the discourses of feminism, entirely absent in *The Best of Everything*, become unavoidable. While the later novels explicitly reject the organized politics of the women's movement, Jaffe's women characters are consistently ambitious, in search of an undefined 'something'.

Beginning in 1975, *The Last Chance* presents a set of characters who are college girls grown up, dealing with the conflicts between career aspirations and romance. Between them, the women embody the options available to their generation; each represents a different route through the possible combinations of marriage, work and children. Ellen is a stay-at-home wife who marries straight out of college; Margot, a single working woman whose television career defines her life; Rachel is a child-free trophy wife and society hostess. Nikki, the most empathetic character in the novel, is the one who comes closest to 'having it all': happily married to a lawyer, she has two college-age daughters and is a successful book editor. The novel begins with the funeral of one of the friends, the narrative hermeneutic being to discover which of the four meets an early death, and, by implication, which of these chosen modes of femininity is the most destructive. The novel charts a year in the women's lives at early middle-age, but is punctuated with nostalgic revisits to their college years in the 1950s.

As the novel progresses, the promise of the women graduates' college ambitions is increasingly undermined. The tensions of sustaining a successful marriage, family and career become apparent, as each woman is frustrated by her circumstances. Strains appear in all their relationships with men, while the working women find their careers increasingly difficult to manage. The novel neatly elides the problems of childcare for the working woman; Nikki is introduced at a successful point in her career, and there is no indication that children represented any disruption to her trajectory. Her daughters are grown, and their early years are casually dismissed: 'She was working full time when the girls were in high school and it never seemed to bother them any' (Jaffe, 1976, p. 24). Despite her love for her husband, the marriage is presented as uncomfortably arranged on her husband's terms: 'it was always the woman who makes the sacrifices, it annoyed the hell out of her' (*ibid.*, p. 23).

The novel is haunted by Betty Friedan's 'problem that has no name'; each of the women in the novel is frustrated by her life choice, although none looks to women's experience beyond her friendship group. While they would all reject any identification with the suburban housewives of Friedan's study, they share and dramatize the 'strange stirring, a sense of dissatisfaction, a yearning' that Friedan describes (Friedan, 1965, p. 13). The one moment of explicit feminist politics in the novel is when the expensive wife Rachel is invited to join a consciousness-raising group. Despite her own declared sense of a luxurious but wasted life, her response to women's liberation is dismissive: 'Rachel thought it ridiculous ... and promised herself not to laugh at them' (Jaffe, 1976, p. 50). The narrative voice endorses Rachel's scorn, the meeting is shown to be full of parodic 'feminist' types. Rachel does not discuss her encounter with feminism with her other female friends, who seem to remain blithely unaware of a women's movement. Instead, each of the protagonists experiments with short-term solutions to the undefined dissatisfaction that permeates the novel: one character takes pills, another a series of lovers, another escapes her marriage to a New York apartment. It is only Rachel who manages a fruitful balance between marriage and her own ambitions; she returns to university as a mature student and college gives her intellectual satisfaction and an improved relationship with her husband. But it is Rachel who is stalked by a sinister presence throughout the novel and it is Rachel's funeral that begins the novel. The only contented woman in the narrative is the one who is destroyed.

The narrative is punitive to each of the women in turn: the devoted wife and mother has an anorexic daughter and turns her husband impotent and mad. The career woman is no more successful; she takes to drink and pills and finally attempts suicide. Nikki, who does manage to combine motherhood, marriage and a career for much of the novel, is driven to leave her husband for a famous lover and a room of her own. But her fragile independence is destroyed by an invasion of burglars and a mugging on the streets of New York; the independent life is too dangerous to sustain. None of the paths the four women take allows them the last chance of the title; any hope for the future is once again deferred until the next generation. Nikki's aspirations are displaced onto her daughters, mingled with regret at her own lost ambitions:

> How different her girls were from her at their age, Nikki thought with admiration and a sense of loss. Not loss of them, but loss of her own youth, her own best years. She had chosen to have marriage and a career; it had been a brave decision in her day, but now as she looked back on her life and compared it with the life her daughters were entering, it seemed as if she hadn't really had all of either part, the job, or the marriage.
>
> (*Ibid.*, p. 46)

Jaffe's 1979 novel *Class Reunion* opens with a questionnaire addressed to the Radcliffe class of 1957, with a set of questions which are very close to a real survey conducted by the American Association of University Women, published in 1976. This report was 'a study designed to show the life styles of a contemporary group of women college and university graduates' (Willis, 1976, p. 31). That survey was addressed to the graduate women who are the fictional heroines of Jaffe's novel, and is preoccupied with precisely the same questions. Both texts are concerned with the use that women graduates made of their education, and address the gulf between the expectations that university offered and the actual experience of the professional world for women. What Jaffe charts fictionally, the American Association of University Women traced with statistics. Faith Willis reported that the majority of women with college degrees did not use 'their education fully in their jobs' (Willis, 1976, p. 2); Jaffe writes about four heroines who fail to fulfil the hopes of their college years.

The novel is centred on a question that could have come directly from the Willis survey: 'Have you fulfilled the expectations you had after you graduated from Radcliffe?' (Jaffe, 1979, p. 4), and goes on to demonstrate that none of the central characters has done so. Like *The Last Chance*, the novel follows a group of friends who first meet in the college dormitory in the 1950s, and traces them over twenty years after graduation. Each woman harbours a guilty secret; each has a 'flaw' which makes her feel inadequate to the contemporary ideal of femininity: Emily is a Jew in a WASP environment, Daphne an epileptic, Christine has an alcoholic mother, and Annabel is quietly sexually active. They all feel themselves to be failing to live up to the expectations of family, and of Radcliffe. The novel is set at a moment of transition in sexual morality, Emily mildly observing that some of her fellow students 'were starting to sleep with the men they were engaged to. They didn't talk about it ... A lot of things were shaking up their world' (Jaffe, 1979, p. 117). The evidence of the 1953 Kinsey Report *Sexual Behaviour in the Human Female*, which covered much of the same period as this novel, had documented that many American young women were indeed less chaste than they publicly claimed.

College represents a brief window of erotic and intellectual opportunity for Emily and her group: 'It was all so romantic, frenzied and short-lived, their wonderful college days' (Jaffe, 1979, p. 20). If it is romance with men rather than with ideas that is initially the real attraction of university, this attitude is shown to change over the course of their degrees. By the time the four women graduate there is a real pride in their academic achievement, coupled with a sense of the obligations that come with a privileged education: 'Their diplomas were truly prizes for perseverance, hard work and intelligence, and they felt proud and excited and special. Graduation was an era marked *ended*, a kind of pledge to go forth and be worthy' (*ibid*., p. 120).

The problem for these women graduates is quite how they can 'go forth and be worthy' in a world that discourages intellectual ambition for women. Emily is warned off medicine, and advised to marry a doctor instead. Just as for the women of *The Last Chance*, the college years offer a glimpse of opportunity and potential that are thwarted in the adult world of life outside the campus. The section that follows the women over the six years after graduation is entitled 'The Sixties: Falling Apart'. Emily and Annabel's experiences of marriage and motherhood turn sour, while the single Chris and Daphne are romantically and professionally unfulfilled. The next episode, 'The Seventies: Together', does describe glimmers of an awareness of the women's movement, but as for Rachel, feminist politics are seen to have no bearing on the real stuff of life. All the women finally marry, and each, in one way or another, gives up her intellectual dreams for love. The representation of marriage in the novel reads as a fictionalization of the American Association of University Women report; marriage for these characters does mean that they cannot make 'full use' of their education.

The novel ends with a daughter poised to succeed her mother as a Radcliffe student. Once again there is the anticipation that the next generation of young women will have it better, but the women's movement and the political activism of the 1960s are not seen to have anything much to do with this. As in other university novels, college represents for Jaffe and her heroines a temporary respite from the realities of inequality. Emily realizes with some bitterness: 'College wasn't your real life. College was a period when you went away and learned skills and found a good husband and then went back to the serious business of living' (Jaffe, 1979, p. 56).

Judith Rossner's controversial novel *Looking for Mr Goodbar* was a best-seller in 1975, and filmed as an erotic melodrama in 1977 (*Looking for Mr Goodbar*, dir. Richard Brooks), and both prompted a debate as to the text's feminist credentials. Like Rona Jaffe's educated and frustrated women characters, Rossner's heroine, Theresa, is a woman who expresses and acts on her sexual desires, but is then narratively punished for them. The novel begins with the confession of Theresa's murderer, establishing from the outset that she is to come to a bad end. Theresa is first encountered sitting alone in a bar and reading, asserting her right to do both: ' "Why shouldn't I?" she says. "I like to read and I like to sit in bars" ' (Rossner, 1975, p. 14). The rest of the novel is preoccupied with whether or not a woman can sustain a life as both a sexual being and an intellectual. The narrative's brutal conclusion with Theresa's violent death suggests not.

Theresa is represented as a damaged woman from the outset. She suffered polio as a child, her spine is curved, and she is scarred from repeated surgery. She also has to contend with the guilt engendered by a Catholic upbringing, and with the ghost of her dead brother. Theresa consequently has a fragile sense of herself, which allows for her to be exploited by men. Her college experience is dominated by a liaison with a married professor of creative writing, Professor Engle. Although college does give her the space in which to assert some ambition and independence, Theresa looks to him to determine what she will do on graduation: 'Martin had never said a word to her about what would happen when she graduated after a conversation the previous fall in which he'd shouted that she would just be throwing away her mind if she went into public school teaching' (*ibid*., p. 77). Nonetheless, that is exactly what she chooses to do, a minor rebellion and a small level of professional status which bring her little satisfaction. Theresa's broken life is imaged in a series of unsatisfactory sexual relationships with men. Theresa is invited by a woman friend to join a women's group, but, like Jaffe's Rachel, she is instantly dismissive. She later expresses a faint glimmering of interest, but, as with Rachel, this is fleeting and she is unable to identify her own situation with that of other women: 'however interesting some of the ideas were to her, she wouldn't be able to sit around with a bunch of women and talk about them' (*ibid*., p. 243).

The narrative implies that it is Theresa's damaged body and psyche that cannot allow her to find a sisterhood and to take support from other women, choosing instead the louche dangers of the singles bar which will eventually lead to her death. The novel does not, however, enter into the world of feminism at all; it is left on the margins of Theresa's experience, and the reader is only offered a brief glimpse of the possibilities it might have offered her. Theresa does articulate a mild regret for the lost opportunity of the women's group, but, as for Rachel, she does not see it as having any real connection to her own life and experience. Rossner, like Jaffe, ultimately suggests that the politics of gender cannot begin to answer the contradictions of the individual woman. While *Looking for Mr Goodbar* does address the practices of feminism, it cannot allow the central woman character to engage with feminist ideas.

The successes of McCarthy, Jaffe and Rossner prompted a swarm of imitators, as publishers began to promote women's fiction in a proven marketable form. The college narrative was a means of packaging the contradictory and multi-layered strands of contemporary women's experiences. Sara Davidson's *Loose Change* purports to be a social history rather than fiction, but her text directly emulates the college fiction's structure of the interwoven set of stories of a group of friends. Davidson's three women students, based on herself and her contemporaries at Berkeley, California in 1961, reproduce many of the elements and narratives found in the novels: Tasha, the art student, just like Daphne in *Class Reunion*, has an affair with a married man and lives with him 'in sin' in Greenwich Village. Berkeley offers, as college does for all these fictional heroines, a world of romantic and intellectual possibility: on her arrival, Sara feels: 'I had arrived at a state of grace' (Davidson, 1977, p. 20). As for Jaffe's heroines, that 'state of grace' is restricted to the college years, and cannot be sustained after graduation. While each of the women do achieve, their professional lives are subordinate to their romances and independence is hard to sustain. As Sheila Ernst has noted:

> In Sara Davidson's *Loose Change* three of the Californian characters appear to be liberated; one is a successful journalist, another a rich art dealer and the third a much envied Berkeley radical having a relationship with a 'top' Berkeley student activist. Each in her own way loses her sense of self in a relationship with a man.
>
> (Ernst, 1987, p. 73)

The narrative charts the three women over a decade from 1961 to 1972, but the most vivid part of the narrative is the college years. Given this historical context, and the claim to be a social history, there is an extraordinary absence of any engagement with the contemporary facts of Vietnam or the civil rights movement. Although the women do participate in demonstrations, these are seen as social events rather than expressions of political dissent. Although she is herself Jewish and angry about racial quotas, Sara can shamefacedly admit 'I didn't like Negroes' (Davidson, 1977, p. 63). Her friend Susie is represented as a political radical and reads Marx, but her commitment comes from an attachment to a man rather than the politics. The only real involvement with a world outside the Berkeley campus that Davidson and her friends experience is through the Peace Corps and travel to Europe. The events of the 1960s are merely a backdrop to the real focus on the emotional dramas of the three characters, the uncertainties of the heroines' romantic and professional lives are not connected at all to the political events of the time. Katie Roiphe has argued that for many Americans, the unsettling of their personal certainties was profoundly bound up with the political unrest of the period:

> added to the anxiety of turmoil at home was the violence of a war brought, for the first time on a large scale, into people's living rooms. The news of kids dying in Vietnam, waving picket signs on college campuses, and running away from home somehow shook people's faith in the natural progression of things, of children growing up, getting jobs, wearing suits, getting married, and living relatively uneventful lives.
> (Roiphe, 1997, p. 92)

As the political events of the late 1960s became inescapable, and as independent and feminist publishers flourished in the 1970s, the subtext of feminist and alternative politics in the college narrative had to become explicit. In Marge Piercy's *Small Changes* (Piercy, 1972) and Marilyn French's *The Women's Room* (French, 1978), the college genre had its blockbusters, both novels were best-sellers which had clear feminist agendas. *Small Changes* was marketed as 'the explosive novel of women struggling to make their place in a man's world' (Piercy, 1972, back cover), and *The Women's Room* was endorsed by Betty Friedan herself, who claimed it as 'The best novel yet about the lives of women' (French, 1978, back cover). The heroines of both these narratives begin as the 1950s suburban housewives of Friedan's study, and go on to find a liberation at university that is unapologetically political and explicitly feminist. Both novels were published after the rise of the Women's Liberation Movement, and appeared at a moment when second-wave feminism was an established phenomenon.

The alternative sexualities and radical culture that were there on the margins of the popular college narrative had moved to the foreground to become the subjects of their own novels. Bonnie Zimmerman has charted the proliferation of the 'lesbian novel of development' in the late 1960s and early 1970s, and notes that education is used as a frequent metaphor for the sexual and emotional development of the lesbian heroine. Zimmerman describes the 'coming out narrative': 'Along her path she is educated socially, sexually and emotionally, often within the environs of an all-female world where the young girl awakens to her true identity, her powers and her sexuality' (Zimmerman, 1983, p. 246). The college dormitory provides an 'all-female world', and is a space for developing female friendships. It is inevitable that the 'lesbian awakening' narrative should neatly fit this genre of women's writing. The elements that Zimmerman describes in the 'coming out narrative' are also to be found in the heterosexual romances of the college novel, which often include a lesbian narrative as one of the narrative strands. The university is a site for early sexual experiences, and offers both a sentimental and an intellectual education in a young woman's search for 'identity'.

Rita Mae Brown's *Rubyfruit Jungle* was the most commercially successful of the 'coming out' variants of the college narrative. First published by a small feminist publishing house in 1973, it went on to become an international best-seller, largely through word-of-mouth recommendations. While the strap-line for the paperback edition trumpeted it as 'A novel about being different – and loving it!', *Rubyfruit Jungle* is not in fact so very different; it employs many of the same devices that recur in heterosexual versions of the college genre. Molly is, as the central female focus in these novels tends to be, an exceptional student, but she is disadvantaged by much more than other more conventional heroines. Illegitimate and abandoned by her mother, she is brought up by her aunt and uncle, who, with echoes of the Joad family in John Steinbeck's *The Grapes of Wrath*, travel to Florida in search of work. Molly learns to read at the age of three, and her stepfather, Carl, recognizes that she is an exceptional young woman: 'You got to treat her with some respect for her brains' (Brown, 1978, p. 39). It is Carl who fosters Molly's ambition to go to college, which is unexpected in a woman who comes from 'Coffee Hollow, a rural dot outside of York, Pennsylvania' (*ibid.*, p. 3). Molly's intelligence gives her a means of moving beyond the confines of small-town life and escaping the drudgery of unskilled work, as Carl puts it: 'You want her to spend her life like us, ... can't even make enough money for a new dress or dinner in a restaurant? You want her to live a life like you – dishes, cooking and never going out except maybe to a movie ...?' (*ibid.*, p. 40).

Molly will clearly escape this fate; she is a feisty young woman and an outstanding student. College is less an emblem of independence and opportunity for the underprivileged Molly than it is a necessary step to 'get out of the boondocks'. As she recognizes: 'I gotta go, I don't get that degree and I'm another secretary. No thanks. I got to get it and head for a big city' (*ibid.*, p. 109). With her family unable to support her, Molly is dependent on scholarships to get to college. While she dreams of film school, New York and California are too far away to be financially possible. Her teacher recommends the 'Seven Sisters' colleges of Vassar and Bryn Mawr (in a nod to Mary McCarthy). The prestigious Duke and Radcliffe also offer her a place, but it is 'the bedpan of the South', the University of Florida, that Molly chooses: 'The only reason I went there was because they gave me a full scholarship plus room and board ... [H]aving no money my choice was determined by material considerations' (*ibid.*, p. 111). Despite being the best student of her year, Molly's choices are constrained.

Molly arrives at college knowing that she is gay, having already explored her sexuality with her closest childhood friends, both male and female. She finds her first gay bar at college, and experiences her first real romance with her college roommate. Faye and Molly share a 'common bond for disruption' (*ibid.*, p. 112), and despise their fellow students for their earnestness. Faye goes through an illegal abortion, a familiar rite of passage in the college narrative; it is Molly's care for her that brings them together. Once their affair becomes public knowledge, the full wrath of the Dean descends upon Molly. She is sent to a psychiatric hospital, and thrown out of the University of Florida for her sexuality, in what has been described as 'a classic lesbian experience' in fiction (Zimmerman, 1983, p. 253). Academic work is no more to Faye and Molly than a means of staying together. While Molly effortlessly makes top grades, her field of study remains vague. Faye has the financial backing of her parents to go to a private college, but Molly's scholarships are withdrawn 'for "moral reasons", although my academic record was superb' (Brown, 1978, p. 131).

Molly hits the road for New York City, the big city where Faye has promised that it 'ought to be a little better', and where a gay community awaits her. Her intellectual confidence is such that she hustles another scholarship for a place at film school: 'I am getting my ass over to N.Y.U. tomorrow and telling those academic robots that they're giving me a scholarship. I'm the hottest thing since Eisenstein; they're lucky to help me in my formative stage' (*ibid.*, p. 168). The only woman in her class, she encounters misogyny from her fellow students and from the academic staff, but single-handledly makes her graduation film and graduates 'summa cum laude', the best in her year. As Molly leaves college for the world of work, her ambition and determination are for the first time muted. The novel ends on a defiant note, but this is tempered by uncertainty: 'I kept hoping against hope that I'd be the bright exception, the talented token that smashed sex and class barriers. Hurrah for her' (*ibid.*, p. 245).

Despite the heroine's proud and out lesbianism, and her sharp wit, *Rubyfruit Jungle* expresses the same tension as the more mainstream college novels. Molly is caught, like all these heroines, between the possibilities of the wider world and nostalgia for home and family. Having cut a successful sexual and intellectual swathe through the cities of Florida and New York, Molly is finally reconciled with the stepmother whose rabid views 'to the right of Genghis Khan' (*ibid.*, p. 242) she had once fled. Her graduation film is focused on stepmother Carrie reminiscing in her rocking chair, and represents Molly's emotional return to the familiar values of home and hearth.

Alice Walker's 1976 novel *Meridian* also has a disadvantaged woman at its centre, but for an Afro-American writer, the pull of family and home has a particular resonance and political charge. Meridian is, like Molly, an outsider in the world of academia; she is a single, black mother, whose access to education depends on scholarships. The writing of *Meridian* was in part supported by the Radcliffe Institute, although 'Saxon College', which Meridian attends, is far removed from the romance and glamour of most Radcliffe-set fiction. Alice Walker herself was a student at the first university for black women students, Spelman College in Atlanta, on which Saxon College is clearly modelled. *Meridian* appears to be a novel centred on the single character of the title, but it reads less as a life narrative than as a set of interlinked short stories, all weighted with the grim history of black women in America. The novel is dialogic, and more complex than the multiple narratives familiar to the college girl form. Meridian's story provides a central thread on which other voices, histories and memories can be hung. Meridian's symbolic status (and academic credibility) as a paradigmatic Afro-American woman is signalled in an introductory dictionary definition of her name that draws out all its connotations of power and transition.

Meridian is drawn into education through the civil rights movement, but it is politics that gets in the way of the upward mobility that university education is meant to give her. Meridian's first sacrifice is to give up her child for the cause, but this is only one of many that she is to make in pursuit of an 'authentic' political life; she chooses to give up her lover and has her 'tubes tied', in a bleak image of sterility. The politicization that comes from the experience of voter registration in the South leaves Meridian unable to move into the secure bourgeois world for which her education has prepared her. She is unable to study 'while others were being beaten and jailed' (Walker, 1982, p. 90). Meridian completes her final dissertation on the evils of property ownership, and lives this principle out in her post-college life. She eschews friends, lovers and possessions, and is wilfully downwardly mobile: 'From being a teacher who published small broadsides of poems, she had hired herself out as a gardener, as a waitress at middle-class black parties, and had occasionally worked as a dishwasher and cook' (*ibid.*, p. 19).

Like most heroines of the college narrative, Meridian is an exceptional student: 'for her area and background her IQ of 140 was unusually high' (*ibid.*, p. 82). Awarded a scholarship endowed by a liberal white family, she initially feels herself 'blessed' to be at college, proud of the 'will' which got her there. Saxon College, however, is about educating young black women to conform to the prevailing conventions of race and femininity: 'The emphasis at Saxon was on form, and the preferred "form" was that of the finishing school girl whose goal ... was to be *accepted* as an equal because she knew and practised all the proper social rules' (*ibid.*, p. 91). Meridian and her friend Ann-Marion, like Molly and Faye, are dissenters in this aspirational world; refusing to sing the school song, they march with the Atlanta civil rights movement, and are jailed along with their schoolbooks.

There is a constant awareness of the disjuncture between the privilege of college life and the poverty found in the American South; Saxon College, 'a school for young ladies' (*ibid.*, p. 25), is surrounded by the ghetto. When a feral 'Wild Child' erupts into the college she cannot be contained; her death is marked by the first student protest in the college's 'long, placid, impeccable history' (*ibid.*, p. 38). The 'Wild Child' is symbolically buried under the 'Sojourner Tree' in the centre of the campus. The tree's name connotes the proud history of black women's resistance, 'Sojourner' invoking the abolitionist orator Sojourner Truth. The tree is also a memorial to a slave whose tongue was cut out by her slave master in a vivid image of the silencing of black women. The tree, planted in the centre of the college, is throughout the novel a recurrent image of suppressed black history. Cut down by the student demonstration, the only image of hope in the novel is that the stump of the tree grows a new shoot. The voice of Sojourner Truth cannot be eradicated.

The novel takes place over a period which begins with the political urgency of the civil rights movement and ends with Meridian's activist lover regretfully musing: 'Revolution was the theme of the sixties ... But all that is gone now' (*ibid.*, p. 192). Meridian refuses either to wholeheartedly embrace violent revolutionary politics, or to let go of the revolutionary spirit, an impasse that leaves her literally paralysed: 'Meridian, for all her good intentions might never be ready for the future' (*ibid.*, p. 123). Meridian is a student at the moment of John Kennedy's assassination, a brief moment of political unity among the student population. She begins the novel surrounded by student activists, galvanized by the events of the 1960s: 'a group of students, of intellectuals, converted to a belief in violence only after witnessing the extreme violence, against black dissidents, of the federal government and police' (*ibid.*, p. 15). While she has witnessed and experienced this violence herself, Meridian agonizes over her memories of her father and family, and cannot bring herself to accept the rhetoric of revolutionary student politics. It is only at a black church that she finds a reconciliation of her own dissent with a wider black history. She sees the churchgoers as 'the righteous guardians of the people's memories' (*ibid.*, p. 205), but a religious faith is not compatible with her radical politics.

The conflict between a loyalty to home and political life has a particularly sharp edge for an Afro-American woman writer. The loss of connections with family life is all the more acute because, as Sandi Russell has explained, Walker's fiction is part of a project for the reclamation of black women's history (Russell, 1990, p. 116). Walker repeatedly represents the histories of Afro-American families, and particularly their women, as the stuff of a hidden black history. Meridian is unable to commit herself to the violent revolution her student comrades promote because she cannot let go of that history; she is 'held by something in the past: by the memory of old black men in the South' (Walker, 1982, p. 14). But while her onetime comrades all lose their youthful political fervour, it is Meridian alone who is 'holding onto something the others had let go' (*ibid.*). Her identification with the dispossessed is such that she experiences psychosomatic fits or trances, episodes which have more to do with guilt than with any mystical experience. Meridian is crippled by guilt from childhood: as a child she is guilty that her mother has sacrificed her teaching ambitions to raise a family; as an adult she is guilty that a college education has given her advantages beyond the expectations of her class and culture.

Meridian is of a generation that has new opportunities, but her respect for black history cannot allow her to forget the past. She is caught between grudging respect for the stalwart courage of previous generations of Afro-American women, and disdain for their resignation and the 'fragility of spirit' that she sees in her mother. Meridian acknowledges that she has options denied to earlier generations: 'her mother's and her grandmother's extreme purity of life was compelled by necessity. They had not lived in an age of choice' (*ibid.*, p. 123). Meridian does live in an age of choice, but what she chooses is to emulate the 'extreme purity of life' of her foremothers. If that choice is masochistic, it represents an uncomfortable compromise between the discourses of political radicalism and black history.

Meridian dramatizes many of the debates about black American experience, interracial relationships and feminism that emerged from the civil rights movement. The narrative is concerned to offer a range of black and female experiences that extend beyond the history of one woman. Meridian's romance with the handsome Truman is paralleled with the story of Lynne, a white Jewish civil rights activist, who provides a model for a discussion of black men's relationships with white women, and of alliances between black and white women. Lynne's committed liberalism and her interracial marriage do not represent a political future for the novel either: the child of her relationship with Truman is killed. The novel finally cannot allow any of the political choices presented in the novel to mark a way forward. Like Meridian, Truman and Lynne are not ready for the future; there is to be no next generation for any of the central protagonists.

Meridian is formally more adventurous than any of the other novels. It rejects social realism and chronology in favour of a patchwork of symbol and fragments, like the quilt that embodies black culture in Walker's short story 'Everyday Use' (Walker, 1984). In 'Everyday Use' a radicalized black woman student returns to claim her heritage in the form of the quilt, but misrecognizes its significance. Her sister and mother recognize it for what it is: an intricately worked but useful object that is made up by women from the small pieces of everyday life. *Meridian* is similarly embedded with fragments, incorporating tales of silenced and abused black women, tales that derive from campus and community mythology and from family histories. These family and community stories sit alongside literary references and reports of political struggles. Two of the chapters consist of poems by the banished Russian poet Anna Akhmatova (in another evocation of an attempt to silence a woman's voice); the novel is studded with stories and epigrams from Afro-American and Native American history. This wide range of references is seen, however, as set apart from the culture of university; Meridian's reading of political theory and her sense of black history are not supported by her academic work.

The women students of these novels can no more envisage their personal experience becoming part of their academic work than Rosamund in *The Millstone* could in the 1960s. By the late 1970s, however, black history and women's studies courses had become part of the academic curriculum and women's groups were an established fact of campus life. Marilyn French's *The Women's Room* and Marge Piercy's *Small Changes* were to become the feminist best-selling versions of the college novel. Merja Makinen has suggested that: 'Feminist literature in Britain and America during the rise of the Women's Liberation Movement initially took the form of the realist "coming to consciousness" novel, a form of bildungsroman, that of the feminist consciousness in the female protagonist' (Makinen, 2001, p. 9). The college narrative can be read as a pre-feminist form of the women's 'coming to consciousness' novel that is rooted in the late 1960s and early 1970s. Jaffe's 1958 novel *The Best of Everything* can also be understood as an early forerunner of the 'coming to consciousness' novel. The college novel, with its structure of individual and collective narratives of transition into adult womanhood, was a form that could be embraced by pre-feminist writers and writers who were antipathetic or indifferent to feminism and also by avowedly feminist novelists like Walker, French and Piercy.

These novels rarely have any direct identification with the women's movement. With the exception of Meridian, Mira of *The Women's Room* and Miriam and Beth in *Small Changes*, all the heroines of these novels encounter feminism in some form, but reject it as having no relevance to their own lives. Nonetheless, the popular 'college novel' deals directly with issues that were very pertinent to women's liberation. The narratives are predicated on a set of women's friendships, and they are preoccupied with questions of sexuality and gender. Contraception, abortion and male power are central motors for the plots; all the heroines have to deal with the fear of pregnancy and have to learn how to acquire birth control. These were all concerns which were on the agenda of the Women's Liberation Movement, as Lesley Hall explains: 'The new wave of feminist militancy ... included free contraception and abortion on demand among the four demands formulated in 1971: women's right to control their own fertility was a central tenet' (Hall, 2000, p. 177).

In the late 1960s and early 1970s, student feminists were reading women's fiction and political theory together, and inevitably took their reading into academic seminars. Katherine Payant remembers the power of a reading experience shared with other women, and the challenge that this form of reading made to traditional notions of the 'literary canon':

> Like many women readers I came to this new writing around 1970, at the same time that I was plunging into the swirling waters of the budding feminist movement. I read my first feminist novels – *Diary of a Mad Housewife* and *Memoirs of an Ex-Prom Queen* – at the same time I read Simone de Beauvoir, Kate Millet, Germaine Greer and Shulamith Firestone. Influenced by my years of literary education, I was not sure if what I was reading was literature, but for the first time in my reading experience I fully recognised myself. Members of my consciousness-raising group read many of these works together, passing along titles of novels to each other.
>
> (Payant, 1993, pp. 1–2)

The college novels were among these titles passed around the feminist readers in women's groups across Britain and America. Their narratives express much the same sense of excitement that Payant expresses for the experience of university and of friendships with other women. Andrea Newman's heroine in *A Share of the World* articulates a sentiment that all these novels share: 'That's the best thing about college ... the freedom to live your own life' (Newman, 1979, p. 32). University is shown in these novels as a temporary utopia, a space in which equality can be briefly experienced, before the compromises of the adult world have to be confronted. The college setting was a means of exploring expanding opportunities for young women; the woman student provided a model for a generation caught between the conventions of a pre-feminist morality and the excitement of new ideas and sexual experiences. In a 2005 interview Rona Jaffe, retrospectively reflecting on her fiction, asserted that the conflicts she had charted in her novels from the 1950s to the 1970s remain true for women in the new millennium: 'Still ... the conflicts are the same today. You have the strong woman living the subservient life ... That's not in the past; it's still around' (La Ferla, 2005, p. 2).

The college novel of the late 1960s and early 1970s continued to dramatize the conflict for young women between ambition and romance. Sheila Ernst has noted that in novels that she defines as 'feminist' in this period, the heroines tend to be overwhelmed by their emotions and the personal overrides the political:

> many of the heroines ... struggle to discover a sense of self and find this struggle most difficult when they are in an intimate relationship ... [M]any of these women *appear* to be leading independent lives with jobs or careers, but intimacy drags them right back into emotional subservience.
>
> (Ernst, 1987, p. 73)

This apparent independence is true in fiction both by feminist writers and by writers indifferent to feminism. The college novel can often explicitly reject feminist ideas, but the genre inevitably shares this sense of relationships with men as damaging to women's ambition and independence. If the majority of these narratives cannot allow their heroines to embrace feminist politics, the characters cannot entirely avoid the impact of the women's movement and radical politics. The structure of the college novel is marked by the interweaving of women's stories and is predicated on a set of female friendships; the genre necessarily charts a collectivity of female experience. The 'group' novel would, however, in the 1980s shift to a focus on a single achieving heroine, and the popular novel go on to feature intrepid women characters who succeed in a world largely without friends.

4

Shopping as Work: The Sex and Shopping Novel of the 1980s

The genre in women's fiction which defined the decade of the 1980s was the sex and shopping novel, also known as the 'S and F novel'. The sex and shopping novel could be generically identified by a cover with a title in 'dripping gold blocking' (Dychoff, 2001, p. 31). While the covers of the college narrative had featured portraits of a group of women, these novels used a single woman, her face half hidden by a shady hat, her glamour signified by bright red lipstick. What distinguished this form of novel from other forms of women's fiction in the decade, however, was its emphasis on the working woman.

The sex and shopping novel crossed over a European and American readership, their authors and narratives determinedly international (in terms of the American and Western European capitals of the world). Their heroines move, whatever their origins, through Paris, London, Milan and New York with great assurance, the power of capital and of international consumer brands enough to sustain them wherever they travel. These novels can be read as the contemporary literary equivalent of the hugely popular prime-time television series *Dallas* and *Dynasty* which were broadcast across the world throughout the 1980s; *Dallas* was first aired in America in 1978, and the last series was screened in 1991, while *Dynasty* ran from 1981 to 1989. These television programmes and the sex and shopping novel shared an emphasis on extreme wealth, and focused on the concomitant lifestyle, in which luxury and glamour were unapologetically celebrated. Both forms of narrative are also centred on powerful women characters, whose dress, self-presentation and households proudly champion conspicuous consumption. However, while the women characters in *Dallas* and *Dynasty* tended to achieve their power and wealth through family connections, usually through marriage or divorce from a wealthy man, their fictional equivalents in the novel are often alone. The structure of the sex and shopping novel is centred on a heroine left to fend for herself but who ends the narrative with triumphant success – a form of narrative that neatly fitted the prevailing contemporary political ideologies of self-sufficiency and individual enterprise.

There is a recurrent trope in these novels of lost and dead husbands and fathers who are lost through a range of narrative devices: divorce, death, desertion or criminal activity. The heroines are left to forge a new life, and the narratives chart their progress towards material and romantic success. This narrative of the successful single woman can be read as a displacement of the contemporary situation of large numbers of women finding themselves alone because of divorce. In America, divorce rates peaked around 1980, while in Britain, divorce had steadily crept up throughout the decade of the 1970s; these novels offered a revenge fantasy of the ultimate triumph, through her own efforts, of the woman left alone.

The sex and shopping novel broke with what had been one of the central conventions of the contemporary romance novel, that the heroine should be less powerful than the hero. This was a form of romance narrative which was defined by a wealthy and powerful heroine. Silhouette (the brand name for the publisher which markets Mills and Boon and Silhouette romantic fiction) had issued a style sheet for potential authors throughout the 1980s which specified that the hero was to be the most wealthy and powerful figure in the romance novel (Philips, 1990, p. 144). The heroine of the sex and shopping genre, however, was not employed by, or in any way subservient to, a hero. Instead, she is a self-employed, entrepreneurial woman, a 'Superwoman' (the title of a 1977 handbook by Shirley Conran) who embodied the potential of enterprise and initiative that was so promoted by both the Reagan and the Thatcher governments of the decade.

The titles of these novels connote serious female determination and ambition: *To be the Best* (1988), *Act of Will* (1987), *Hold the Dream* (1985) (all novels by the English writer Barbara Taylor Bradford), *I'll Take Manhattan* (1986) and *Dazzle* (1991) (novels by Judith Krantz) are examples of the range of titles written by women which held out the promise of achieved material success and wealth for women readers. As Judith Shulevitz has pointed out, this sub-genre of the romance narrative brought together many of the conventions of romantic fiction with plots which centred around high finance and business enterprise:

> [The] so-called sex-and-shopping genre ... [is] a catchy but deceptively broad term: Susann wrote morality plays about fame and its vicissitudes; Sheldon writes gothic narrative against a fuzzy backdrop of celebrity and high stakes finance. Krantz's novels read like Harvard Business School case studies on the retail experience, filtered through gauzy, if sexually explicit, Harlequin style romance.
>
> (Shulevitz, 2000, p. 206)

While Shulevitz may have a point in her suggestion that the 'sex and shopping' novel 'is a catchy but deceptively broad term', it was nonetheless a form which had a limited life span, and which answered to a historically specific dominant ideology. The popular success of the genre was not to last for long after the end of the decade of the 1980s and into the 1990s, like the American television programmes *Dallas*[1] and *Dynasty* which ended their runs in 1991 and 1989 respectively. Shulevitz does here identify the sex and shopping novel as a recognized fictional genre, and one which conflated contemporary discourses of commerce and finance with those of glamour and romance. In this new form of romantic fiction, the traditionally 'feminine' sphere of 'gauzy romance' comes together with what had previously been constructed in the romance novel as a 'masculine' world of business, enterprise and commerce. Whatever their setting or the nature of the business, in the sex and shopping novel it is women who achieve success in the field of 'high stakes finance'; although the categories of management and craft skills were in fact the least likely occupations for working women, according to the 1976 Willis study of graduate working women: 'Only 16 per cent of women are in the professional category, five per cent in the manager and administrator category and kindred worker category' (Willis, 1976, p. 7). Nonetheless, these are precisely the areas in which women are seen to excel in fiction in the 1980s. The heroines turn their expertise in the arts of 'femininity' to professional advantage: the range of enterprises in these novels includes fashion and jewellery design, publishing, and international chains of hotels and department stores.

These narratives answered to a fantasy that skills traditionally associated with femininity, such as shopping, interior decoration, dress design and home-making, could be transformed from disdained hobbies into significant commercial concerns. Their heroines' successes in these fields suggested that the contemporary political climate offered a potential for women to make the transition from low-paid or voluntary workers into professional businesswomen.

In the British context, Sheila Rowbotham has argued that while the right-wing policies of the Conservative government, itself led by a powerful and successful woman, were detrimental to the majority of women, it did appear to allow those women with capital to prosper materially:

> In practice neither women nor poor families were favoured by Thatcherism ... On the other hand, the cuts in direct taxation during the early 1980s and the impact of unemployment on inflation added to the prosperity of families with high incomes, while women who were in a position to buy property, rise in one of the better-paid professions or the media or set up their own businesses could do well.
>
> (Rowbotham, 1997, p. 479)

It is precisely these 'successful' women that the sex and shopping novel both celebrated and promised, their narratives suggesting that 'setting up' a business was the way to success, that from modest beginnings, enormous wealth could be achieved. In the early 1980s, in both Britain and America, this was a fantasy that appeared as a real possibility, with the success of companies such as the Body Shop, the Sock Shop and Mrs Field's Cookies. These were enterprises that were women led, and which had all started from small and domestic beginnings, but which were to go on to become global brands.

The political shifts in the economic and employment policies in Britain and America had meant a 'feminization' of the economy, but that 'feminization' was less about supporting and encouraging women workers than it was an extension of the 'trend towards low-paid, insecure and non-unionised labour' (Haywood, 1997, p. 141). The sex and shopping narrative suggested that these economic policies could be made to work for the benefit of women, and that insecure and low-paid work (which remains a rite of passage for all the heroines of these novels) could be the launch pad for greater things. The plots and resolutions of these novels held out the promise that all women workers could 'do well' and that the most humble or insecure forms of work could become the basis for a powerful commercial enterprise.

Judith Krantz's 1978 novel *Scruples* established a prototypical heroine and plot for the sex and shopping novel. In the first of Krantz's 'ten best-selling tales of female glamour through high fashion and the media' (Shulevitz, 2000, p. 206), Billy Ikehorn turns her skill and pleasure in shopping into a business opportunity. Set in Beverly Hills, Billy is first approvingly introduced in terms of her material wealth; her possession of luxury items and the details of her financial investments are carefully itemized, her wardrobe a signifier of her financial status:

> Billy Ikehorn Orsini ... brought her vintage Bentley to a stop with an impatient screech in front of Scruples, the world's most lavish speciality store, a virtual club for the floating principality of the very, very rich and the truly famous. She was thirty-five, sole mistress of a fortune estimated at between two hundred and two hundred fifty million dollars by the list makers of the *Wall Street Journal*. Almost half of her wealth was tidily invested in tax-free municipal bonds, a simplification little appreciated by the IRS. ... Billy's tawny wool cape was lined in golden sable. She pulled it around her as she looked quickly up and down the sumptuous heart of Rodeo Drive.
>
> (Krantz, 1978, pp. 2–3)

Scruples earned Krantz 'the highest ever advance sale for paperback rights to a novel ($3.2.m)' (Sutherland, 1981, p. 74) and went on to become a television mini-series. Billy's name has an interesting gender ambiguity, suggesting an ambivalence in the construction of a financially successful woman. In the combination of a male name with a diminutive, there is a suggestion of a masculine hard-headedness, which does not compromise the traditional attributes of femininity. Billy is introduced as a properly extravagant consumer, but is nonetheless shown to be sensibly investing her fortune. Billy is the widow of a millionaire, and the novel goes on to tell the retrospective tale of her rise to wealth, and of her careful custody and enlargement of financial capital. Krantz is keen to establish that her heroine has both class and wealth: Billy is the daughter of 'the very best of Boston families', although, importantly, her wealth does not derive from family money. It is the training of a 'good family' that provides her with the cultural capital from which she goes on to make her fortune; it is Billy's exquisite taste which makes her business enterprise successful. She puts her knowledge of elegance and style, acquired in Boston, Paris and New York, to work by setting up a fantasy store in Beverly Hills: 'an outpost of the elegance and grace and refinement that, until now, had existed only in Paris' (Krantz, 1978, p. 234).

Billy reconciles the contradictory values of the Reagan and Thatcher ethos; she combines a competitive work ethic with a proper respect for aristocratic heritage. Like many of the heroines of these novels, Billy eschews higher education in favour of a form of finishing school, a training in the etiquette and tastes of the privileged (the multiple heroines of Shirley Conran's *Lace* meet at a Swiss finishing school). The novel is concerned to demonstrate Billy's intelligence; she is accepted by the best universities in the country, but instead chooses a training in cosmopolitan etiquette and style with 'a family of the ancient royalist aristocracy' in Paris. Billy and her rise to wealth thus embodies a magical synthesis of new money and traditional values, a reconciliation of family values and the virtues of individual enterprise that was such a marked feature of the contemporary populist politics of both Britain and America. Stuart Hall has described the British manifestation in these terms:

> Thatcherite populism is a particularly rich mix. It combines the resonant themes of organic Toryism – nation, family, duty, authority, standards, traditionalism – with the aggressive themes of a revived neo-liberalism – self-interest, competitive individualism, anti-statism.
>
> (Hall, 1983, p. 29)

The heroines of the sex and shopping novels come to embrace the politics of individual enterprise and ambition, their entry into the world of finance and commerce marked by a recognition that sisterhood is less financially rewarding than self-interest. One of the heroines of Shirley Conran's *Lace* (Conran, 1982) founds a publishing empire based on her disenchantment with both feminist politics and women's magazines. The success of her publishing venture VERVE! allows Judy Jordan to be worth several million dollars and to wear Maud Frizon shoes and designer outfits from Chloé. Although the heroines of the novels are often presented as initially in a state of crisis, their narratives chart their progress until they finally arrive in a world in which the interior décor is sumptuous, the clothing is designer and their social circle consists of people of extreme wealth and economic power.

The heroine of Judith Gould's *Sins* (Gould, 1983) is another magazine publisher, but Hélène does not stop with a single magazine; she heads an empire of fashion titles. The novel's subtitle, 'A novel of ambition and desire', and its narrative clearly relish the opportunity to write a woman who has none of the redeeming features of traditional femininity, but who is ruthless in her ambition. Crossing continents and decades, the novel is as relentlessly ambitious in its scope as is its heroine. The narrative begins in a boardroom in Manhattan, and then shuttles between contemporary America and flashbacks to post-war Europe, in an affirmation of the post-war progress of the Western world. The historical sweep from wartime France to contemporary America is, however, largely expressed in terms of fashion: the 'New Look' is the most notable aspect of post-war Paris, while a visit to Germany in 1954 is marked by the fact that the women wear Persian-lamb coats. Hélène is a child of occupied France; her experience of Paris under the occupation fuels her courage and determination, and provides her with an unassailable justification for her subsequent ruthlessness and ambition. Hélène begins with nothing, but her European taste (which is represented as an innate gift) and her modest dressmaking skills become the foundation of a multi-million dollar business concern. The New York office of her empire is a model of unapologetic conspicuous consumption: 'the reception area was spacious and lavishly appointed. Here the dollar-and-cents value of the empire was translated into tangibles for all to see. No expense had been spared' (*ibid.*, p. 23). Hélène herself is naturally 'extremely elegant'; she is regularly dressed in mink and adorned with diamonds, and carries a case that 'had cost two thousand dollars' (*ibid.*, p. 331).

The novel is populated by characters who are extremes of wealth, talent and beauty; all are extremely financially successful, none more so than the leading protagonist. Hélène is a thoroughly amoral heroine. She becomes mistress to a French aristocrat and blackmails her lovers and persecutors to fulfil her dream of founding a magazine devoted to taste and style. Her affair with a French Comte supplies her with a charming house in Paris and a collection of exquisite jewellery (described in loving detail). Her ageing musical genius husband conveniently dies and leaves her with the financial capital to become a publishing magnate. Hélène's subsequent lovers are aristocrats and billionaires, her friends are all extraordinarily talented photographers, designers and stylists. The final romantic hero is not only an English Duke, but also the 'third richest man in England' (*ibid.*, p. 135). For Hélène, like Billy, her personal beauty and knowledge of fashion provide the means to open up access to the parties, the restaurants, and the great hotels and houses of London, Paris, and New York. These novels are full of the details of ornate furnishings and decoration, in a world that is to be found only on television and in the pages of glossy magazines. *Hello!* was first published in England in 1988 and celebrated the fashions and the domestic interiors of the enormously wealthy and aristocratic in remarkably similar terms.

Publishing in the 1980s was dominated by takeovers and mergers, and successful popular novelists became commodities to be exchanged by rival companies, in a position to command huge advances. The paperback rights for Judith Krantz's *Princess Daisy* (1980) were sold to Bantam books for $3.2 million (Greenfield, 1989, p. 148). As publishers made more use of advertising strategies than they ever had before, new titles and successful authors were marketed as glamorous products. Backed by promotional campaigns, such novelists became celebrities in their own right, their achieved wealth and success emulating the designer lives of their heroines. Best-selling novelists such as Jackie Collins, Shirley Conran, Judith Krantz, Barbara Taylor Bradford, and particularly Danielle Steel, were promoted as figures whose own lifestyles and self-presentation promised the achievability of dreams of glamour. Their soft focus and styled images in author photographs suggested that any woman with a typewriter and a room of her own could have it all. The enormously prolific Danielle Steel, who produced between two and six novels each year between 1981 and 1989, was perhaps the most glamorous of all. Educated in France, with a background in public relations and three husbands behind her, Steel was well placed to act out the lives of her heroines. Steel's novelist heroine Natasha Walker embodies a contemporary mythology of the successful woman writer, which, apart from the hair colouring, clearly owes much to Steel's own persona:

> A long lanky blonde, with her hair falling over one eye, sat in a tiny bright yellow room pounding away at a typewriter ... And the framed covers of her last five books hung crookedly on the far wall, scattered among equally askew photographs of a yacht moored in Monte Carlo, two children on a beach in Honolulu, a president, a prince and a baby ... [S]he had written five novels and two movies, and in the literary world she was a star.
>
> (Steel, 1980, p. 91)

Steel's heroines, like Billy in *Scruples* and Steel herself (who had a family background in Eastern Europe), combine an American ambition with the traces of a vaguely European nobility. Isabella, of the 1980 novel *To Love Again*, reconciles aristocratic heritage and commerce and European tradition with American modernity. An Italian princess, she has married into 'the tabernacle of Roman couture, the pinnacle of prestige and exquisite taste in the eternal international competition between women of enormous means and aspirations' (*ibid.*, p. 2). Summarily deprived of her husband and fortune through a kidnapping, Isabella is left with nothing but the (not inconsiderable) proceeds of her jewellery, and moves to New York, arriving at a Park Avenue apartment in a Rolls Royce. This is a recurrent structure in Steel's novels; the heroine loses everything, and must begin again from nothing, a narrative that neatly articulated a prevailing ideology that success could be founded on individual initiative rather than privilege. Having built up the design company once again, her own exquisite taste ensuring its success, Isabella ends by triumphantly entering an exclusive New York restaurant, and so rejoins the world of successful entrepreneurship and achieved wealth:

> The soft pink lighting warmed the familiar faces, faces one usually saw in fashion magazines or on the covers of *Fortune* or *Time*. Movie stars, moguls, publishers, authors, heads of corporations. The very good at what they did, and the very rich because they were.
>
> (*Ibid*., p. 258)

Ien Ang has suggested that the houses and character types popularized through programmes such as *Dallas* came to connote a form of visual pleasure that was to become a global phenomenon:

> The hegemony of American television (and film) has habituated the world public to American production values and American mises-en-scène, such as the vast prairie or the big cities, the huge houses with expensive interiors, luxurious and fast cars, and last but not least, the healthy – and good-looking men and women, white, not too young, not too old. Such images have become signs which no longer merely indicated something like 'Americanness' but visual pleasure as such.
>
> (Ang, 1985, p. 55)

The lovingly detailed descriptions of beautiful people, cars, restaurants, jewels and clothing found in these novels offer the reader a written equivalent of this visual pleasure. The details of clothes and furnishings that are such a feature of these novels affirm an unabashed celebration of consumption, and particularly of expensive and exclusive branded luxury items. Steel approvingly describes a New York apartment with a lingering emphasis on the impracticality and expense of its design:

> The living room was enormous, ice-white with dollops of richly textured cream, smooth white fabrics, white leather, white walls, long mirrored panels and much chrome. There were stark glass tiles that seemed suspended in thin air, delicate lighting, a white marble fireplace, and plants that hung airily from the ceiling to the floor. The large handsome modern paintings were the only splash of bold colour in the room.
>
> (Steel, 1980, p. 123)

The cultural knowledge that is articulated here, and the painstaking attention to the details of interior design and clothing that is so recurrent in these novels, often reads as close to the captions to articles in glossy consumer magazines. The pleasures of shopping for clothes and décor are endorsed and validated in these novels as a particular form of knowledge, and the narratives convert such consumer knowledge, the pleasures of shopping, into the transferable skills necessary for building a business empire. The shopping in these fictions (of which there is a great deal) is not simply concerned with the pleasures of consumption, but shows their heroines turning the skills of shopping and consumer knowledge into a profession. Shopping becomes literally a form of work; the heroine's rise to success is almost invariably through some form of retailing, the department store featuring large in these novels. *Scruples* is more about the heroine's love affair with a store than with any of the men in the narrative. Judith Michael's Katherine in *Possessions* (a title that in itself suggests the significance of commodities) learns the struggle to become an independent working woman as a window dresser in 'an exclusive department store that catered to the whims of wealthy customers' (Michael, 1984, p. 6). Faced with a disappearing husband (in this case he has absconded with his firm's accounts), Katherine has to forge a life for herself and her two children. Once she has learnt the rules of commerce and enterprise in a humble job in retailing, Katherine can go on to convert her hobby of jewellery making into a million-dollar enterprise. Shirley Conran's successful heroines in *Lace* learn their crafts as fashion journalists and hoteliers by starting out in lowly jobs in catering and the retail trade.

It was indeed in the retail and catering industries that the majority of women workers in Britain and America found employment throughout the 1980s, most often in non-unionized and exploited occupations. The post-Fordist employment policies of Thatcherite Britain and Reagan's America had produced a shift from productive labour into 'service' and leisure industries and promoted flexi-time (often part-time) forms of work, forms of work which were familiar to women. But as Lynne Segal pointed out at the time, these conditions were not necessarily in the interests of women workers: 'the expansion of part-time and "job-splitting" opportunities, which Thatcherism is supporting, makes it possible for women to do paid work on top of heavy domestic burdens' (Segal, 1983, p. 211). It was the catering and retail trades which saw the greatest rise in female employment during the 1980s, and the insecure and low-paid jobs that they offered represented the worst of the 'feminization' of contemporary employment policy. While the sex and shopping novel suggested that converting such forms of work into a successful career was a matter of individual achievement, in practice these were occupations which offered little opportunity for advancement. While women's employment was rising, very few women could achieve in these fields. Rowbotham has explained, echoing Willis's findings, that while women's employment had seen a '5 per cent increase on the previous decade ... expansion was mainly in junior management in retail, hotels, catering and local government. Top women were a tiny minority' (Rowbotham, 1997, p. 495).

This 'tiny minority' of successful career women are presented in these narratives as role models, their stories offering the possibility that any informed and enterprising woman worker could move from the shop floor into the board room, that an insecure and junior position could lead to higher things. Their premise is that the contemporary shift in employment policies had opened up opportunities in which women workers could shine. Ian Haywood has argued that Thatcherism 'was a "New Right" philosophy which ... based its appeal on the mentality of the entrepreneur, the owner of a small business, and the self employed artisan and skilled working-class sector' (Haywood, 1997, p. 139).

The entrepreneur, the owner of the small business, and the self-employed woman are precisely the heroines of the sex and shopping genre, and they are entirely complicit in this New Right ideology. These heroines are, to a woman, 'Right-Wing Women' (in Andrea Dworkin's term), each clearly achieving through her embracing of and success within the terms of free-market capitalism. Writing in 1983, Dworkin asserted that: 'women struggle, in the manner of Sisyphus, to avoid the "something worse" that can and will always happen to them if they transgress the rigid boundaries of appropriate female behaviour' (Dworkin, 1983, p. 119). Nonetheless, these fictional heroines are by no means the 'domesticated females' helpless against male power that Dworkin describes in her book. Dworkin counterposes the 'self-loathing, fear, and humiliation' of the Right-Wing Woman with the radical feminist, who demonstrates, she argues (with some tautology): 'self-determination, dignity, and authentic integrity'. None of the women in these novels can be read as experiencing self-loathing, even in their initial crisis; all the heroines begin with confidence in their own abilities, and end their narratives committed to self-determination, dignity, and, within their own terms, integrity. If the heroines of these novels could hardly be described as feminists, they are shown to struggle, but they are also shown to transgress the boundaries of 'appropriate female behaviour', as successful and ambitious entrepreneurs. Work becomes integral to the heroine's sense of herself, and career achievement central to the construction of the happy ending of the romance narrative. As one heroine expresses her gratitude to an investor in her jewellery-making business:

> '... you've given me the freedom to work. I don't have to borrow; I can work in my own home in the daytime or at night; I can try different techniques and styles because I have the tools for them. Do you know what this means to me?' Tears filled her eyes. 'It's as if you've given me a life. The tools to shape a life ...'
>
> (Michael, 1984, p. 178)

In the British context, with a woman prime minister in power, and apparently unassailable, the 1980s seemed to be a decade which did demand of women that they should have it all: romance, a family and a glamorous and powerful working life. Thatcher herself endorsed and promoted the female skills that feminists such as Dale Spender had identified as 'invisible' labour

(Spender, 1982). The language of female assertion was in the mainstream, embodied in a woman prime minister, but this was not the language of feminist theory. Stuart Hall and Martin Jacques have pointed out that Thatcherism paid particular attention to the centrality of women's domestic role (Hall and Jacques, 1983), but as Thatcher herself demonstrated, the language of home economics could easily be made to slide into the language of enterprise and capital. In an interview, Thatcher evoked women's traditional skills without challenging their limited applications in the domestic sphere. She argued instead that the domestic labour of women could be seen as a model for business management:

> many, many women make naturally good managers ... each woman who runs a house is a manager and an organizer. We thought forward each day, and we did it in a routine way, and we were on the job 24 hours a day.
>
> (Interview with Margaret Thatcher, quoted in Rowbotham, 1997, p. 473)

Barbara Taylor Bradford, 'possibly the world's most popular novelist, probably Britain's second wealthiest woman, definitely the country's richest author' (Hattenstone, 2000, p. 4), explicitly made an analogy between the first woman prime minister, her fictional heroines and herself as a successful novelist in a newspaper interview. Taylor Bradford was in the 1980s a British version of Danielle Steel, whose persona and success as a writer became as important as those of her heroines. Her novel *A Woman of Substance*, published in 1980, told the story of a servant girl who became a business tycoon. The financial success of the novel allowed the author's own story to mirror the achievements of her fictional heroine, Emma Harte, who, like Billy of *Scruples*, makes her fortune in retailing and opens a department store. Taylor Bradford, like her heroine and like Margaret Thatcher, seemed to embody the potential opportunities for femininity in the 1980s; all three came from relatively humble (and Northern) backgrounds, and all became powerful and wealthy women. Taylor Bradford was herself described by one journalist as: 'Our Barbara, the Yorkshire lass who once scoured her mother's front steps, has grown into this formidable woman who can make or break multi-national publishing companies' (Hattenstone, 2000, p. 4). Nonetheless, while asserting her right to be a formidable woman, Taylor Bradford's expectations were that both she and her heroines should maintain the traditionally feminine virtues. Like Thatcher, and like her heroines, she expected women to achieve in the public sphere, while simultaneously maintaining responsibility for the domestic: 'I think a woman should be able to cook a meal and look after family affairs, I'm very old-fashioned like that. I wouldn't let a maid touch the wooden furniture. Only I polish it' (*ibid.*, p. 4).

Sheila Rowbotham identifies this tension between domesticity and enterprise as one of the central contradictions for women in the decade: 'The enterprise culture was full of contradictions for women, both ideologically and practically. An unfettered market-oriented individualism clashed head on with the moral authority of hearth and home in Conservative ideology' (Rowbotham, 1997, p. 499). These contradictions were not restricted to those women who embraced the spirit of enterprise, however, but also began to inform the culture of feminism. As Rowbotham explains, the period from the late 1970s saw an upsurge of attempts among women and feminist organizations to marry the principles of sisterhood and enterprise:

> Alternative networks among business, managerial and professional women mushroomed during the 1970s to offset the male advantage of 'old boy' contacting, and with them went books and magazines which picked up on the self-affirming message in feminism and applied it to individual enterprise.
>
> (*Ibid.*, p. 445)

The dividing line between feminist commitment and individual enterprise, and between the self-affirming messages of popular novels and those of the committed feminist press, were to become increasingly blurred over the course of the decade.

Terry McMillan is a rare phenomenon, as an Afro-American woman who writes best-selling popular fiction which is read across racial and national boundaries. McMillan was nurtured by the Harlem Writers Guild, and is one of the black American writers that Sandi Russell cited in 1990 as an emergent 'new and exciting' voice (Russell, 1990, p. 153). Russell praised McMillan for her depiction of the 'dogged determination to survive' in Afro-American women. The doughty heroine of the 1987 novel *Mama* (McMillan, 1987) has a struggle to raise her five children, and manages to ensure that her daughters will not have to struggle as she did. Her children are assured entry into the black middle classes; one daughter becomes a schoolteacher, another a journalist.

McMillan's gutsy heroines were later to become more a celebration of black women's entry into the enterprise culture than icons of resistance and survival. In a 1991 interview in the feminist magazine *Spare Rib*, McMillan stated: 'I believe that good story telling should give people hope' (Grant, 1991, p. 8). Her subsequent novels have been very much about women's achievements, and celebrate forms of female success which endorsed rather than challenged the dominant orthodoxy of individual enterprise. *Waiting to Exhale* was the novel which put McMillan in the best-seller category. The novel charts the movement of a group of independent Afro-American women into the middle-class lifestyle that the heroine of Alice Walker's *Meridian* was so committed to repudiate. McMillan's heroines have none of the political agonizing and guilt that Meridian suffered at her success, but instead relish the comforts that their achievements can provide. Unlike the disadvantaged settings of *Mama* and *Disappearing Acts* (McMillan,

1990), the four women in *Waiting to Exhale* (McMillan, 1992) begin from relatively affluent positions; they are all college-educated, financially secure, and inhabit 'nice neighbourhoods'.

Waiting to Exhale borrows from the college novel structure, with its four-pronged narrative of a group of friends, and charts their success in business and in romance. The opening narrator, Savannah, works for a television company, and is criss-crossing America in search of love. She has 'everything she needs': a secure job, a car and a nice apartment (*ibid.*, p. 2), and can afford a collection of Afro-American art. Savannah financially supports her mother, who is dependent on food stamps, and she despises her sister for her lack of entrepreneurial spirit. By the end of the novel she has found love and promotion at a professional conference in Las Vegas, and resolves to devote herself to promoting black education programmes. Her friend Bernadine is a deserted wife, whose dream of a catering business is disrupted by marriage and children. Her wealthy husband is an embodiment of black business success, and has left her with a luxury house and car, and all the kitchen equipment necessary to set up her own business. Her financial settlement on their divorce is enough to allow her to make major contributions to black charities, particularly those that promote black enterprise. One of these is 'Black Women on the Move', an organization that provides assertiveness training for Afro-American businesswomen. Robin, a successful insurance saleswoman, uses her assertiveness course to acquire a man. The fourth member of the group, Gloria, runs a flourishing beauty salon that caters to the successful black women professionals that the novel represents. The novel ends with the women poised to travel to London, their financial and romantic problems resolved by their determination and enterprise.

By 1996, McMillan could wholeheartedly embrace black women's (and her own) entrepreneurial success. *How Stella Got Her Groove Back* (McMillan, 1996) was another best-selling American fairy-tale of the rewards of enterprise, defined in the *New Yorker* review (quoted on the inside front cover) as: 'A sexy handbook of self realization'. The heroine, single mother Stella, has none of the struggles of Mildred in *Mama*; she is instead surrounded by expensive consumer goods, a member of a luxury gym, and is a hard-working 'fancy-schmancy analyst for one of the world's largest investment banking institutions' (McMillan, 1996, p. 33). If Stella is bored by her job, she makes a 'shitload of money' and is wealthy enough to afford a luxury holiday in Jamaica. She has it 'all': a small son she adores, a luxury apartment, and a large independent income. All she lacks (like the women of *Waiting to Exhale*) is a man worthy of her achievements. This is remedied on the holiday, where Stella meets a much younger Jamaican man and imports him back to America. She ends the novel reassuring herself: 'you have earned this you deserve this you can take this to the bank' (McMillan, 1996, p. 445).

Terry McMillan represents a novelist who had first been endorsed by feminist and Afro-American readers, and who went on to become a mainstream commercial and popular success. If popular women novelists such as Krantz, Steel and Conran had taken on some aspects of feminist ideas and now wrote in career success as a defining element in the romance narrative, so feminist novelists took over the genres and conventions of the popular romance and attempted to make them their own. Like the heroine of Margaret Atwood's *Lady Oracle* (Atwood, 1977), whose writing career managed to encompass, if not reconcile, the penning of both feminist theory and bodice-ripper romances, throughout the 1980s Lisa Appignanesi combined the editing of theoretical documents such as *Desire* (Appignanesi, 1984) at the Institute of Contemporary Arts in London, with writing Mills and Boon titles under the name of Jessica Ayer.

The dividing line between feminist commitment and individual enterprise, and between the self-affirming messages of popular novels and of the feminist literary press, blurred in the decade. There was a belated recognition from publishers of something that had been true for a long time, that women were the largest consumers of fiction. There was a boom in publishing for women and success for feminist presses. Marilyn French's *The Women's Room* was a best-seller in both Britain and America in 1983, and the small feminist publisher The Women's Press had a best-seller with Alice Walker's *The Color Purple* in the same year. The success of feminist book fairs, the beginnings of women's studies courses, and the commercial viability of feminist publishing houses, and particularly of Virago Press, seemed to assure that feminist ideas were central to publishing. Mainstream publishers began to introduce feminist lists (Pandora Press was launched as a branch of the then Routledge and Kegan Paul) and 1985 saw the launch of two new, explicitly feminist monthly magazines to support *Spare Rib* (the first British magazine of the women's movement, which began publishing in 1972), *Women's Review* and *Everywoman* (Winship, 1987). None of these committed feminist publications, nor their more mainstream counterparts, however, was to survive into the 1990s.

In 1978, Valerie Miner, as part of a feminist writing collective, could declare an intrinsic relationship between women's writing and feminist practice: 'What does fiction have to do with politics? We are sisters, colleagues and comrades to each other. I read this book as a declaration of that coalition' (Miner, 1978, p. 61). The rallying cry of committed feminist writers, publishers and journalists, that writing by feminists was necessarily a feminist and political act, and that there was a clear relationship between feminist fiction and politics, could in the 1980s no longer be taken for granted. Anne Cranny-Francis has argued that there is a clear distinction to be made between a feminist appropriation of 'popular literary forms' and the women writers of genre fiction who, she claims, work 'conscientiously within the dominant ideologies of gender, race and class' (Cranny-Francis, 1990, p. 1). Her concern in her study of feminist genre fiction is with those feminist writings that do not admit 'compromise'. Throughout the 1980s that distinction became less and less easy to make; a feminist book could no longer be judged by its cover. Virago Press began to depart from its familiar and tasteful green covers with illustrations that deliberately echoed the novels of popular publishing houses. Zoë Fairbairns's 1983 feminist historical novel *Stand We at Last* was first published by the feminist press with a cover that emulated the historical sagas of writers such as Catherine Cookson and Barbara Taylor Bradford. The novel was taken up by the mainstream paperback publisher Pan Books a year later.

Fairbairns was, with Miner, one of the contributors to the 1978 collection *Tales I Tell My Mother*, to which she wrote the introduction. The collection of short stories was the product of a feminist writing collective, and Fairbairns here clearly expresses her commitment to and familiarity with the political worlds of both feminism and socialism:

> Collectivity is a word that is bandied about a lot in the women's movement. Sometimes, 'collective' is just a trendy euphemism for the same old committee. Sometimes it's an excuse for not doing anything. At its best though – and it has been good for us – it really can mean a group of equals, united by a genuine determination to get on with the job.
>
> (Fairbairns, 1978, p. 3)

By 1987 the same collective had produced a new collection of short stories, but nine years later, the writers were no longer in a collective and no longer working as a group. The new collection did not contain the essays from each writer on the relationship between politics and fiction that were so integral to the first volume. Instead, the foreword (written by a male editor) proudly celebrates the development of the individual writers' careers, and their commercial successes with mainstream publishers:

> All of the writers have signed with large commercial publishing houses, and successfully launched themselves on serious writing careers ... To celebrate their individual success, and by way of marking the development of feminist short story writing over the last ten years ... a new collection was brought together. Of course, the authors were working quite separately by now, each extending feminist writing on both sides of the Atlantic.
>
> (Sinclair, 1987, p. viii)

The shift from a feminist politics of collectivism to one of individual achievement that can be seen in these two volumes of feminist short stories is echoed in Fairbairns's 1987 novel *Closing*, an uneasy novel about the future of feminism in a Thatcherite world of market values, in which the feminist heroine has her feminist convictions challenged. Theresa is a disillusioned veteran of feminist publishing (based to some extent on the experience of the magazine *Women's Review*) who comes by the end of the novel to embrace the management language and selling ethos of the decade. Fairbairns takes on the generic form of the sex and shopping saga, with multiple and overlapping narratives which spin between a group of women who meet on a management course for women: an environment which neatly embodied the tensions between feminist independence and free-market enterprise.

Fay Weldon, whose own fiction had appeared in shiny embossed covers in emulation of the blockbuster novels of Jackie Collins, also took over established popular forms. *The Life and Loves of a She-Devil* (Weldon, 1983) took the familiar feminist tale of a mutinous wife, and turned it into a carnivalesque fairy-tale of revenge. Published in 1983, it borrowed the typeface and gilt lettering familiar from the popular sex and shopping novel, and went on to be a successful television series and a less successful Hollywood film. In 1987, Weldon wrote a serial novel for a popular woman's weekly magazine, clearly relishing the opportunity to tell a shaggy dog story and to write in the episodic tradition of Charles Dickens. Originally commissioned by a populist mainstream magazine in an attempt to reach women audiences beyond the self-defined readership of feminist fiction, the serial was later published as a novel under the title *The Hearts and Minds of Men*; however, there is no acknowledgement in either the hardback or paperback edition of its origins, and the serial-novel was to become a recognized part of Weldon's oeuvre. Despite her own scathing remarks to a fictional niece on popular romance fiction (which was published in paperback with the same typography and gilt lettering as on the cover of *The Life and Loves of a She-Devil*), Weldon had learned much from what she refers to as 'the ... hyped twin houses of *Scruples* and *Lace*'. Nonetheless, she goes on to describe the genre in these terms:

> The blinds are frilly and expensive and very firmly pulled down. You're not supposed to look around too closely, once inside. You may not want to much (and in any case, your comments aren't called for. You're supposed to pay your money at the door and leave at once) ... They are calculated to divert and impress and often do – but do not take them seriously, Alice, and know them for what they are.
>
> (Weldon, 1985, p. 23)

In retrospect, it is less easy to know the sex and shopping novels of the period for 'what they are' than Weldon here suggests. The discourses of women's empowerment and success that had been forged in the consciousness-raising and women's groups of the 1960s and 1970s were, in the 1980s, mapped onto the rhetoric of entrepreneurial spirit and self-improvement that marked the political discourses of the period. And the sex and shopping novel was one of the forms which brought them together.

The 1980s were a decade in which the once relatively separate fields of popular fiction for women readers and feminist literature borrowed from one another, and in which the discourses of feminism and the Thatcherite rhetoric of enterprise could be seen to have points of convergence. As Beatrix Campbell recognized in 1987, 'Right-Wing Women' could not be entirely immune to feminist ideas in this period:

> Women's relationship to the political agenda has been touched not only by Thatcherism (and Thatcher herself) but by feminism. Feminism may not describe the politics of Tory women, but Tory women more than most have a gendered politics, and these days that cannot exist outside the frame of feminism. Thatcherism and feminism are two of the forces which have impacted on the lives of women in the 1970s and 1980s. Feminism inhabits the same household as femininity … Women are everywhere in a weak position and yet are not weak. Women are subordinate and yet are strong. That describes the Tory woman.
>
> (Campbell, 1987, p. 298)

The paradoxes that Campbell expresses here are articulated and narrativized in the genre fiction for women of the decade. The problems confronting women are worked out and resolved in the sex and shopping narrative within the terms of a conservative rhetoric, but they are not without a considerable dash of feminist discourse.

Feminist novelists and publishers throughout the 1980s emulated many of the design features and the conventions of the successful blockbuster novel and produced fictions which articulated a concern with the future of women's liberation in an age which exalted the free market and individual enterprise. Popular novelists such as Shirley Conran, Danielle Steel and Judith Krantz, whose writing made it very clear that they would have no truck with the politics of feminism, nonetheless expressed a language of female empowerment that could veer perilously close to the demands of the Women's Liberation Movement. By the end of the 1980s, many feminist writers had shifted from the earnest collectivities of the 1970s and early 1980s, to embrace mainstream and popular forms of fiction. The personal had indeed become political, but the discourses of women and work, by women writers across the political spectrum, had in the novels of the 1980s transmuted into a politics of personal ambition.

Note

1 *Dallas* was revived in 2012.

5

Keeping the Home Fires Burning: The Aga-saga and the Domestic Romance of the 1990s

As the new millennium approached, there was an ideological turn away from the untrammelled enterprise and consumerist excesses of the 1980s and an emergent espousal of ecological and spiritual movements. A widespread rejection of the ethos of the Thatcher and Reagan years culminated in the elections of the centre-left governments of Tony Blair's New Labour in Britain and Democrat Bill Clinton in America. Popular culture came to embrace more 'caring' values. As fashion and popular discourse apparently reacted against the commercial culture of the decade, the heroine whose independence was predicated on consumption no longer represented such a desirable version of femininity.

There was an identifiable shift in popular fiction against the celebration of unabashed consumerism that had marked the sex and shopping novel, and a move towards a search for 'authenticity'. In British and American fiction, the 'authentic' came to be signified by the country, and by village or small-town life. The 'rural' became a metonym for a more honest lifestyle, an ideal which was set against the shallow associations of shopping in the city. The settings of popular women's fiction moved from the capital cities, which had been the focus of the sex and shopping novel, and into rural environments. Sincerity and tradition rather than glamour and wealth became the mark of the ideal partner and lifestyle. Romance is more muted in these novels, their heroines tending to be married or in long relationships, and while they may have emotional and sexual adventures, there is not the excitement and urgency found in novels centred on the single 'career woman'.

The 'Aga-saga' was a defining 'woman's' genre in 1990s Britain, recognized by librarians, readers and publishers as a new form of writing by and for women. It represented a new form of caring and feminized fiction that turned its back on the Ambition (the title of an emblematic novel of the decade (Burchill, 1989) that had marked the popular novel of the 1980s.

The recurrence of typefaces and cover designs marked these novels as belonging to a group and as an identifiable genre in contemporary women's writing. The Aga-saga was immediately recognizable from its cover. Invariably white, it featured a tasteful watercolour illustration depicting either a domestic still life – a kitchen table arranged with a combination of a hat, gardening trug or vase of flowers – or a landscape featuring a lone woman in a cottage, or sitting in an English country garden. These are images of women in a domestic setting, in retreat from the world of the city and paid employment.

The Aga-saga is distinguished from other forms of romance fiction by featuring a female protagonist who is middle-class and middle-aged, by the foregrounding of domestic life and by a rural setting. The domestic romance is full of the details of country life, with loving depictions of domestic architecture, and the details of the kitchen and the country garden. Like women's magazines, the genre provides a cultural space which foregrounds women's preoccupations, but these are firmly located within the family and domestic sphere. In line with the typical class background and age of their heroines, Aga-sagas tend to focus on the tastes and concerns of the more upmarket monthly women's magazines, *Good Housekeeping* and *Ideal Home*, rather than the more widely selling women's weekly popular magazines. As their generic title suggests, the main focus of the Aga-saga is the home and kitchen.

These novels are full of the details and pleasures of the home environment, their heroines preoccupied with the concerns of the home-making pages of women's magazines: the decoration of a house, the presentation of a meal, the entertainment of guests, the care of the garden and of children. The details of furnishings, table settings and recipes are often so precise that they could be used as models by the reader. As the cover illustrations celebrate the art of domestic arrangements, so the narratives foreground the small pleasures to be found in domestic labour. The details of bowls of fruit and flowers, the charm of a piece of material or china, are described with careful attention. The plot of the Aga-saga is similarly fuelled by issues that could have come from the articles and problem pages of a woman's magazine. Difficulties with adolescent children, disillusionment with a husband, the tedium of domestic life and failed ambitions are the stuff of which these novels are made. The central focus of the Aga-saga, no less than the college narrative, is a heroine's ill-defined but very real sense of frustration and disillusion.

As Alison Light has argued, romance fiction offers readers: 'a world of fancy and faery inspired by an extravagant longing to go beyond what we have and what we know to be the case, to transform our workaday selves through the enhancement of adventure or the giddy metamorphoses of love' (Light, 1994, p. xi). The Aga-saga is neither read nor marketed as romance fiction, but the genre conforms to many of these same pleasures. The heroine begins from a very workaday self, weary from responsibilities to children, partners, and, less often, work; over the course of the narrative she aspires to transform herself, or at least her environment.

The Aga-saga is a genre exclusive to women authors and readers, but unlike the sex and shopping novel, Mills and Boon and Silhouette romances and the later 'chick-lit' novels, it has not generally been decried as romantic trash. Black Swan Publishers, one of the main imprints for the genre, boasts in its catalogue that it offers 'a selection of fine titles'. The Aga-saga achieved a measure of literary critical respectability, the novels reviewed in the broadsheet newspapers and the authors interviewed in magazines and at literary festivals. This reputation has much to do with the perceived age and class of its authors and readership as middle-aged and middle-class. Unlike the majority of genre romance fiction, the Aga-saga is author rather than imprint-led. The novels inevitably include an authorial biography, in which the details of the novelist's education, marriage, place of residence, offspring and family animals often read as very close to those of her heroines. The novelists themselves often write lengthy acknowledgements and dedications, in which husbands, children, grandchildren and friends are gratefully celebrated. The authors of the Aga-saga and their biographies serve as a validation of the aspirational fantasies offered in their fiction. The novels and their writers affirm that childrearing and creative accomplishment are compatible and achievable for women, and reassure that romance and ambition can survive after marriage and into middle-age.

The Aga-saga can be read as a form of post-marriage romance, a fiction that promises, unlike the standardized plots of Mills and Boon and Silhouette romance, that marriage need not mean the end of courtship and romance, nor of an independent identity for the heroine. Laura, the heroine of Titia Sutherland's 1994 novel *Running Away*, expresses her frustrations and needs in these terms: 'I feel inadequate ... but it's not to do with work or no work. I've lost my sense of identity and I want to find it again ... I'm not trying to be difficult, but I must do this soon, or I'll become impossible' (Sutherland, 1994, p. 27). Laura fulfils the promise of the novel's title and escapes, accompanied by the strains of Vivaldi, to a remote country cottage in order to pursue her 'sense of identity'. Her departure is carefully planned, but she does not share this with her family; in leaving them with a fully stocked freezer and directions to the supermarket, her conscience is cleared for a fulfilment of her own needs. In Laura's escape from the family, she experiences being desired by a man other than her husband, flirts with the possibility of an affair (but desists, as is the case for the majority of these heroines) and finds a publisher. And finally she returns home to a newly appreciative husband and children, her identity confirmed by a shot of rural isolation. This is the standard narrative arc of the Aga-saga; all include variations of these elements of frustration, escape and return.

As the titles suggest, with their emphasis on place rather than personal identity, the Aga-saga tends to be located in a mythical, organic community. Their settings tend not to be regionally specific; although a county or state may be invoked, the community is defined much more by its local history and community mythology than by precise geographical location. These novels are most often set in a nostalgic world of church going, fêtes and home-baking competitions in a fantasy of village life, the cosy rituals of rural communities that have been affectionately satirized by Anita Burgh's deft 'Tales from Sarson Magna' novels (Burgh, 1994 and 1995), and also by the television series *Midsomer Murders*. The novels are set in a small rural community in which everyone is known, and any departure from convention is observed, much as Dorothea experienced in George Eliot's *Middlemarch*. Clive Bloom sees the 'Aga-saga' as in the tradition of the morality tale, updated for the late twentieth century:

> the village tales of moral decline or family virtue that flourished before the 1920s and vanished thereafter (until stripped of their Christian and temperance virtue and reincarnated as the modern 'Aga-saga' tales of immoral doings in middle England).
>
> (Bloom, 2002, p. 16)

The village, small town or pastoral setting is an intrinsic element of the Aga-saga. The closest that these novels get to the urban is a small country town or a cathedral city. Fleeting appearances from the urban population may occur, but these threaten to disrupt the comfortable certainties of rural life. The heroine may travel, but it is to a rural environment (often in Italy) and usually to a place with family connections, unlike the capital city travels of the jet-setting heroines of the sex and shopping novel. The protagonists of the Aga-saga may be called into the nearest city or town, but they return with relief to a familiar hearth and landscape.

The Aga-saga can be read as a later version of the country-house romance novel of the 1950s (see Philips and Haywood, 1998), in which the heroine is more likely to be in love with her partner's house than with her partner himself. The heroine of Mary Sheepshanks's 1995 novel *A Price for Everything* is disillusioned with her husband, but devoted to his house, as the back-cover plot outline cheerfully admits: 'Sonia … loves the family seat rather more than she does her husband' (Sheepshanks, 1995). Sheepshanks's novel addressed the problem (as did many popular women's novels of the 1950s) of how to maintain a country estate and mansion at a time of economic recession. If this was not a dilemma for many women outside a certain class, it did represent an aspirational fantasy; in these novels the custodianship of the house becomes a metonym for the preservation of tradition. The uncomfortable marriages that such novels depict and the financial difficulties that the heroine has to contend with suggest that these traditions are under threat, and that the rural idyll may be a way of life that can no longer be sustained.

Joanna Trollope was the pre-eminent novelist of these fictions in England, the undisputed 'Queen of the Aga-saga'. Trollope's novels have acquired a literary respectability that has seen them televized by the BBC, with all the production values of a 'classic serial' and casts of established actors and the author fêted at literary festivals and interviewed in the broadsheet press. Trollope's popularity spawned a host of imitators, in which publishers trawled their lists for women writers of a similar age and class, who could be packaged and marketed in emulation of her commercial success. Trollope's novels are full of the details of country houses and cottages, of dinner parties and elegantly appointed kitchens and sitting rooms. As one reviewer has said of her work: 'One of the pleasures of reading Trollope is certainly that of luxuriating in houses beautiful' (Turner, 1995). Trollope is the editor of an anthology celebrating country life, *The Country Habit* (Trollope, 1993a), and her novels are similarly tributes to the rural, the pastoral settings of her fictions providing a context for their heroines of continuity and tradition. The dramas of the novels, however, suggest an uncomfortable recognition of the fragility of that tradition, and how easily it can be damaged. Trollope's fiction is always centred on marriages, and the threats of affairs and boredom that can end them.

Husbands and partners in these novels can no longer be relied upon, either economically or personally, to support the lifestyle and activities of the traditional domesticated wife. In *The Rector's Wife*, the wife of the title recognizes that her husband has failed to satisfy her professional ambitions for him (and so has failed her), but the narrative cannot allow that she might take them over for herself. The novel was written in 1991, when the ordination of women was very much on the church agenda, but that this vicar's wife might herself become a rector is never a possibility; there is a brief reference to women priests, but this is summarily dismissed as an option. The heroine's intellectual aspirations are instead fulfilled through an affair with a visiting academic. Unusually in these narratives, she does not return to her husband; he is instead conveniently dispatched in a car accident. Her status as the rector's wife in the community, the vicarage home and a small stipend are allowed to remain intact, the husband continuing to support the family even after his death. The rector's wife's only status outside her marriage is through her job as a supermarket assistant, in what is clearly only a part-time and temporary excursion into the life of a working woman. It is strongly signalled that this is not the heroine's appropriate lot in life, and that a replacement (and more ambitious) husband will shortly appear.

There is a wide variation in these novels of the means by which the heroine asserts a stand for recognition. In Trollope's novels they include: a relationship with another woman (*A Village Affair*), an affair with an exotic lover (*A Spanish Lover*), involvement with a cathedral choir (*The Choir*). In other novels the offer of a country cottage (Philippa Gregory's *Perfectly Correct* and Titia Sutherland's *Running Away*) is in itself enough to allow the heroine to demand her independence. Whatever the individual circumstances may be, there is always a narrative device which removes the heroine from her usual habitat, and the structural effect is the same: the absenting of the central female presence from the context of home and family. The heroine does not so much find herself in her solitude or in the throes of an illicit passion so much as she relishes the impact of her departure upon her partner and family. Her removal from the centre of family life forces a recognition of the pivotal role that a wife and mother plays within the home. The narratives concentrate less on the pleasures of the heroine's independent life than on the fragments she has left behind. By the end of the novel, both the heroine and her family have come to appreciate the significance of her contribution to family life; an acknowledgement of the indispensable female presence can only be achieved by its withdrawal. Once the contribution that women make to the smooth running of domestic life has been acknowledged, then the structure of family life can be returned to its normal patterns.

Female ambition is expressed only in very limited terms in these novels. The heroines often do have some employment or a creative skill, but these often take the form of a 'feminine' accomplishment: writing poetry, water-colour painting, an ability with languages, an interest in church architecture or singing. The work that these women do is most frequently represented as a mere extension of a hobby; not the kind of salaried employment that could sustain a family but a part-time interest that demonstrates that the heroine has brains. The heroine's working or creative ambitions are not taken with much seriousness, her talent or ability represented as charming rather than professionally viable, enough perhaps to provide a small income. Sonia, of *A Price for Everything*, is a painter; her creativity is typical of these novels in the suggestion that she lacks the ambition (and perhaps aptitude) to achieve professional status: 'somehow her promise had not been quite fulfilled ... [S]o far she had lacked the drive and determination that were also necessary if she was to reach her potential as an artist' (Sheepshanks, 1995, p. 9). It is never stated, but the implication is clear, that it is the advent of children that has sapped this potential.

One of the fantasies that this genre answers to is the 'plight' of the middle-aged woman. Although the 'empty nest' syndrome is never directly named, it is a recurrent feature of these narratives that there are teenage children who are sullenly retreating to their bedrooms or who have left home and no longer require mothering. The strongest sense of loss in Elizabeth Buchan's *The Good Wife* is for a daughter leaving home for a gap year before college; her mother inhabits 'an emptier house than it had been for years, in which the movement of things and people had dwindled' (Buchan, 2003, p. 304). The Aga-saga is a form of fiction that does answer to a real and painful situation that is an experience for the majority of women, but one which is rarely addressed in a culture that unquestioningly celebrates the maternal. In these novels, the feelings of women at the point of their children's departure from the family home are taken very seriously. These are novels of reassurance, asserting that once the immediate maternal role is over, a woman still has a significant role to play.

It is an unspoken convention of these novels that the husband and father does not properly understand or share such feelings. This may be expressed as a widening rift in the marriage, a drifting apart or an apparently unaccountable extra-marital affair, but all these narratives chart the erosion of a marriage in which the assumptions and expectations of husband and wife are no longer shared. There is a displaced recognition here that the masculine role in the late twentieth century is no longer secure. Men in these novels have lost their potency, their ambition and interest, often embodied in the loss of a business. It is more often frustration with the man in her life rather than with herself that sets the heroine on the quest for fulfilment.

The genre does acknowledge women's disappointments in children and in men, and their narratives do present painful conflicts between generations and genders. These novels do not offer seamless representations of family life; the fissures and frustrations of childrearing and of relationships are acknowledged, as are their pleasures. The novels usually enter at a point at which the fictional family is in a state of transition. The children tend to be young adults rather than small children. Child characters are rarely sentimentalized, just frequently not there, conveniently stowed away in schools, colleges and untidy bedrooms, the better to allow the heroine an unencumbered space in which to find 'herself'. Inexplicable yearnings, illicit love affairs and frustrated ambitions (on the part of both husbands and wives) are the motors for the plots of these novels, but the reasons for these vaguely defined dissatisfactions are never confronted. The Aga-saga finally reasserts a relatively becalmed image of cosy domesticity, in a celebration of the warmth and comfort of the family.

As Joanna Trollope has confirmed, the Aga-saga novelist does not see herself as a writer of reassuring fictions: 'What exasperates me most about my public image are the words 'cosy' and 'smug' applied to my novels, because I think they're rather bleak, and about the pain and destructiveness caused by self-fulfilment of a not particularly outrageous kind' (Loudon, 1995). These novels may be bleak in their depiction of a marriage that has lost any heart, but the Aga-saga did not acquire its generic nickname for nothing. The heroine's search for self-fulfilment is indeed never particularly outrageous, and the narratives are very keen to underline the 'pain and destructiveness' that such a search may cause to husband and children. At the heart of the narrative is a reassuring image of the domestic that is invariably coded as feminine. The heroine's frustrations and search for fulfilment might initially appear to dissent from the demands of the feminine role, but ultimately, the plot resolutions and the generic constraints of the form reaffirm a domestic ideal of femininity that finally leaves the traditional structures of gender and class unchallenged.

The titles of Elizabeth Buchan's novels suggest women who might be prepared to leave their insensitive husbands behind, and to assume responsibility for their own happiness. However, the revenge enacted by the eponymous wife in *Revenge of the Middle-Aged Woman* is strangely muted, despite the loss of her house, job and husband to another woman. Rose begins the novel as a happily married woman, and a successful books editor for a broadsheet newspaper. Work, however, proves to be a treacherous place: 'one had to become rather protean, undercover and dangerous to survive' (Buchan, 2002, p. 5). Rose is to discover over the course of the narrative quite how undercover her colleagues can be. A trusted woman colleague has lured her husband away, and her boss replaces her with the same younger woman. While Rose revels in the natural world of her garden, the office space is for her an enclosed and alien place: 'The walls of the building shut out goodness knew what weather' (*ibid.*, p. 44).

It is her house and garden that provide Rose with a sense of security and continuity. She unapologetically takes a 'delight in domesticity ... The ritual of sweetening and cleansing a house was as old as time and I liked the idea that I was one in a long line of women to perform it' (*ibid.*, p. 30). The novel is full of the pleasures of polishing the kitchen, of cooking meals and tending to the garden, acts of nurturing that her adult children no longer require from her. The family is dismissive of Rose's work: 'The family scoffed at the term "study" and at the idea that I needed one' (*ibid.*, p. 85), and she herself sees the upkeep of the house and family as entirely her responsibility. Her husband, Nathan, is a deputy editor on the same newspaper, but it is her job to 'sooth' him and to remind him to telephone his children. As with so many of these heroines, Rose's middle-age and the loss of her centrality in family life is confirmed by the loss of her grown-up children to their own lives.

The narrative charts Rose coming to terms with the loss of all the anchors that had determined her place in the world. With the loss of her husband she also loses the kitchen, the garden and the family (even the family cat dies); the nurturing that has framed her existence is no longer required. The loss of the house and garden that she has so lovingly tended is represented as more acute than the loss of her husband. Rose's response to her husband's and colleagues' betrayals is to rise above it all, by behaving 'beautifully' and forgiving. She ends the novel prepared to recreate her garden and kitchen in another context, newly appreciated by her children and disloyal husband. An old lover reappears, his olive grove in Tuscany presenting Rose with new opportunities for gardening and for cooking. Rose's role as a domestic goddess, although profoundly unsettled by the events of the narrative, is not challenged, merely reconfigured.

In Buchan's *The Good Wife*, Fanny may begin the novel frayed by the demands of her husband and family, but she begins and ends the novel as exactly that, a good wife. While Fanny's husband runs the country as a Member of Parliament, she runs the household and supports him personally and politically. Fanny is clearly politically very competent, and she runs surgeries for her husband's constituents while he is at Westminster and advises him on political strategy; but, like the rector's wife, there is no suggestion that she might herself harbour political ambitions. Fanny is the daughter of a wine importer, and is herself a skilled wine taster. This expertise was once used professionally, but as marriage and motherhood erode her working life, it becomes a mere social asset, allowing Fanny to discuss fine wines at parties.

By any standards, the demands on Fanny are excessive; she is required to be a good constituency wife, answerable to the expectations of the Party as well as to her family. The uncomfortable house which Fanny refers to as 'my territory' is also run according to her husband's needs. As their grown-up daughter leaves home, she is left with his adult nephew and his alcoholic sister, Meg. Fanny's sharp mind and wit are cluttered with the details of domesticity; she constantly worries about curtains, shirt collars and the need to stock the fridge. Throughout the novel there are intimations of rebellion against the role that the constituency and her family demand of her. Fanny and her husband attend a production of *The Doll's House*, but as Nora shuts the door of the family home behind her, the line that resonates for Fanny is 'I don't believe in miracles any more'; she reads Nora's departure as an expression of disenchantment rather than one of resistance.

The novel begins with Fanny questioning her happiness: 'Not a question, perhaps, that a good wife should ask' (Buchan, 2003, p. 1). She chooses to repress the question throughout the novel, and resigns herself to the 'dull ache of small martyrdom' (*ibid.*, p. 8). The narrative is nonetheless scattered with moments that suggest this martyrdom is hardly 'small' and which express real desolation. Observing her cleaning lady with her head in the oven, Fanny remarks that this is a position that 'not a few political wives (any wife?) had from time to time considered' (*ibid.*, p. 17). Fanny is allergic to her wedding ring, a physical embodiment of the discomfort of her marriage, but she continues to wear it. When her husband has an affair with his research assistant, Fanny resolves to suffer in silence. The cost of sustaining her marriage is her compliance with the demands of the political wife: 'I would do my best. I would clamp my mouth shut, stitch up my wounds, fight back and demand Will's sexual ... loyalty. In return I would place myself by his side: smiling, entertaining, supporting' (*ibid.*, p. 172). The novel is haunted by figures of failed wives and mothers. Fanny's own mother, Sally, has left her daughter and husband and escaped to raise horses in America. The alcoholic Meg has lost both her husband and her child and lives a life of quiet desperation until she dies in a drunken fall. These women act as a terrible warning to Fanny and serve to confirm her resolve to continue as an unquestioning Good Wife.

Fanny's one moment of freedom is a trip to her father's home town in Italy to scatter his ashes. There she has time to 'seek out' her 'secret self', and to return to her professional skills. Fanny's sexual attractiveness is reconfirmed (in an episode that is a regular feature of these novels): she is desired once again by her first love, an urbane Italian wine merchant.

Loyal to her husband, and interrupted in a kiss by his sister, Fanny resists seduction; her love affair is finally with the house in Italy rather than with the man. Fanny returns to her marriage, confirmed in the belief that her marriage depends on her simulation of happiness: 'It struck me that the politics of a successful marriage involved never asking too straight a question, and in never answering it fully, always leaving that tiny margin of unknowing' (*ibid*., p. 293). This is written without any suggestion of irony, but, nonetheless, the 'faint sensation of despair' that Fanny acknowledges in herself haunts the novel and its ending. As there is in Rose's story, there is a strong sense of unease that accompanies the novel's reaffirmation of Fanny's domestic role, and a lingering awareness of how easily the apparent security of the wife can be threatened.

In Kathleen Rowntree's 1992 novel *Between Friends*, the heroine is so concerned to preserve her family, marriage and way of life that she silently suffers the knowledge of her husband's affair with her best woman friend. The narrative suggests, and the conclusion confirms, that it may well be best for women not to confront painful and difficult knowledge, but instead to sustain an illusion of family happiness. This stoic self-sacrifice is rewarded by the return of the husband, and any recriminations from the heroine are dutifully suppressed. It may cost women to suffer the strains of contemporary life, but family and marriage must be preserved and it is ultimately, so these novels imply, in the best interests of women to do so.

Philippa Gregory's heroine in *Perfectly Correct* is the inverse of these betrayed wives, as the 'other woman' in a triangular relationship. Louise is younger and sassier than the conventional heroine of the Aga-saga. She is child-free and an avowed feminist, but her story follows precisely the same pattern of reconciliation to the domestic life. After a relationship of nine years, she too is dissatisfied and a move to the country prompts a reassessment of her values. Louise has all the trappings of a sophisticated and independent woman: an academic job, a married lover and a house of her own, inherited from an aunt. By the end of the novel and the romantic resolution, she has lost all of these. Despite her professed feminist principles, 'sisterhood' is not enough to prevent Louise from having a long-term affair with her closest friend's husband. All her intellectual capital and professed sophistication are exposed as fraudulent when she is confronted by the traditional values of a longstanding rural family.

Louise's carefully constructed independence is challenged by the appearance of an elderly woman who seems to be a traveller in her garden. The irascible Rose turns out to be the real owner of Louise's house, the hero's aunt, and to be the genuine bearer of feminist history. Despite her association with the Suffragette movement, Rose is entirely dismissive of Louise's work: 'that job of hers is a bit of nothing. What she needs is a good man' (Gregory, 1996, p. 91). The 'good man' proves to be the local farmer, Louise's neighbour. Their romance is paralleled with Louise's attempts to write a feminist analysis of D. H. Lawrence's short story 'The Virgin and the Gypsy'; her initial antipathy to Lawrence's representation of masculinity ends with a new appreciation of 'men who prize their assertiveness' (Gregory, 1996, p. 291).

The romantic hero is, like Lawrence's Gypsy, a man of nature and the soil: 'He looked like a giant, like some old Sussex chalk giant, conjured from the rain, the storm' (*ibid.*, p. 146). Andrew is a farmer, whose 'natural' alliance with the land and long family connection to the local area provide the heroine with the solidity and continuity that her independent feminism is shown to lack. Andrew has 'the confidence of a man who lives in his own house, his father's house, with his own land stretching for miles all around him' (*ibid.*, p. 89). Family history and rural traditions are shown to be more important than Louise's principles; the world of feminist academia is represented as shallow and rivalrous. The feminist sisterhood is ruthlessly parodied, and the one political action that Louise's women's group undertakes ends in a farcical bacchanalia.

The novel expresses a real tension over the discourses of feminism. While it has no qualms at savagely satirizing feminist activists, there is a real understanding of and sensitivity to feminist history (Gregory is herself a historian). Toby, Louise's married lover, is incapable of recognizing the significance of Rose's papers; an episode in which he dismisses the records of Sylvia Pankhurst's work is well informed and moving. Toby is revealed as a fraudulent 'new man', who attempts to exploit Rose's association with the Suffragette movement for his own ends, as insensitive to her history as he is to his wife and mistress. But the novel's celebration of women's history does not extend to a feminist politics. Miriam, Toby's wife and Louise's closest friend, is a staunch champion of women's rights, and works in a women's refuge. It is Miriam, however, who wistfully articulates the novel's sense that feminist politics are no longer relevant to contemporary women: 'at the start in the 80s there was a genuine feeling that poverty and abuse of women could be solved. Since then, post-Thatcher, there's a sense that poverty and cruelty is natural' (*ibid.*, p. 71).

Rose's final legacy to Louise is not in the end feminist history but romance. She makes a pyre of the papers that document her involvement with Sylvia Pankhurst, and instructs her nephew to light the fire. Louise never reads these papers, and watches their torching with only mild regret. Rose has left the country cottage to the couple, on condition that they marry. Louise's romance allows her to trade up from a small cottage and a Rayburn to an Elizabethan mansion with an Aga in the kitchen. She ends the novel, despite her professed feminism, as a typical Aga-saga heroine, recognizing that the real work of life is to be a wife and mother, and that fulfilment lies in the country tradition and in family, rather than academic, history.

The charms of 'village' life might seem to have less purchase on the American imagination than on the English, but small-town life is used as a transatlantic equivalent to the British rural village, and comes to stand for tradition and integrity in much the same way in American versions of these novels. In Martha Stewart, America produced the uber-Aga-saga heroine. Martha Stewart made a career out of celebrating the 'homemaker' (rather than the 'housewife', a term which evokes all the connotations of Betty Friedan's unhappy suburban women). Stewart was herself a woman who was capable of managing a business empire while simultaneously very publicly baking cookies and adorning her table with handmade decorations. With her advice on decoration, table settings and gardens, Stewart taught her readers how to enact the lifestyle and how to dress the settings of the domestic romance. The collapse of the Martha Stewart dream did little to scotch the myth of the contented homemaker; Stewart's imprisonment for fraud hardly damaged her empire of magazines and franchises.

Anita Shreve is an American equivalent of Joanna Trollope, as a chronicler of middle-aged marriages who has not been denigrated as a writer of genre fiction and maintains a reputation as a 'literary' writer. Her 1993 novel *Where or When* is unusual in that it has a man overseeing the Aga (or at least supervising the cooking), but it follows the generic pattern of the Aga-saga in its narrative of a failing marriage, an apparently inexplicable passion and in the focus on the home and kitchen. The descriptions of food and its preparation in the novel are so detailed that it is possible to reconstruct the recipes. Charles may cook elaborate dinners, but it is his wife, Harriet, first seen baking bread, who is responsible for the children and for the day-to-day running of the house: 'Harriet mows the lawn, keeps the exterior tidy and painted' (Shreve, 1993, p. 20). Charles is able to listen to the songs that belong to the era of his lost love, secure in the knowledge that Harriet will know the whereabouts of their children.

The story of their marriage is played out in a Rhode Island community where everyone knows everyone else; Charles has to buy stationery to write to his lover at an anonymous mall in order to escape speculation from the local shopkeeper. This community is, however, suffering the effects of the economic recession. Charles's business is a victim of the recession, and the family house is under threat. It is made clear that Charles is not alone in the community as a man who has lost his professional status and financial security: 'he is but one of many ... the list is long. Each with bombed out fantasies ... Each scrambling now just to keep his home' (*ibid.*, p. 18). Charles is emasculated by the threat of unemployment, and by the demands of domesticity, but his inevitable love affair is presented as a rekindling of a lost passion rather than as a response to the loss of masculine authority.

Charles is clearly in the grip of a mid-life crisis: he buys a Cadillac and plays the songs of his teenage years repeatedly, while his wife looks on with some concern. His love affair with his childhood sweetheart is not, however, presented as a symptom of this crisis, but rather as a romantic destiny. Charles's adultery is seen as no more a betrayal of his wife than is his failure to maintain the family and home: 'He hardly knows which is worse – to tell her that he loves another woman or to tell her that he can no longer provide for her as he has promised to' (*ibid.*, p. 151). Charles's culinary skills, his appreciation of music and reading of French philosophy are all expressions of his own conviction that he is more than a small-town insurance salesman. Romance offers a means of reaffirming and rekindling childhood dreams; Charles's renewed affair with his summer-camp love allows them both to escape from the adult constrictions of parenthood and marriage. The lovers' reunion is a moment stopped in time; the place where they first meet is: 'exactly the same. Nothing ever stays the same ... but somehow this has done so' (*ibid.*, p. 83). The magic of love is seen to have the power to stop the process of ageing and the advance of modernity; Charles writes to his lover: 'I want to make love to you and have it stop time' (*ibid.*, p. 108).

Sian, his love object, is in a similarly stale marriage. If her husband is in touch with the land as a farmer, his business is also failing. Sian, like so many of these heroines, has a creative talent that is not sufficient to support the family; she publishes volumes of slim poetry and has a part-time academic job. For Sian, the affair is a reaction against the drudgery of family life: 'My fantasies are simple ones and are products of what I think is a kind of emotional exhaustion – the result of trying to hold myself and my family together all these years' (*ibid.*, p. 120). The emotional exhaustion of Harriet, Charles's wife, is not dwelt upon. When Charles leaves her, she is left to organize the family Christmas and to explain his departure to the children. The novel ends tragically, like Trollope's *The Rector's Wife*, with Charles's death in a car crash. His death allows an escape from the recriminations of his family, and from the bank's foreclosure on the mortgage, and allows the narrative to evade the effects of Charles's pursuit of love. It is Sian's voice which ends the novel, her grief given more weight than Harriet's, in a confirmation of an ideal love affair which remains eternally untainted by the demands of family and adulthood.

March, the middle-aged heroine of Alice Hoffman's *Here on Earth*, is also in pursuit of her first and lost love. Returning for a funeral to her small Massachusetts home town of Fox Hill, March is in flight from her marriage to the mild Richard, and impelled by the memory of her passionate childhood romance with the strange Hollis, a baleful presence throughout. The novel is a knowing tribute to Emily Brontë's *Wuthering Heights*: Hollis's early history is just like Heathcliff's, the story of an orphan boy brought to the family home by the heroine's father. Just as Cathy does, March develops an intense connection with the boy, but, as in *Wuthering Heights*, a wealthy local family train her to respectable marriage with their son, Richard, who stands as the Edgar Linton figure in the novel.

The parallels with *Wuthering Heights* are precise: March, like Cathy, is removed from Hollis because of an injury to her foot; Hollis, like Heathcliff, is cruel to dogs. Strung alongside the passion of this *Wuthering Heights* narrative, however, is the familiar story of a bored wife with a teenage daughter escaping to a rural community. March is a jewellery designer, an occupation which had 'started out as a hobby' (Hoffman, 1998, p. 44), but which cannot be developed because her work is obstructed by her marriage to Richard. As is the case with all these heroines, March's skills and talents remain undeveloped. Her pregnancy with Richard's child is experienced as stifling; she feels: 'trapped in some deep, irrevocable way ... She was affixed to this place and to her own body; anchored by flesh, blood and her own exhaustion' (*ibid.*, p. 58). Once her daughter has grown, it is her affair with Hollis that disrupts her attempt to return to her work.

Fox Hill, the site of her passion for Hollis, is another small-town community which runs on Harvest Fairs, library committees and gossip. March is pulled back into her childhood world and acknowledges: 'I need a break from my life, that's what I've realized' (*ibid.*, p. 113). Richard becomes a largely distant voice on the telephone; March's passion for Hollis is, as romance was for Charles, a means of returning to her unencumbered youth. Hollis sees her as someone who is not defined by her roles as a wife and mother and allows her to redefine herself temporarily: 'back then she was a girl who didn't know any better; she wasn't somebody's wife, somebody's mother' (*ibid.*, p. 135). In the midst of her affair with her childhood love, she not only absents herself from her daughter and her husband but also from her domestic duties: 'March can't seem to deal with the trivial details of domestic life, they seem beyond her somehow, small but impossible tasks' (*ibid.*, p. 181).

Fox Hill is not, however, an entirely cosy community. The woods outside the town are sinister and the Massachusetts weather is bitter, as is the romantic hero. The novel is haunted by damaged men: the heroine's brother is a Branwell figure, haunted by the fire which killed his wife and drinking himself to death. His son is neglected and taken over by the sinister Hollis. Hollis himself, like Heathcliff, is a cruel and demanding lover; he has become a wealthy man who is now deliberately running down the family home of his rival for March's affections. March may not die, like Cathy, but her relationship with the cruel Hollis is a trap of dependency. March summons up the courage to finally leave him, and Hollis, like Charles, is killed in a car crash. It is left ambiguous as to whether his death is an accident or suicide. March's ending is similarly ambiguous; she leaves Fox Hill, but any reunion with her husband or daughter occurs off-stage. March is not permitted a happy ending; the passionate love of her childhood provides no escape from a bleak marriage, and proves to be as stifling. It is strongly suggested that it is with the kind Richard that she belongs, and that any attempt to escape is to prove dangerous.

Adriana Trigiani's novels are more reassuring about the prospects for marriage, but the tensions of domesticity for women are still very evident. Her series of narratives featuring her heroine Ave and her romance and marriage to the rural Jack are all set in Trigiani's own real Virginia hometown of Big Stone Gap, but Big Stone Gap has little of the sinister edge found in Hoffman's Fox Hill. Trigiani's fiction offers affectionate and comic evocations of a small community which is populated by a large cast of eccentric but lovable characters, but which is nonetheless threatened by the global economy and by male unemployment. In the first novel of the sequence, *Big Stone Gap*, the heroine, Ave Maria, is an outsider, by virtue both of her Italian origins and of her spinsterhood, although she was born and has lived in the small town all her life. A brief excursion to college to train as a pharmacist is the only time she has ever left Big Stone Gap. Big Stone Gap is a neighbourhood which runs on bake sales, sewing circles and gardening clubs, in a nostalgic celebration of small-town life. This is a community that looks after its own, the women providing baskets of pies and cakes for the ageing and invalid. As in other fiction in this genre, the details of domestic interiors and of recipes are so precise that they could be used as instructions. These are novels that are intended to be read in the kitchen; the second novel includes a full recipe for 'Cousin Dee's Peanut Butter Balls' (Trigiani, 2002b, p. 33).

At the opening of the first novel, Ave Maria aspires to a world outside the Virginian mountains: 'the idea of living in Big Stone Gap for the rest of my life gives me a nervous feeling' (Trigiani, 2002a, p. 4). At the age of thirty-five, Ave is college educated, and a practising pharmacist. There are clear intimations of a yearning to escape the confines of small-town life: she goes to foreign movies; the mobile library provides glimpses of other worlds and knowledges. She plans her escape to Italy to track down her long-lost family, but instead the community pulls together to bring the family to her. In this first novel Ave only leaves the State of Virginia on her honeymoon. The characters in the novel are constantly reminding Ave of her single status, and urging her to marry. As her trusted handyman tells her: 'Ye ought to git murried Miss Ave. Womens ain't supposed to works like 'at' (*ibid*., p. 32).

The romantic hero, Jack, is instrumental in preventing Ave from leaving the town. He is first encountered as Ave appreciatively eyes up his mother's 'clean, spare stone house' and sunny kitchen; she is attracted to the house and the man simultaneously. Both are embedded in the community and represent family continuity: 'the quiet dignity of the MacChesneys of Cracker Holler' (*ibid*., p. 137). The community conspires to bring Jack and Ave together, and on her marriage, Mrs MacChesney's house and kitchen are to become Ave's domain. Ave's full acceptance into the community is withheld until her marriage; as she ruefully acknowledges: 'Around here, being married makes you a prize' (*ibid*., p. 45). The pull of the community is what keeps Ave in Big Stone Gap, and her romance finally confirms she will never leave, that this is 'the place I most want to be ... I know where I belong' (*ibid*., p. 318).

By the second novel of the series, *Big Cherry Holler*, Ave is married to the man of the mountains, Jack, and moved still further into a rural environment, deeper into the Virginia Mountains. The novel begins in the kitchen, where Ave is first seen baking at her mother-in-law's stove, in an image of a female tradition of domestic labour. The past is presented with unabashed nostalgia, Ave's present image of her husband and daughter is refracted through the frame of the past: 'They look like an old photograph' (Trigiani, 2002b, p. 9). As a wife and mother to a small girl, she is now fully integrated into the world of school and parenthood, waiting for her daughter as her mother once waited for her. These continuities are, however, under threat; the chill winds of globalization have impacted on the community, the pharmacy is expanding beyond a neighbourhood store, the second generation are moving out of the town, and the local mine has been taken over. The threat of unemployment puts a strain on the marriage, as Jack can no longer be relied upon to do 'what a father does best', that is, protecting his wife and daughter (*ibid.*, p. 320). The closure of the mine represents a loss of continuity and of male pride for Jack and for the wider community: 'My husband is out of work. But it's worse than that; Jack's identity and heritage is tied to the coal in these hills in a deeply personal way. The MacChesneys have been coal miners for as far back as anyone can remember' (*ibid.*, p. 10).

On marriage, Ave had relinquished her stake in the pharmacy, and has returned to work part time; she recognizes then quite how much she has missed her professional life: 'The job was something that was all mine, and I liked that. I missed being needed for my skills and my knowledge of medications. My job fills me up in ways I never knew until I left it behind' (*ibid.*, p. 41). Her pleasure in her working life and her ability to financially provide for the family represent clear threats to Jack's masculinity and to the marriage, although the narrative avoids making this link directly. Instead, the rifts in the marriage are represented as an indefinable distance between the couple: 'something is wrong. Something has shifted' (*ibid.*, p. 13). Ave perceives her marital problems to be the consequence of her own failures as a wife and mother: 'I think everything is my fault ... I am the woman in this family; I'm supposed to make everything work. What I can't seem to say aloud is that I'm failing' (*ibid.*, p. 21).

As Ave confronts her disappointment with her marriage, her ambitions beyond Big Stone Gap resurface: 'I was going to leave ... seek my happiness, have a life of adventure before it was too late ... Why do I have that old boxed in feeling?' (*ibid.*, p. 68). The narrative thereafter follows the familiar trajectory of the Aga-saga as Ave escapes to her family in Italy. There, she is desired by another man, but does not succumb to his seduction. Reaffirmed in her feminine attractiveness, she rediscovers a sense of herself and comes to terms with her own family roots. Ave is then able to return wholeheartedly to the marriage.

As the community of Big Stone Gap rallied to bring the couple together, so they conspire around Ave to bring her errant husband to heel. Jack's possible affair is never quite confirmed; like Fanny, Ave prefers not to confront the knowledge, dismissing her suspicions and asserting his friendship with another woman as a symptom of 'My husband's mid-life crisis' (*ibid.*, p. 211). Ave assumes responsibility for all the tensions in their relationship: 'I made you feel bad about yourself' (*ibid.*, p. 260). While the narrative ends with a reassertion of Ave's commitment to community and family, there is a wistful sense that this is not quite enough. Ave hopes for more for her daughter, a wish that the next generation of young women will have it better: 'Don't be like your mother and your grandmother whose name you share. Do better' (*ibid.*, p. 157). The next novel, *Milk Glass Moon*, sees Ave continuing to reflect on her failures as a wife and mother as her daughter grows up, a child who is destined, like Ave herself, to remain in Big Stone Gap. It is ironic that among the many celebrity endorsements of Trigiani's 'Big Stone Gap' novels is one from Sarah Jessica Parker, who, as Carrie Bradshaw in the contemporaneous television series *Sex in the City*, came to embody the single woman in the big city. Trigiani's nostalgic reconstructions of rural community life clearly exerted a pull that extended well beyond the housewives and small-town communities represented in these fictions.

The domestic romance of the Aga-saga represented a rejection of the stressed and competitive lifestyles of the 1980s and a retreat into the rural and the domestic. That withdrawal is not, however, without its problems; there is in these novels a recognition that the tensions and strains in both marriages and communities are in part financial. In the late twentieth century, the excesses of the 1980s had been followed by an economic recession in both Britain and America. The family home came to embody the warmth, comfort and support that women had once been expected to supply single-handledly. The 1980s ethos of working hard in a gruelling and competitive world has not gone away, despite the bucolic fantasies of the 1990s, but as the sex and shopping novel of that decade had demonstrated, women had joined it too. Although the genre might seem to address the symptoms of women's discontent, its rural and domestic locale means that it cannot do anything but elide and displace the causes of familial strain. The Aga-saga belonged to a contemporary discourse of the family; as the stresses and strains of employment, property ownership and financial insecurity had their effects on personal relationships, the family and the rural community came to stand as images of a defence against the challenges of the post-modern and post-industrial globalized world.

The Aga-saga may appear to have taken on board the feminist expectations of a generation of women writers, it may even feature a feminist heroine, but the conventions of the genre do not allow for anything more than an acknowledgement of the contemporary tensions in expectations of the feminine. There is always a recognition in these novels that women do have ambitions beyond the confines of home and hearth; their heroines are always in search of something more than the family and the domestic, and the narratives do show them striking out. But their aspirations are always resolved within the terms of the family, and only very rarely disrupt the security of the family home. The heroine may take a lover (who may be a man or a woman), she may publish, paint, travel abroad or escape to an isolated cottage. Whatever the fictional quest might be, it is finally achieved without any major disruption to the family structure or to her marriage. These heroines cannot 'find' themselves outside the family unit, but in one way or another will always return to the domestic front. While the narratives begin from an expression of a woman's dissatisfaction with domesticity, ultimately gender roles in this genre are allowed to remain entirely undisturbed.

The women characters in these novels cannot quite forgive their husbands for not supporting them and for not surviving the impact of economic recession better. The husbands in these narratives are all metaphorically emasculated in some way, and not necessarily by their wives' infidelity: the betrayed husband in *Where or When* loses the use of his arm; Fanny's politician husband in *The Good Life* loses his parliamentary seat; the proud miner, Jack, in Trigiani's novels is made redundant. Not even a man of the soil can be depended upon to support a family; farmers and miners lose their land, their jobs and their traditional role as providers for the family. On the margins of all these narratives are communities of men who have lost their jobs or whose businesses are failing. These novels represent marriages and communities in which the male wage is no longer secure; the sanctuary of the family, the home, is often in peril, the mortgage on the house under threat. There is, however, a stubborn refusal on the part of these heroines to readjust to changes in traditional gender roles. In the late twentieth century, as 'masculinity' could no longer be relied upon to provide for the family, so 'femininity' could no longer be entirely depended upon to provide the safe haven that John Ruskin expected of Victorian women in 1871. The Aga-saga heroines are not entirely unquestioning in their wifely support of their man 'in his rough work in the open world' (Ruskin, 1990, p. 136). The heroine may initially resist this dutiful role, but her resistance ultimately proves to be half-hearted; in the end, she continues to retain responsibility for the household and the domestic chores, while simultaneously propping up her husband's sense of self and the family finances. She may feel frustrated and unappreciated, but the heroine finds resolution in a temporary escape, and returns to the family, reconciled with her husband and her conventional role.

In temporarily removing herself from the family and the domestic, by making her absence felt, the Aga-saga heroine can return to a husband and family who come to recognize quite how much she does. The Aga-saga fulfils a fantasy that the 'invisible' work that women do can and should be acknowledged and rewarded. The Aga-saga is generically dependent on the presence of, if not an actual Aga, a symbolic presence glowing at the centre of family life. Whatever the strains and conflicts presented in these novels, the narrative resolutions continue to assume that the Aga, located in the kitchen, should be lit and maintained by a woman.

6

Shopping for Men: The Single Woman Novel

In the last years of the twentieth century, and into the twenty-first, the television heroine Ally McBeal became a metonym for what was assumed, in media discourse, to be a sociological phenomenon – the narrative of the late-twenty- to thirty-something single career woman, desperately in search of love. Ally's fictional sister was Bridget Jones, whose anxieties, expressed in *Bridget Jones's Diary* (Fielding, 1996), were seen to embody a new form of femininity. As one newspaper columnist assessed the second volume of *Bridget Jones's Diary*, *The Edge of Reason*:

> Bridget is not just some fictional comedy character ... Bridget is a somewhat exaggerated but otherwise accurate-to-the-letter example of a specific social group (thirty-something professional single women) ... [I] t is blindingly clear that Fielding has identified a phenomenon which will not go away, and, if anything, is multiplying in strength.
>
> (Watson, 1999, p. 27)

But Bridget Jones is precisely a fictional character, and she is very much the product of a genre of popular fiction for women readers.

Bridget Jones's Diary is one of the novels that Dominic Head cites as a text that 'strike[s] a chord in the public consciousness by virtue of their engagement with the present'. He judges Bridget Jones as a character who 'has been rightly seen to typify new social moods' (Head, 2002, p. 6). Helen Fielding's Bridget Jones was not, however, alone; the anxieties Bridget has about herself and her romantic life featured in a number of novels that preceded the publication of *Bridget Jones's Diary*, and the success of Bridget Jones led to a recognized genre in publishing. Bridget is only one heroine among many who feature in the range of novels that have been disparagingly termed 'chick-lit'. The chick-lit novel has a heroine who takes her independence and working life for granted. Their plots, however, continue to be framed in the terms of a traditional romance narrative, one of the generic conventions of which is a happy romantic resolution for the heroine.

In the terms of one of these novels, these are narratives which describe the lifestyle of 'an exhibit in an ethnological museum. "Unmarried urban woman, late twentieth century", the label would read. "Note the mating-display rituals of scarlet lipstick and short skirt"' (Sisman, 1998, p. 2). Although their narrative structures reproduce many of the same features, the single woman narrative does not entirely belong to the genre of the Mills and Boon or Silhouette romance; the quest for romance centres around a heroine who is already, and in her own right, financially independent. These are novels in which the rituals of scarlet lipstick and of fashion are central, preoccupied as they are with consumption and style. In a 1970 essay, 'Consumer Society', Jean Baudrillard argued that:

> Today we are everywhere surrounded by the remarkable conspicuousness of consumption and affluence, established by the multiplication of objects, services and material goods. This now constitutes a fundamental mutation in the ecology of the human species. Strictly speaking, men of wealth are no longer surrounded by other human beings, as they have been in the past, but by *objects*.
>
> (Baudrillard, 2001, p. 32)

The chick-lit novel invariably represents a woman of (relative) wealth who relishes a world of consumer choice, who is in a position to participate in the 'multiplication of material goods' and who takes some pride in the fact. As one heroine puts it: 'I'm successful, in a fashion. I earn enough money to go on shopping binges at Joseph every three months or so, and I own my own flat' (Green, 1997, p. 3). The single woman novel is a genre which takes great pleasure in conspicuous consumption, and which plays with the opportunities afforded by the multiplication of consumer goods for women who are in a position to afford them. In order to be in a position to consume, the central characters of these novels are independent, privileged young women, usually university-educated, and with jobs in the glamorous end of the middle-class professions, often in the media: Tasha of *Straight Talking* is a television producer (like Bridget Jones); Libby of *Mr Maybe* works in public relations. Although the heroines rarely demonstrate any career ambition (ambitious women are frequently derided and often characterized as rivals to the heroine, both professionally and in love), their jobs are important to them. Unlike the ambitious 1980s sex and shopping heroine, this is largely because it is work that provides the salary to support an urban lifestyle. If the heroines frequently bemoan their limited incomes, their lifestyle is largely dedicated to consumption. They are women who have confidence in themselves and, to a large degree, in their appearance, a confidence that is validated by their ability to afford designer labels. Tasha, for instance, prepares for an evening out, secure in the knowledge that 'the finishing touch is a dab of MAC taupe lipstick. I do look good' (Green, 1997, p. 161). While this is undoubtedly about the heroine preparing to be an object of the male gaze, there is also a considerable pride in the consumer sophistication of the lipstick's brand name, and in her ability to afford it.

The reader of these novels is addressed as a woman who shares the heroine's metropolitan lifestyle of restaurants and shopping. Often written in the first person (as in Jane Green and Tyne O'Connell's series of novels), the tone is one of shared confidences. The reader is assumed to be a skilled consumer, to have a familiarity with designer labels, and is expected to have the knowledge to recognize the sophisticated brand names that fill the pages of these novels (even when these references are coded, as in 'D&G', 'Calvins' or 'Manolos'). These are novels written for young women who are skilled and experienced in contemporary discourses of consumption; their design suggests that they are clearly targeted at the readers of such consumer and lifestyle publications as *Elle* and *Marie Claire*. Their covers echo the covers of such magazines, and often refer to the colours and patterns of each fashion season, as in the shocking pink, lime green and leopard skin cover of Jane Green's 1997 novel, *Straight Talking*.

As Rachel Bowlby has charted, consumption has been associated with women since the development of the large department stores in Europe in the late nineteenth century (Bowlby, 1985). Sean Nixon extends this argument to take account of male consumption in the late twentieth century, and explains that:

> The very spectacle of consumption – the windows filled with goods, the lighting, the displays, the other shoppers, the places to meet – has ... historically been signalled as a feminine domain, and associated with femininity. From the department stores at the turn of the century with their clientele of middle-class ladies, to the 'consuming housewife' of 1950s advertising, the dominant imagined addressee of the languages of consumerism has been unmistakably feminine. Consumption, associated with the body, beautification and adornment in particular, has historically spoken to a feminine consumer, producing her as an 'active' consumer but also as a 'spectacle' herself – to be looked at, subject to a predominantly masculine gaze.
>
> (Nixon, 1992, p. 151)

The heroines of these fictions are certainly active consumers, but this is not only in the interests of creating themselves as 'spectacle'; their pleasure in consumption is not limited to fashion and beauty goods for their own adornment, but extends to the consumption of men themselves. In these novels, masculinity becomes a spectacle for women; the hero of Freya North's *Chloë*, William, is referred to literally as an object of desire ready for consumption; the heroine and her friend discuss him as being 'ten times more scrumptious than ... egg- mayonnaise granary sandwiches. In fact, make that fifteen ... as divine as the fudge brownies? Easily' (North, 1997, pp. 326–7).

These narratives are concerned with the heroine's deployment of consumer skills in order to seduce a man, but those skills are also used in the commodification of masculinity itself. Shopping for men in these novels is not only about employing consumer skills in order to identify (or even to create) an appropriate partner for the heroine, but it is also about the opportunity to select from a range of different men. Alice K of Caroline Knapp's *Alice K's Guide to Life* is racked with anxiety about the 'dating' process, but nonetheless has a demanding points system by which she assesses the wardrobe, tastes and cultural capital of her suitors:

> Cashmere. Alice K. liked a man who cared about his socks – five points ... Elliot M. grew up in Chicago – ten points for cosmopolitan background ... Throughout the evening, she also discovered that Elliot M. exercised regularly (five points ...), liked good food and wine (ditto) ... Lying in bed, Alice K. tallies up the numbers. Not bad, she thinks, although there's still a lot of outstanding information, some nagging doubts. For instance, Elliot M. drove a Volkswagen Jetta (fine), but had the radio tuned to a classic hits station (not so fine) ...
>
> (Knapp, 1994, pp. 43–4)

The plot descriptions on the back covers of these novels often involve a list of male names, one of whom will be revealed in the narrative as the hero. The title of Jane Green's *Mr Maybe* indicates that the search for a romantic partner has become a matter of consumer choice for the contemporary young woman. The heroine, Libby, is a successful and financially independent PR woman, whose expectations of a male partner are that he will be able to match her in the consumption of designer labels. The potential hero is 'Mr Maybe' rather than 'Mr Right' because he is desirable, but impoverished and inappropriately dressed.

The desirability of men is assessed in these fictions through the male characters' display of the appropriate commodities; more important than their career trajectory or their politics (Libby is happy to switch from Conservative to Labour supporter) is the possession of the right labels. The conflation of man, property and commodities is a recurrent device in these novels; a potential male partner in *Mr Maybe* is assessed in these terms: 'He was everything I'd ever been looking for. He was a property developer, which is a bit boring I know, but he wasn't boring. He was handsome, well dressed, had a beautiful flat in Maida Vale, a Mazda MX-5 ... Well, the list goes on and on really' (Green, 1999, p. 8).

The hero of Robyn Sisman's novel *Perfect Strangers* is perfect precisely because he is absent, known only through the objects that surround the apartment that the heroine has swapped with him in New York. His desirability is signified through the commodities and design of his flat that the heroine inhabits without ever having met him: 'The living room had white walls, parquet floors and pretty pastel fabrics ... One end had been turned into a study area, with bookshelves, a leather club-like sofa and a sleek, modern desk with a fax and a computer on it – a Mac 6400, she noticed. Not bad' (Sisman, 1998, p. 43). It is not just the computer here that is 'not bad', but also the apartment and its owner, even though he is absent. This same trope of the ideal, but physically absent, hero was also to appear in contemporary romantic films. In *Sleepless in Seattle* (1993, dir. Nora Ephron), the heroine emulates the narrative of the 1957 film *An Affair to Remember* (dir. Leo McCarey) in pursuit of a hero she has never met. The heroine of the 1995 film *While You Were Sleeping* (dir. John Turteltaub) becomes engaged to the ideal man, who is in a coma for much of the film. This structural device in which an absent hero is the focus of desire allows for a fantasy projection of an ideal mate and simultaneously enables the heroine to become the central figure in a romance narrative.

Laura Zigman's 1998 novel *Animal Husbandry* was hailed in Britain and America as the transatlantic version of *Bridget Jones's Diary*, and Zigman as a new Helen Fielding, although the fast-paced sassy tone of the novel is far closer to the New York of Candace Bushnell's Carrie Bradshaw of *Sex in the City* than it is to the very English insecurities of Bridget Jones. Jane, like Bridget Jones, works as a television researcher. She is, again, like Bridget and Carrie Bradshaw, flanked by her best women friends and a gay male intimate, a regular cast of characters in these novels. While Jane and her friends inhabit a New York world of media professionals, it is the dissection of relationships rather than work that preoccupies them all. The heroine's first date with the novel's romantic interest is in a shopping mall. Jane assesses male partners in terms of their clothes; as a male suitor appears at her apartment, she considers him an appropriate accessory to her lifestyle: 'He was wearing a baseball cap ... Champion sweatshirt, basketball sneakers ... [W]hen he leaned up against the wall, it occurred to me how good my apartment suddenly looked' (Zigman, 1999, p. 80). The most romantically charged moment in the novel is not to do with a relationship, but is the moment of finding a rent-controlled apartment; the language used here is evocative of an erotic encounter: 'the perfect apartment ... I felt a thrill and a calmness I had never known before ... My joy knew no bounds' (*ibid*., p. 97).

Jane's group of friends, like Alice K, have a daunting list of check points to assess their potential partners in terms of consumption, measuring their suitability according to the cut of their wardrobe, shoes and hair. Their narratives of broken relationships are interspersed by quotes from a range of philosophers and popular scientists, all selected for their analysis of human relationships. Jane is a consumer of self-help books, and goes shopping for Freud and Darwin to shed light on her own failed romances. It is through consumption that she maps her emotional life; her broken heart is measured in a list of necessary expenses, in which Jack Daniels whisky and Häagen-Dazs ice cream figure large.

The assessment of clothing, interior design and food consumption in these novels frequently borrows from the language of lifestyle and women's magazines. There is a direct cross-over between fiction and journalism in this genre of women's writing, in which the personal column, autobiography and fiction merge across different media. Helen Fielding's *Bridget Jones's Diary* began as a newspaper column, as did Candace Bushnell's *Sex in the City*, which became a novel, and then a television series. As Zoë Heller has pointed out, what she terms 'girl columns': 'enjoyed a great surge of popularity in the nineties ... [E]very British broadsheet had a jaunty female correspondent in its pages, providing weekly glimpses into her private affairs' (Heller, 1999, p. 11).

Kathryn Flett was among these 'jaunty' female writers and her 1999 memoir *The Heart-Shaped Bullet* began as a weekly Sunday paper column. The book may be subtitled 'A True Story', and be an autobiographical account of the end of her own marriage, but it works within a discourse of contemporary femininity that is shared with the fictional narrators of these novels. Design, style and skilled consumption are central to *The Heart-Shaped Bullet*: Flett consistently assesses people in terms of their tastes and shopping habits; her future husband is approved because 'he loved Bath Olivers (which he bought from Harrods)' (*ibid.*, p. 56). The breakdown of their relationship is charted in the exchange of his increasingly unsuitable gifts to her; her love for him is expressed in the care with which she chooses furnishings for their flat. Flett articulates her anxieties about the marriage, and expresses her disdain for comfortable coupledom, entirely in terms of commodities and a stratification of brand names:

> was it really any different if, instead of a neat modern home on an estate in the 'burbs, with a World of Leather three-piece suite, a copy of TV Quick on the IKEA coffee table, a Ford Probe in the drive, a Blockbuster video and a curry on Fridays, a nice M&S-catered dinner party on Saturdays with a few of your best friends, at which the men talked about Manchester United and the women talked about Princess Diana, you instead chose to live in an *Elle Decoration*-style loft in the centre of London, with a copy of *Blueprint* on the Conran Shop coffee table, a 4WD in the residents' parking bay, an Indonesian takeaway and a video (with subtitles) on Fridays, a nice dinner party with a few of your best friends on Saturdays, catered by, say, the Real Food Store, at which the men talked about Arsenal and the women talked about Princess Diana's psychotherapy habit? These things were, when it came down to it, just a matter of style.
>
> (*Ibid.*, p. 69)

As Pierre Bourdieu has pointed out, 'these things' are by no means 'just a matter of style', but are an assertion of class difference and assumed superiority. Flett herself modestly acknowledges that her own lifestyle is closer to Conran than IKEA; her comprehensive knowledge of brand names distinguishes her own taste from that of the 'ordinary' consumer, and is in itself a display of distinction. As Bourdieu has put it: 'The competition for luxury goods, emblems of "class" is one dimension of the struggle to impose the dominant principle of domination' (Bourdieu, 1984, p. 232).

Flett, as onetime editor of a style magazine and consumer writer, might be expected to be concerned with questions of style and taste; she is, as a style journalist, exactly what Bourdieu defines as a 'taste-maker', an 'ardent spokesman in the new bourgeoisie of the vendors of symbolic goods and services' (*ibid.*, p. 310). Kim Izzo and Ceri Marsh also come from journalistic backgrounds in magazines; their 2002 *The Fabulous Girl's Guide to Decorum* is a strange hybrid of fiction and etiquette manual. An introduction describes their text as 'both a celebration of the fully formed Fabulous Girl and a primer for the Fabulous Girl in training' (Izzo and Marsh, 2002, p. 13). The fictional heroine is, like the authors, a magazine journalist. While the advice given to the single 'Fabulous Girl' is not unlike that given by Beryl Conway Cross in the 1956 *Living Alone*, the Fabulous Girl is a much more skilled consumer than her predecessor. She is advised to read 'fashion magazines from around the globe both for pleasure and to keep up with what's going on in the world of style' (Izzo and Marsh, 2002, p. 22), to get to know shopkeepers and so 'keep up to date with merchandise' (*ibid.*, p. 87). The reader is provided not only with a list of wardrobe, cosmetic and household essentials, but also with a roster of professional 'people' she will need to employ to sustain her 'fabulous' lifestyle. The contents of her handbag, music collection and fridge are proscribed as 'What the Fabulous Girl needs' in her home. The most 'important space', however, is her wardrobe (*ibid.*, p. 251). The Fabulous Girl's 'Perfect Day' is a day out with her best Fabulous girl friend at 'the nicest shopping district in town' (*ibid.*, p. 136). Her romantic life is just as subject to the rules of consumption as is her wardrobe; potential suitors are sorted into categories, the search for a lover described in terms of rummaging through a sales rack.

This authoritative command of lifestyle choices is not restricted to writing by magazine journalists such as Flett and Izzo and Marsh. The same preoccupation with branded commodities is repeatedly echoed in fiction, and often in remarkably similar language. The heroine of Jane Green's *Straight Talking* expresses her disdain for an ordinary married couple in terms of their choice of comestibles:

> Marks & Spencer canapés ... they look pretty, so people think they're being so clever and smart by serving them. And this was a Marks & Spencer, cheap-sparkling-white-masquerading-as-champagne-and-mixed-with-cassis kind of party. The boring kind.
>
> (Green, 1997, p. 15)

The first-person narrator of *Straight Talking*, Tasha, is anxious to demonstrate her knowledge of contemporary style throughout the narrative. Like Flett, she presents herself as someone who is in a position to recognize 'emblems of class'. Tasha works for a daytime television magazine programme, owns a designer-label wardrobe and has friends who can afford designer lingerie and to eat with her in fashionable restaurants. Tasha is presented with a choice of three men over the course of the narrative, but the hero declares himself to the reader, if not immediately to the heroine, by his style credentials. The hero is himself a retail designer, as the heroine admiringly confides to the reader: 'In fact, you've probably had a cappuccino in one of his restaurants, or possibly admired a staircase he's designed in your favourite designer store in town' (*ibid.*, p. 76). The hero and heroine's partnership is destined at the end of the novel to be an alliance of shared tastes and cultural capital, as Bourdieu has explained: 'Taste is a matchmaker, it marries colours and also people, who make "well-matched couples" initially in regard to taste' (Bourdieu, 1984, p. 243).

The eponymous heroine of *Chloë* has the consumption of men made easy for her by an inheritance from an earthly, rather than fairy, godmother. A small legacy provides Chloë with an independent income and instructions to search England, Wales, Scotland and Ireland for 'a small patch that you can at last call Home' (North, 1997, p. 20), an itinerary that offers the heroine a choice of four different men. Godmother Jocelyn is clearly established as a woman of means and taste, connoted by the luxury brand names that she has left behind: a Dunhill handkerchief, a Hermès scarf, Mitsuko scent. Her legacy to Chloë is not only one of property, but also one of cultural capital. The presiding spirits of the novel, and the heroine's confidantes, are Mr and Mrs Andrews; Chloë's taste for Gainsborough's painting is also her godmother's bequest. The painted couple are also made present for the reader by a reproduction which prefaces the novel; a reference to high art which confirms not only the cultural capital of the heroine but also that of the novel's author, who is described as holding 'a Masters Degree in History of Art from the Courtauld Institute'. The choice of 'Mr and Mrs Andrews' is significant; as John Berger has pointed out, Gainsborough's painting is a portrait of: 'landowners ... [whose] proprietary attitude towards what surrounds them is visible in their stance and their expressions' (Berger et al., 1972, p. 107). Mr and Mrs Andrews provide for both heroine and reader an image of secure bourgeois and propertied marriage; they clearly represent what the godmother anticipates for her goddaughter, and the heroine for herself.

Although Chloë is established as an attractive and independent young woman (she has a flat in Islington, a boyfriend and a career in higher education), the novel begins from the assumption that there must be more to life: 'Chloë; time to free yourself from the self-obsessed shackles of the lowly paid and not very good inner London Polyversity where you've shouldered the role of student-communication-liaison-officer for four thankless years' (North, 1997, p. 16). Each destination on Chloë's journey holds out the promise of a different lifestyle, and offers her a new kind of man. Each man and location is presented as a candidate for Chloë's definition of 'home'; each site offers a certain charm, and is described in great detail and in language that would be appropriate to an estate agent or an interior design magazine. In Wales: 'The farmhouse was neither old nor particularly picturesque. It was a sensible structure well suited to its purpose' (*ibid.*, p. 61). The man who comes with this household is, like the house, a sensible structure well suited to his purpose; although startlingly handsome, his job as a farmhand renders him inappropriate as a life partner. Neither man, lifestyle nor house can provide the bourgeois comforts that the heroine implicitly requires.

Ireland also offers attractions, but not the security demanded for the heroine. The location is 'a fat little cottage, white-washed and with green doors and frames. It was dark inside but gloomy for an abundance of ornaments ... (which) offered glints of colour from every direction' (*ibid.*, p. 137). The man who accompanies this environment is similarly over-ornamented and gloomy; as a fine artist, he has pretensions that do not sit comfortably with Chloë's bourgeois aspirations. It is, unsurprisingly, England which finally offers the home and man who are most 'heimlich' for the heroine. William is not an artist but a craftsman, both his profession and his environment appropriate to the heroine's expectations; he lives in a delightful Cornish cottage which is furnished with simple but emphatically stylish charm. The hero is a ceramicist, who is first encountered through his craft, the suggestion being that the man must be as covetable and as tasteful as the objects he creates: 'Their creator could only be as beautiful as they were, and William's ceramics were quite the most lovely things she had ever seen. Genuine, secret, and so very strong, quiet and serene' (*ibid.*, p. 390).

The stories of Chloë and William are paralleled throughout the novel, as Chloë encounters his work at different destinations, their shared destiny made evident in their shared aesthetic tastes. William's desire for Chloë is couched in terms of the aesthetics of his craft; she becomes an aesthetic object, ready to be moulded by him: 'he ... remembered again her russet curls vivid against the grey of his glaze. At once he had an idea for a vessel ... Something fairly slender but subtly curving, smothered with *terra isgillarta*, the rich slip he would then burnish until it shone almost wet' (*ibid.*, p. 9). The narrative is at pains to point out that William is a successful craftsman; his work is flourishing commercially and is approved by the appropriate style magazines; his pots have featured in *Homes and Gardens* and *Country Life*. The romantic alliance of hero and heroine is neatly predicted by one of Bourdieu's classifications of class distinction, their romance dramatizing a merger between the heroine's bourgeois cultural capital (embodied in Chloë's inheritance) and William's skills as a craftsman. As Bourdieu puts it: 'artists, craftsmen and art-dealers, who earn their living from industrial and commercial profits, and are close in those respects to other small businessmen, are set apart from them by their relatively high cultural capital, which brings them closer to the new petite bourgeoisie' (Bourdieu, 1984, p. 123).

The consumption of men is not always as easily managed narratively as it is for Chloë. If identifying a hero from a range of different men proves to be difficult, then it is always fictionally possible for the heroine to create her own ideal man. By endowing a man, even the most unlikely candidate (one hero begins as a trainspotter), with the requisite fashion items and the cultural capital of style magazine knowledge, it is possible to construct a perfect partner. Jane Gordon's *My Fair Man* refers in its title and in a epigraph at the beginning of the novel to *Pygmalion*, but there the resemblance to George Bernard Shaw's play ends. If Professor Higgins's transformation of Eliza Doolittle is designed to demonstrate that class is not a product of nature but of culture, Gordon suggests that class is entirely a matter of style, and that style can be acquired through consumption. The heroine literally steps over the hero in a Covent Garden doorway, in an encounter that heightens her possession of cultural capital and his lack of it. She is coming out of the opera, en route to a fashionable restaurant; he is selling *The Big Issue*. Hatty, the heroine, offers the hero a crash course in what Sean Nixon has called: 'forms of popular knowledge open to men – knowledge concerning adornment and style' (Nixon, 1992, p. 166). Gordon's novel demonstrates that these forms of popular knowledge are not restricted to men, but have become available to women through style journalism. Jimmy's transformation is effected through the acquisition of the requisite designer brands and is possible only because Hatty has acquired a comprehensive understanding of fashion through style journalism. As soon as the hero enters the heroine's world, he is supplied with 'a white Paul Smith T-shirt, some Calvin Klein Y-fronts and a pair of ... button-fly jeans' (Gordon, 1998, p. 55), and immediately becomes an object of desire.

The hero is transformed through the terms of style magazines into an object that could appear on their pages. At the hairdressers he is presented with:

> a copy of a glossy magazine called *FHM* that was full of big pictures of lager, aftershave ... and a lot ... of the kind of clothes he was now wearing ... He looked ... like something out of the magazine that was propped open in front of him. The beautiful – slightly homoerotic – image of the boy in the Kouros ad, or the model in the full-page ads for Calvin Klein jeans.
>
> (*Ibid*., pp. 89–90)

Through the heroine's consumption of male style products (she buys him a wardrobe and a library of style magazines), the hero, Jimmy, becomes an object worthy of consumption himself. To finally become a worthy partner for the heroine, however, it is necessary that he should succeed in his own right, and achieve as a successful novelist. The novel's romantic dénouement occurs on his territory rather than hers, at the launch party for his book at the Newcastle dockside, in his home base rather than the cosmopolitan London which he has conquered, and which is her world. Jimmy nonetheless achieves to the point that he becomes the toast of London society, and appears as a celebrity in the same magazines which created him:

> It seemed as if everywhere she turned she saw Jimmy. The *Big Issue* cover had just been the start of his media exposure. He had subsequently featured in a variety of magazines and papers from *GQ* to *Gay News* ... his beautiful face popped up in the People columns of *YOU*, *Hello*!, *Tatler*, *Harpers* and *Vogue*.
>
> (*Ibid*., p. 319)

The 'makeover' narrative is not restricted to women writers. The hero of Robert Llewellyn's *The Man on Platform 5* is transformed into a metropolitan success, largely through the purchase of designer clothing, just as he is in Gordon's *My Fair Man*. Like Hatty, Eupheme, Llewellyn's heroine, offers fashion advice and cultural knowledge which she has gleaned from style magazines; *The Face* and *ID* are recurrently cited as authoritative sources of information on the stylistic requirements of acceptable masculinity.

Although both these Pygmalion narratives offer a gender reversal of the Professor Higgins role, in that it is the heroine who initiates and is the agent of change (and, importantly, provides the cultural and financial capital), the romantic resolution invariably involves the hero achieving success on his own terms. Like Jimmy, Ian succeeds, on his own terms, to become an object of respect and admiration for the heroine. The computer geekiness of 'The Man on Platform 5' is finally legitimated when he becomes a millionaire with a new computer program he has written. The initially impoverished hero of *Mr Maybe* finally confirms that he is Mr Right because he is public-school-educated, owns Ralph Lauren shirts, and has achieved a publishing deal for his novel. It is a structural invariable of these novels, just as it is for Mills and Boon romances, that the hero should demonstrate his professional success before the obstacles to romance can be overcome. Success for women in these fictions is conferred not by their own achievements but by those of a male partner.

The narrator of these fictions will often deliberately distance the heroine from any suggestion of feminism, while simultaneously endorsing her successful career. Libby of *Mr Maybe* despises her consort's socialist-feminist friends; Hatty's feminist posturings are humbled and dismissed by the end of *My Fair Man*. Suze, the advertising executive of *Perfect Strangers*, is typical in her response to the accusation (and it is a recurrent feature of these novels that the designation is assumed to be an accusation) that she is a feminist: '"*Feminist*?" Suddenly Suze was furious. Her head snapped back ... "It's not feminist to think men and women can treat each other like human beings"' (Sisman, 1998, p. 224).

It is hard to recognize what it is that is not feminist about this statement, but it is a denial which is repeated in some form in all these novels. Suze here expresses a paradoxical desire to be taken seriously as a woman, while denying that there is any political dimension to that demand, a paradox that recurs throughout the narratives. Kathryn Flett's memoir articulates precisely the same contradiction:

> I wasn't exactly what you'd call Political, and hadn't ever described myself as 'a feminist' but I didn't lose much sleep about the possibility of being able to compete with men (or women, come to that); it was simply a given. Obviously I had to have a career in place before I even thought about marriage.
>
> (Flett, 1999, p. 21)

The heroine of *Straight Talking* seems to address the reader in the language of female solidarity, but makes it quite clear that she is firmly distancing herself from any feminist position, and that her fellowship with women is a poor substitute for partnership with men:

> You can always recognise a fellow member of the sisterhood ... Once upon a time, in their twenties, the sisterhood were men's women. All their friends were men ... But now in your thirties you've changed. You've become women's women. There's a weary air about you ... I'm assuming you're a member of the sisterhood ...
>
> (Green, 1997, pp. 8–9)

Female friendship is instead expressed in terms of shared tastes and consumption patterns; these novels invariably feature a scene in which the heroine and her closest friends go shopping together. The most emotional moment in *Straight Talking* is a scene in which the heroine and her friends try on designer wedding dresses, each choosing their dress before they have found a prospective groom: 'the four of us made a pact. Whoever is the first to get married has to dress the bridesmaids in Armani' (*ibid*., p. 250). Flett's account of her own wedding day is dominated by descriptions of the style and cost of her dresses. There is a conflation and a confusion in these novels between romantic desire for a man and for the commodities of luxury and fashion which he is expected to provide. The man here becomes an accessory, a commodity to be selected in accordance with an already-written style agenda.

There is a very traditional fantasy of femininity in these novels, which is articulated in terms of commodities; there is an attempt to simultaneously ironize the dream, with the contemporary edge of a recognized brand name, and to admit to it. The heroine of *Straight Talking* confesses to the conventional nature of her aspirations, but while she archly suggests knowingness, the fantasy remains unchallenged, as it is in all these novels:

> I was never supposed to be single at thirty years old. I was supposed to be like my mother, wasn't I? Married, a couple of kids, a nice home with Colefax and Fowler wallpaper and a husband with a sports car and a mistress or two. Well, to be honest, I would mind about the mistresses, but not as much as I mind being single. What I'd really, really love is a chance to walk down that aisle dressed in a cloud of white.
>
> (*Ibid.*, p. 1)

The title of Marian Keyes's *Lucy Sullivan is Getting Married* suggests a similar unreconstructed fantasy, as the plot begins from the desire and pursuit of a husband. Although presenting their heroines as modern and independent, these are novels which ultimately accept a subservient status for women and a form of gender relations that belong to a pre-1960s generation. Lucy Sullivan, like Bridget Jones, fails initially to recognize the right male object of desire because he is approved by her mother, and is too close to home to initially appear desirable. While the heroines may be independent career women, their desire is still for a male provider. Just like Bridget Jones, Lucy ultimately comes to recognize that Mother knows best.

While the population and census belie the phenomenon of the independent woman's problems in finding love, these novels powerfully evoke a sense of dissatisfaction in young women's lives, a dissatisfaction that, it is assumed, will be answered by a man. The difficulty facing the heroines of these narratives is not that of finding a man, but of finding a man who is in a more powerful position than their own. As the heroine of *What's A Girl to Do?* suggests: 'Like most *fin de siècle* girls I was looking for someone who could offer me more than I could offer myself' (O'Connell, 1999, p. 168). Flett wistfully articulates the impossible combination of desires that are recurrently echoed in these novels:

> Why did I feel I *deserve* something more, actually *believe* that the noxious concept of Having It All was a divine right? What I sought – a successful career, a wonderful man, perfect children, a beautiful home, inner peace, intellectual stimulation, exotic travel and knees like Princess Diana – was, I knew, at least in part an agglomeration of powerful but pernicious glossy magazine fantasies, but the fantasies were too powerful to be resisted, even by a woman who helped to peddle them.
>
> (Flett, 1999, p. 23)

The regularity with which various versions of these anxieties recur in contemporary popular women's writing suggests that these irreconcilable demands are material contradictions confronting the expectations of femininity in the late twentieth century. As expressed in these fictions, it would seem that contemporary femininity is expected to be simultaneously glamorous and maternal, cosmopolitan and homemaker, modern, working women and stay-at-home wives. Young women seem, too, to be demanding this impossible ideal of themselves; as Flett succinctly puts her wifely ambitions: 'cool, modern, Nineties, urban, rural, full-time working career woman, wife and mother' (*ibid.*, p. 69). It is consumption that is presented in these novels as a means of reconciling these conflicting demands and of achieving a resolution. Because the contemporary woman consumer is presented with an apparent infinite variety of lifestyle choices, she is expected to select among them and so find contentment. Lauren Langman has argued that the pleasures of consumption offer a multiplicity of modes of being, and that shopping provides a:

> commercially produced fantasy world of commodified goods, images and leisure activities that gratify transformed desire and provide packaged self-images to a distinctive form of subjectivity. A decentred selfhood has become a plurality of intermittent, disconnected, recognition-seeking spectacles of self-presentation.
>
> (Langman, 1992, p. 40)

These are narratives which are indeed about packaged self-images and which celebrate the commodification of desire, but the spectacles promoted in these novels cannot be read as disconnected, nor the heroine's selfhoods as decentred. There is a distinct logic to this fictional world of commodified goods and images, and a distinct set of rules to the understanding of feminine self-presentation. There are recommended modes of being in these narratives, which are rewarded by romance, and which rest on the approved rules of style magazine recommendations. And those rules are not without implications; as Bourdieu puts it:

> Through their slyly imperative advice and the example of their conspicuously 'model' life-style, the new taste-makers propose a morality which boils down to an art of consuming, spending and enjoying. Through injunctions masquerading as advice or warnings, they maintain, especially among women ... a new form of the sense of moral unworthiness.
>
> (Bourdieu, 1984, p. 311)

The dissatisfactions of contemporary femininity that are recurrently expressed in these novels could be read as just such a sense of 'moral unworthiness'.

Rob Shields, following Michel de Certeau, has also argued that consumption can be a form of agency. He suggests that: 'There is a need to treat consumption as an active, committed production of self and of society, which rather than assimilating individuals to styles, appropriates codes and fashions, which are made into one's own' (Shields, 1992, p. 2).

The heroines of these novels are certainly active and committed consumers, and their consumption is undeniably concerned with the production (or, rather, construction) of self. Nonetheless, the anxious repetitions with which this consumption is reported and the prevalence of brand names, suggest that that construction can only exist within a limited lexicon of consumer products. There is a strict hierarchy of labels in these narratives: Marks & Spencer and IKEA are despised; Joseph and the Conran Shop celebrated. Fashion and style products are cited to connote a particular lifestyle; goods are bought not only for pleasure, but also so that they should be recognized as signifiers of style and class. In these novels, skilled shopping can confer those properties onto a man and transform him into a hero.

The heroines of these novels assume all the gains of the twentieth-century women's movement, taking their work and independence for granted, but leaving traditional gender relations and patriarchal structures profoundly unchallenged. The Fabulous Girl is, according to her creators: 'confident in her status as an equal to men in all facets of life. However, she does enjoy old-fashioned gestures of gallantry' (Izzo and Marsh, 2002, p. 78). The expectation in these fictions is that while these heroines expect to have an independent career and income, and to consume without hindrance, simultaneously the romantic hero is expected to be the provider. A requirement of the Fabulous Girl's love object is that he should be more socially and professionally respected than she is herself. The heroines in these novels are all searching for a version of Carrie Bradshaw's Mr Big, a man who is more of an achiever than the achieving heroine. *Having It All*, the title of a 1991 Maeve Haran novel, is, in the contemporary popular narrative of single women's lives, about having it both ways.

7

Resentful Daughters: The Post-Feminist Novel?

The front cover of the 1997 novel *Bright Angel Time* carries a review by Esther Freud, which describes it as: 'One of the most shocking and powerful books about childhood I've ever read. There is a whole generation of people waiting for this particular story to be told'. Both Freud, herself the author of the 1992 *Hideous Kinky*, and Martha McPhee, author of *Bright Angel Time*, have written narratives about charmingly wayward but ultimately irresponsible mothers who drag their daughters unwillingly through the vagaries of their alternative lifestyles. Both novels are written in the first person and in confessional mode – the confidences of a young woman who has survived. Freud and McPhee are not alone in their writings in this form, or on this subject; the last years of the twentieth century and the first years of the twenty-first saw a spate of novels by young women writers that were concerned primarily with relationships between mothers and daughters. If the successful working mothers of Rona Jaffe's fictions are nonchalant about their daughters' upbringing in the 1960s and 1970s, those novels do not give the daughters any right of reply. The next generation of women writers were to be acerbic about the experience of being brought up by a generation of ambitious women, and unforgiving in their assessments of their mothers.

Melanie Klein has much to say on what the Kleinian psycho- analyst Nini Herman has termed the 'mother/daughter dyad'. Herman describes some of the women patients she encountered in her own therapeutic practice as exhibiting 'sequences of grudges and life-poisoning resentments against their mothers and by extension the world at large' (Herman, 1989, p. 18). These novels could be read as triumphant narratives of just such a 'sequence of grudges', in which the heroine finally comes to terms with her resentment towards her mother and so prevents it from becoming 'life-poisoning'.

For Kleinian theorists the relationship between mother and daughter is one that is fraught with aggression and conflict. 'Girl's envy ... fear of ... hatred and aggression towards mother' each has its set of own index entries in *The Selected Melanie Klein* (Klein, 1986). While Sigmund Freud did address the issue of mother and child conflict, he was not particularly concerned with the gender-specific issues of the relationship between mother and daughter. Conflict between the generations was for Freud an unavoidable consequence of parental responsibility; painful though that conflict might be, he understood it to be an essential stage in the child's journey to maturity and as an inevitable process in order for the child to achieve independence. In one of the few essays in which he addresses femininity directly Freud argues:

> It is the special nature of the mother–child relation that leads, with equal inevitability, to the destruction of the child's love; for even the mildest upbringing cannot avoid using compulsion and introducing restrictions, and any such intervention in the child's liberty must provoke as a reaction an inclination to rebelliousness and aggressiveness.
>
> (Freud, 1986, pp. 422–3)

Melanie Klein's later account of the early stages of the Oedipal conflict reconfigured Freudian theory to pay closer attention to gender difference and to the maternal role. Klein articulates the girl's relationship with her mother as violent and damaging, and as a form of conflict that begins from early infancy:

> in order to explain how women can run so wide a gamut from the most petty jealousy to the most self-forgetful loving kindness, we have to take into consideration the peculiar conditions of the formation of the feminine super-ego. From the early identification with the mother in which the anal-sadistic level so largely preponderates, the little girl derives jealousy and hatred and forms a cruel super-ego after the maternal imago.
>
> (Klein, 1986, p. 80)

These are novels which do directly address the 'formation of the feminine super-ego' and which chart the perceived damage that mothers can do to their daughters. The fictional mothers in this genre can be read as cruel 'maternal imagos', and the writing of the novels understood as narratives of triumphant fantasy in which the daughter overcomes the failures of the mother. However, while there are undoubtedly elements of Kleinian theory to be uncovered in these texts, and it would be relatively easy to undertake a Kleinian reading of each of these novels, this would not account for the fact that this is a genre that developed at a particular historical moment and which belongs, as Esther Freud recognized in her review of *Bright Angel Time*, to a specific generation of women.

Molly Ladd-Taylor and Lauri Umansky have pointed to a late-twentieth-century preoccupation with the 'bad mother' in popular culture. Representations of bad mothers, in popular fiction and in the news media, they suggest, have come to inform political and social discourse in contemporary America:

> 'bad' mothers have moved noticeably toward center stage in American culture. The stereotypes are familiar: the welfare mother, the teen mother, the career woman who has no time for her kids, the drug addict who poisons her fetus, the pushy stage mother, the overprotective Jewish mother, and so on. But mother blaming goes far beyond these stereotypes. It can be found in custody disputes, political speeches ... It can be found as well in the guilt feelings of working women who have internalized the 'bad' mother label.
>
> (Ladd-Taylor and Umansky, 1998, p. 3)

Such versions of the 'bad' mother can also be found as recurrent figures in contemporary women's fiction; many of these familiar stereotypes are to be found as characters across the range of women's writing in both Britain and America. The first-person narration of a resentful child has become an established genre of contemporary fiction, albeit one that remains largely unacknowledged. There is now a generation of women writers who deal with the tensions between two generations of women, who are alert to any form of bad parenting, and particularly to the failures of the mother.

The resentful daughter narrative can be understood as a form of what Freud identified as 'the neurotic's family romance', in which the daughter replaces 'both parents or the father alone' (Freud, 1984, p. 224) with a fantasy substitute. While Freud privileged the father as the focus of a fantasy substitution, these novels act out a literal replacement of the unsatisfactory mother. In these narratives, a group of friends, a sibling, a therapist (and in one case an advice manual) take over the nurturing role that the heroine's biological mother has failed to fulfil.

Suzanna Danuta Walters has noted of representations of mother and daughter relationships in popular culture:

> In our culture, mothers and daughters are the slightly tawdry 'B' movies to the de Mille extravaganzas of mother/son passion and torment. Never achieving the stature of the 'Oedipal spectacle', the mother/daughter nexus nevertheless wanders through our cultural landscape in a sort of half-light, present and persistent, but rarely claiming center stage.
>
> (Walters, 1992, p. 4)

The fiction which charts this nexus similarly exists in a 'sort of half-light' insofar as these are novels which are read in their thousands, but which never quite make it into the literary canon of women's or feminist writing. The resentful daughter genre of fiction can be understood as a sister genre to the male child confessional narrative, a form that was hugely popularized by the phenomenal success of Dave Pelzer's *A Child Called It* (Pelzer, 2000). Both genres are often marketed with similarly sepia-tinted covers illustrating a small child. The narratives of Pelzer and other male writers, such as Augusten Burroughs's tale of his childhood abandoned into the hands of a maverick psychotherapist (Burroughs, 2002), or Tim Guest's account of growing up in an ashram (Guest, 2004), are viscerally angry narratives of extreme abuse, at the hands of adult men and women (not exclusively the mother), and are claimed to be largely based on autobiography. A female version of an appalling childhood at the hands of an unstable mother is Julie Gregory's memoir, *Sickened*; like Pelzer's texts, this is presented as a 'true story', and Gregory's story is authenticated by the inclusion of medical reports and an introduction from a psychiatric expert.

The resentful daughter novel is, however, an avowedly fictional form. Rather than the anger that fuels these memoirs, the novels are marked by a sulky resentment that is less about physical and mental abuse than it is concerned with a mother's irresponsible lack of maternal attention. The relationship between mother and daughter from the point of view of a resentful young daughter is a genre of fiction that emerged in the 1990s, and which has since proved a media and publishing phenomenon. Oprah Winfrey's Book Club, 'one of the most staggering phenomena in the history of collective reading' (Hartley, 2002, p. 4), has the power to instantly create a best-seller and did so when it promoted Janet Fitch's 1999 novel *White Oleander*. Fitch's novel is the narrative of a young girl abandoned to a series of foster parents by her poet mother who is in prison (this was later to become a film, starring Michelle Pfeiffer as the errant mother – *White Oleander*, 2002, dir. Peter Kosminsky). Rebecca Wells's account of a mother distinctly lacking in Southern Comfort, *Divine Secrets of the Ya-Ya Sisterhood*, sold 2.5 million copies and was filmed in 2002 (dir. Callie Khouri) with the poster tag-line 'Mothers ... Daughters. The neverending story of good vs. evil'. *Divine Secrets of the Ya-Ya Sisterhood*, and its prequel, *Little Altars Everywhere*, are perhaps the most successful of these narratives to date, and Wells's status as a publishing phenomenon made her novels a subject of the marketing study *The Tipping Point*. The novel owed its success, according to Malcolm Gladwell, less to its literary qualities than to word of mouth among women readers, and particularly to the phenomenon of the reading group. As Gladwell puts it:

> *Ya-Ya* was what publishers refer to as a 'book-group book'. It was the kind of emotionally sophisticated, character-driven, multi-layered novel that ignites reflection and discussion, and book groups were flocking to it. The groups of women who were coming to Wells's readings were members of reading groups, and they were buying extra copies not just for family and friends but for other members of the group.
>
> (Gladwell, 2000, p. 173)

Gladwell thus attributes the success of Wells's novels to the 'critical role that groups play' in tipping the point into a word-of-mouth success. What he does not acknowledge is that there was a specific gender and generational constituency for that group of readers. The book-group culture could be understood as a contemporary version of consciousness raising, in which reading groups, which tend to be dominated by women, come together to share experiences under the guise of discussing a particular novel. As Jenny Hartley found in her research: 'Groups ... gain from the intimacy and trust which flourish in the congenial atmosphere. Members talk each other not only through books but often, over the years, through some of life's rougher patches' (Hartley, 2002, p. 130).

Wells herself reported that attendance at her book readings was made up of particular generations of women readers:

> I started noticing mothers and daughters coming. The daughters would be in their late thirties, early forties. The mothers were of the generation who went to high school during World War Two. Then I noticed that there started to be three generations coming, twenty somethings as well.
> (Wells, quoted in Gladwell, 2000, p. 170)

The generation of women who went to high school during the American involvement in the Second World War would have been the mothers who emerged into adulthood in the post-war reconstruction, and who would have been in their thirties or early forties at the highpoint of the 1960s.

Although Wells's novel begins in 1959, she makes no reference to this context, her characters exist in a fantasy land created by a group of ageing and nostalgic Southern Belles. The Ya-Ya Sisterhood is a group of women, friends since childhood, whose friendship overrides any other loyalty, and whose motto is 'SMOKE, DRINK, NEVER THINK' (Wells, 2000, p. i). The success of *Divine Secrets of the Ya-Ya Sisterhood* followed Wells's earlier novel, *Little Altars Everywhere* (Wells, 1992), which charted Sidda's childhood in all the gruesome details of her mother's rivalrous neglect. *Divine Secrets of the Ya-Ya Sisterhood* begins with a prologue introducing Sidda as a small child waking from a nightmare and in search of her beautiful mother, Vivi, who cannot be roused from her 'bourbon soaked sleep' (Wells, 2000, p. i). The narrative proper begins with the adult Sidda triumphant; she is happily engaged and a successful stage director (Wells is herself an actress and playwright), her production fêted by *The New York Times*. While loaded with Jungian and religious references, the thrust of the novel is to chart the tensions, past and present, between Sidda and her mother Vivi. Vivi is presented as intensely rivalrous, and vicious towards her daughter. The lavish wedding which ends the novel is again a triumph of the daughter over her mother, as Sidda's marriage is held out by her father as the hope for the future of the family. The ageing members of the Ya-Ya Sisterhood are left alone to dance together.

Esther Freud's *Hideous Kinky* (written four years before *Divine Secrets of the Ya-Ya Sisterhood*) is about a woman who has abandoned the post-war world of conformity in England in search of an alternative way of life in Morocco with her two small daughters. The young narrator of *Hideous Kinky* begins the novel in transit, in a camper van en route to Marrakech. Their evening meal is 'soup with carrots and potatoes in a metal pot on a camping stove'. This earthy food is in stark contrast to the meals of the daughters' imaginings; they dream of 'cornflakes, white bread, spaghetti hoops, Liquorice Allsorts and 99s' (Freud, 1993, p. 230).

Their mother is oblivious to these conventional childhood desires; she remains throughout the novel a shadowy figure whose attention is never focused on her daughters. The novel is resonant with the narrating daughter's images of perceived abandonment. Losing her navy blue knickers while swimming in a lake (the knickers an image of one of the last vestiges of respectability and English school life) the narrator attempts to attract her mother's attention away from her lover: '"Mum ..." I shouted over the water. I knew she wouldn't hear me. Tears as warm as the lake trickled down my face' (*ibid.*, p. 70).

The mother's own idea of adventure is presented as no less childlike, if more exotic, than that of her daughters. Mum is recurrently distracted from motherhood by alternative cultures and by men. She is grumpy when the narrator suffers a nightmare (like Vivi in *Divine Secrets of the Ya-Ya Sisterhood*); when her daughters once again attempt to attract her attention, she does not respond: 'Mum didn't answer. She was sitting cross-legged with her back very straight. Her eyes were closed ... "She's meditating", Bea said. "Oh"' (*ibid.*, p. 79).

The children are deeply unimpressed by the cultures and landscape of Morocco, and are dismissive of any interest in alternative philosophies. As their mother begins to express an interest in Sufism, her younger daughter wearily pleads: '"Oh Mum, please ..." I was prepared to beg. "Please don't be a Sufi"' (*ibid.*, p. 99). Throughout the novel the young narrator and her older sister, Bea, take on responsibility for their mother, reminding her of their need for schooling, and pragmatically checking her more unrealistic schemes. The sisters' shared culture is one of nostalgia for the home comforts of England; they share a yearning for the ordinary, in a fantasy life which is very modest in its demands: '"What do you want most in the whole world?" ... Bea closed her eyes ... "Mashed potato ..." she said, "and a Mars Bar ... What would you like to be then?" ... "I don't know. Normal I think"' (*ibid.*, p. 33).

It is Mum who is seen to consistently disrupt her children's attempts at normality. The novel ends with an image of Mother's unreliability: as she and the children board a train to return to the perceived safety of England, her daughter does not trust her not to jump off again.

Hideous Kinky has autobiographical elements, as evidenced by the front cover which carries a portrait of the author as a young girl by her own father, Lucian Freud. While both Esther Freud and Rebecca Wells do recycle aspects of their own life histories in their novels, their shared themes, of a daughter's yearning for the conventions of traditional family life and of resentment against a mother, are echoed in a series of contemporaneous novels that make no claim at all to autobiography. Martha McPhee's *Bright Angel Time* shares with *Hideous Kinky* and with Rebecca Wells's novels a child's point of view, giving the narrative voice a disingenuousness which can be coruscating in its appraisal of adult behaviour.

The opening lines of *Bright Angel Time* present 'Mom' as a woman in search of 'freedom', having been left by her conventional husband with three young daughters. The departure of the father is also seen by her daughters as the loss of their mother: 'When Dad left, Mom left' (McPhee, 1997, p. 167). 'Mom' is transformed into 'Eve', who is now experimenting with New Age therapies and with relationships with a new kind of man. Her first appearance acts as a metaphor for the naïve trust in strangers that marks her perceived behaviour over the course of the novel: 'Mom learned to fall backward into the arms of strangers without hesitating or looking over her shoulder. She learned to fall freely, with her muscles relaxed and her mind open' (*ibid.*, p. 1). Mom begins the novel, opening in 1970, as an image of the clean, scrubbed and happy housewife, with a distinct echo of Marilyn Monroe in the description of her figure:

> Mom had curly hair, golden curls the color of sand. She was thin, with a big bust, a gap between her teeth ... She wore taffeta dresses with big flowers and no sleeves. Some had matching jackets, some had matching sweaters. The colors were living colors that make me think about summer: peach, lemon, strawberry. Her skin was ivory and smooth and there was no hair on her legs or under her arms. It was comforting skin, the type that showed no signs of stress, honest sincere skin.
>
> (*Ibid.*, p. 2)

This desirable image of a co-ordinated and high-maintenance femininity, and the comfort it provides, is undermined as the novel progresses. There is a brief indication of Eve's frustrated ambitions, and the social expectations that she subsume them into domesticity: 'She'd been educated. Four years of college. They taught you how to be a wife ... Her mother taught her how to be a wife ... Her father laughed at her idea for secretarial school' (*ibid.*, p. 165).

Mom's transition from maternal figure to 'Eve', a woman with her own agenda, is marked by the changes in her dress as she travels with her lover and her children to the West Coast: 'She stood tall and thin, her hair a mat of tangled curls, in a flower-print shirt and new blue jeans' (*ibid.*, p. 57). As Eve embraces liberationist ideas in her thinking and her appearance, so she is perceived by her daughters as having 'let herself go'; throughout the novel her politics are associated with a lack of care and of personal grooming.

There is an emphatic denunciation of adult sexuality in the descriptions of Mom, and a strong sense of the loss of the containment of the family home: 'Black grime wedged under Mom's fingernails. She wore a T-shirt with a caption reading STAMP OUT SEXISM in bold letters ... Mom's breasts bulged through her too small bra' (*ibid.*, p. 98).

There is here a visceral disgust at the mother's mature sexuality, an Oedipal loathing that is particularly directed at the mother's lover. Anton, Eve's dubious lover, is seen by her daughters as entirely responsible for her transition into feminist politics and for Mom's abandonment of the respectable twin-sets and values of suburbia. Anton is pilloried and satirized throughout the novel; his paternal nurturing, it is intimated, is distinctly suspect. His form of feminist politics is dismissed as weird and irrelevant; he offers Eve: 'his idea of women's liberation. He started the local chapter of NOW and organized sit ins in pubs that excluded women' (*ibid.*, p. 2). It is, however, only through the figure of Anton that feminist ideas are referred to at all in the novel. His appreciation of their mother as a woman cuts no ice with her daughters. Anton's belief in her is written in a narrative voice that slides from the daughter's perspective to the mother's, and so is refracted through the mother's own naïve distortion, which is tainted by sexual love:

> He thought her mind was wonderful, magical. He loved to hear her talk about Virginia Woolf, to recite Emily Dickinson. He believed there wasn't anything she couldn't do ... Mom could be this equal for him, if she'd only let herself go – forget what society had taught her to be. Doris Day.
>
> (*Ibid.*, p. 167)

It is precisely the loss of their Doris Day mother that the daughters so resent, and they will not let her forget the demands of her traditional role. The novel ends, like *Hideous Kinky*, with the daughters united in a sisterhood of sibling solidarity, surviving together, but lost by their irresponsible mother.

Astonishing Splashes of Colour, Clare Morrall's 2003 novel (a surprise nomination for the Booker Prize in that year), takes its title and opening epigram from J. M. Barrie's *Peter Pan*, the story of a boy who never grew up; the cover depicts a childlike painting of a young woman floating. The first-person narrator is similarly locked in childhood; she is still known by her childhood nickname of Kitty, and reads children's books for a living. As an adult she is unable to leave the parental home and to commit herself to her own marriage. While this is largely attributed in the novel to the loss of her own child in pregnancy, and her subsequent inability to become a mother herself, the overriding sense of loss in the novel is not for the baby, but for a lost mother. Margaret, the assumed missing mother, was once a college student, whose studies were (as for Eve in *Bright Angel Time*) curtailed by marriage and motherhood. There is a vague awareness that the dimly remembered mother may herself have been frustrated in her ambitions, but this is only addressed in terms of a child trying to make sense of her own narrative:

> 'But did she finish her degree?' I asked. I knew the answer already, but have never been happy with the answer. I want it changed. 'Did she go back to the university and finish?' ... My father wants me to believe they lived happily ever after. My mother, Margaret, probably with a promising academic career ahead of her, surrendered it to get married and have six children.
>
> (Morrall, 2003, p. 81)

The woman whom the heroine assumes to have been her mother and believes has abandoned her young family finally reappears to attend the funeral of her own parents. She is represented with all the signifiers of dress and appearance that connote the 1960s hippy, as Kitty sourly remarks:

> Her eyes, very bright and intense, project a kind of fury ... She is wearing a faded pink corduroy pinafore over a purple blouse, which is made of a flimsy, chiffon material. Underneath the long skirt, you can see grey socks and flat sandals. On her head is a floppy cloth hat, with a blue paisley pattern. It is slightly grubby, giving her a neglected appearance. She looks like a bag-lady. A woman of seventy acting as if she's Alice in Wonderland.
>
> (*Ibid.*, p. 194)

The reasons for the woman's fury are not a matter of concern to Kitty, and there is an unacknowledged irony in that an adult woman who calls herself by her childhood nickname, and whose inquisitiveness is entirely focused on her childhood, is herself not without a touch of Alice. It is only when the narrator recognizes that her biological mother is not this actual woman, but a memory of a woman who is dead, that Kitty can begin to develop a life of her own, a life that is still presaged as bleak and tentative. Kitty's memory of her actual lost mother is another embodiment of 1960s hedonism. She is evoked only by the eccentricity of her dress and by the manner of her death. Both mother figures are seen as having abandoned Kitty for an illusion of liberation, and have so thwarted her own ability to become an adult woman and a mother herself.

Louise, the narrator of Kathleen Tessaro's 2003 novel *Elegance*, is, like Kitty, unable to grow up. When we first meet Louise she is wearing a 'pair of flat Mary-Janes with Velcro fastenings ... faded and scuffed' (Tessaro, 2003, p. 14). Like her shoes, Louise's sexless marriage suggests a wilful girlishness and a refusal to be an adult woman. Her husband, who, it transpires, is gay and disinterested in her sexually, refers to her as 'pumpkin'.

Louise lives out the classic Freudian family romance, in replacing her inadequate mother with the far grander Madame Antoine Dariaux, author of the eponymous *Elegance*, an advice manual on feminine etiquette and apparel. *A Guide to Elegance* by Madame Genevieve Antoine Dariaux is an actual book, published in 1964, and is a literal A–Z of the important things a woman should know, beginning with 'Accessories' and ending with 'Zips' (Dariaux, 1964). The dating of *Elegance* from the early 1960s and the pervasiveness of Madame Dariaux's advice (the book is directly referenced in epigrams which precede each chapter) suggest that this book within the book is the voice of a surrogate mother. Louise's lack of confidence and her unfulfilled marriage could, it is strongly implied, have been averted with the certainty and sage advice of this guide, the 'Holy Grail' (Tessaro, 2003, p. 21) of feminine knowledge.

Madame Dariaux's authoritative and certain voice on the requirements of femininity becomes the beacon of guidance that Louise's mother failed to be. Louise rejects both her mother and her woman therapist (who dresses badly and is therefore not to be taken seriously) in favour of Madame Dariaux, who is first encountered as a poised image of femininity in a photograph at the National Portrait Gallery. The novel is structured around snippets of advice from the manual, and Madame becomes the wished-for mother, a fount of feminine wisdom: 'she'd become real to me and even when I resented the unfailing accuracy of her wisdom, she never let me down' (*ibid.*, p. 23).

Louise's own mother, it is suggested, has let her down, because she has failed in her duty to instil a professional femininity in her daughter. Although her mother is educated and professionally successful, Louise cannot forgive her for her lack of elegance and style:

> I think of my own mother and of how she hated shopping, dressing up or looking in mirrors. Not only did she not aspire to elegance, but I believe she suspected it as a pursuit ... Pale and bespectacled, with short dark hair she cut herself, she preferred to spend most of her time in Birkenstocks and plain, loose trousers ... [I]n the male dominated world of science in which she excelled, fashion was of little practical use.
>
> (*Ibid.*, p. 39)

Louise's (unnamed) mother, 'dressed in thick moccasins she'd made herself and ... her favourite Greenpeace tee-shirts', is clearly a feminist (although the term is never used in the novel). She is contrasted unfavourably with the mother of a school friend, who is represented as an ideal housewife, in a traditional image of femininity which neatly reconciles the contradictory demands of homemaking and fragile beauty. There is a knowing hint of Oedipal rivalry between the mother and the younger Louise, but the father is such an insubstantial figure that this hardly registers in the narrative. Louise describes her father as a perpetually absent figure: 'The most enduring image I have of my father is of distraction. His mind was always elsewhere ... "I have a list of things to do today" was his constant refrain ... And he'd be off' (*ibid.*, p. 152). Louise's sense of neglect is, however, entirely attributed to her mother.

The surrogate mother, Madame Dariaux, who trains Louise in the skills of femininity so neglected by her biological mother, becomes an enabling fairy godmother, who recommends the consumption of clothes and lingerie, and in sorting out Louise's wardrobe, sorts out the problems of her life. Louise's transformation from frumpy child-bride into a sexually aware, adult woman takes the form of a magazine makeover, in which a roll call of brand names and a proud display of shopping skills announce her initiation into the world of 'Elegance':

> I'm wearing a black pencil skirt from Kookai that's almost exactly like this season's Prada ... and a pair of painfully high pink mules which are the spitting image of the Manolo's ... in this month's Vogue ... My lipstick is Mac, my toenail polish Chanel ... And I'm as hot as they come.
> (*Ibid.*, p. 229)

The attainment of 'Elegance' is devoid of any intellectual or personal development, but is acquired through the consumption of fashion items; it is about style rather than any attempt to restore or to nurture personal relationships. As a superior consumer and a better-dressed woman than her mother, Louise is finally able to reconcile herself with adult femininity, and so, like Sidda, she can finally triumph over her mother.

In all these narratives of spoilt, wilful and neglectful mothers, whose whims and irresponsibility are shown to have damaged their daughters, the great unspoken is the feminist movement. Feminism is not addressed as such, but it is persistently there in a coded form. The mother figures of these novels are in search of some form of liberation, whether this takes the shape, as it does in these narratives, of whisky, academia, unsuitable men or hippy travels (or any combination of these). In the eyes of their fictional daughters, however, these mothers have chosen a form of self-assertion that is personal, but never political. There is no recognition that these individual mothers, educated and middle class as they all are (and this is stressed in each novel), belonged to a generation of women who would have been mothering at the high point of the women's movement. Mothers behaving badly in the 1960s and early 1970s (the approximate dating of all these fictional childhoods) was not only a political statement at this time, but also a fashionable one. None of these fictional mothers, however, attend political meetings or conferences, or voice their aspirations in terms of a politicized feminism, and they and their daughters never refer to the Women's Liberation Movement.

As Ladd-Taylor and Umansky have argued: 'We cannot afford to let the cipher of the bad mother stand in for real confrontations with the serious problems of our society' (Ladd-Taylor and Umansky, 1998, p. 23); the discourse of the 'bad mother' is one that has all too easily been co-opted by the politics of the right, and by an anti-feminist agenda. The ciphers who are the 'bad mothers' in these novels belong to the generation of second-wave feminism; women who would have been experimenting with different forms of femininity, and who had expectations that things could be different for their daughters. Their claims to independence are nonetheless entirely individualized in these narratives, grudgingly seen as a matter of personal neglect and of abandonment by their fictional daughters.

The paternal figure is not a significant figure in any of these novels; there is no expectation that fathers might share the burdens and pleasures of domesticity and childcare (if, as rarely, they do, this is presented as highly suspect, as in *Bright Angel Time*). Fathers are markedly absent from these narratives; they are either dead, drunken or divorced, sometimes idealized, but not physically present in the narrators' childhoods, and are never sufficiently there to be blamed. The resentment at what the heroines see as an unsatisfactory childhood is focused entirely upon the mother; as Germaine Greer has wryly commented of popular journalism: 'The father, be he absentee or abusive, gets off scot-free. It's not "your mum and dad" who really "fuck you up", just your mum' (Greer, 1999, p. 199).

These fictional heroines cannot forgive their mothers for not being the traditional mother figure; in Nina Herman's phrase, they are women who have been 'too long a daughter' (Herman, 1989). These narratives can be understood as post-feminist novels only insofar as they represent the voice of the generation of daughters of the second wave of feminism, but as one guide to post-feminist theory has put it: 'Post-feminism does not mean feminism is over' (Phoca and Wright, 1999, p. 3). For these novels it does: the politics of feminism is entirely dismissed as irrelevant to contemporary female experience, and femininity is expressed in these narratives (particularly in *Elegance*) not as a matter of assertion or equality but of consumption. These are not novels that challenge gender roles but, instead, reconfirm them by reasserting a desire for the mother to stay in the home. There is a shared loathing among the narrators for the forms of food and dress assumed by their mothers, and a strong sense of loss that the maternal figure is not what she once was. What the young heroines share in these novels, to a remarkable degree, is a desire for the return of the traditional housewife and mother of the 1950s and early 1960s. The uncomplicatedly happy and domesticated 1950s housewife in Britain and America was, however, as Elizabeth Wilson and others have shown, a myth (Baker, 1989; Wilson, 1980; Philips and Haywood, 1998). Nonetheless, these fictional daughters would begrudge their mothers the relative independence, ambitions and sexual choices that the second generation can now assume for themselves.

The fictional daughters of these apparently irresponsible mothers of the 1960s and 1970s are uniformly resentful; a whole range of novels written by the young women of the late 1990s articulate the mother and daughter relationship as one of rivalry and bitterness. These daughters resent their mothers' relationships, their friendships, their academic careers, their spirit of adventure. These assertions of independence are written about as forms of personal indulgence, and are not recognized as part of a political groundswell of female assertion from which the next generation of women was to benefit.

Resentment at the generation of 'baby boomers' would go on to gather momentum in the first years of the twenty-first century, particularly in the aftermath of an economic crisis in which the benefits that had accrued to the post-war generation could no longer be taken for granted. With the election of a Conservative-led coalition government in Britain in 2010, that resentment took on a directly political edge with the publication of the Conservative politician David Willetts' *The Pinch: How the Baby Boomers Took Their Children's Future – and Why They Should Give it Back*, a title which directly held the post-war generation responsible for the recession in which their children were to grow up: 'The charge is that the boomers have been guilty of a monumental failure to protect the interests of future generations' (Willetts, 2010, p. xv).

The title and narrative of Linda Grant's novel *We Had It So Good* (Grant, 2011)) echoed this *mea culpa* of the 'baby boomer' generation (both Willetts and Grant were born in the 1950s). Her novel traced the fortunes of a couple who have benefited from a grant-aided education, career opportunities at the BBC and affordable houses in Islington. Their children despise them as self-indulgent hippies. Grant's own website firmly points to the culpability of the parents: 'their fortunate generation has always lived in a fool's paradise' (www.lindagrant.co.uk).

Resentment at the 'monumental failure' (in Willetts' phrase) of the generation who were young in the 1960s and 1970s was also a regular theme of plays by both women and men. Stephen Beresford's first play, *The Last of the Hausmanns*, was produced at the National Theatre in 2012. It dramatized the conflict between a child of the sixties, Judy, and her resentful daughter and son who scorn her radicalism and accuse her generation, much like Willetts, of squandering their future. As Mark Lawson noted in *The Guardian*, Beresford's play was one among a trend in contemporary drama, a genre he named the 'baby bust' play. According to Lawson, the baby bust genre was characterized by a

> sense of a middle-class ceiling – that the postwar generation have pulled the ladder up after them – is central to the criticism of the baby boomers. A recurrent theme in what we might describe as the 'baby-bust' genre is selfishness. The products of the 1960s, it is suggested, have monopolised and exhausted the assets of society: not just the oil and mineral reserves but the money and the culture. Because they have abolished the idea of retirement – and may aim to remain in

> employment until death – there will be no jobs for their children and therefore no homes.
>
> (Lawson, 2012)

Lawson cites Mike Bartlett's *Love, Love, Love* and April De Angelis's *Jumpy* as other examples. Both were produced in the same year as Beresford's play, and both at the Royal Court Theatre in London. *Jumpy* dealt with a radical woman – a feminist who was one of the Greenham Common protestors – from the next generation to that of Judy in Beresford's play. The play traces the tensions between her and a resentful daughter who rejects her mother's feminism and radical politics. *Love, Love, Love* trod much the same ground as Grant's *We Had It So Good*, in presenting a smug couple whose adult children perceive them as having betrayed their youthful radicalism (and the next generation) for a comfortable bourgeois existence, which was supported in part by the state.

In the aftermath of the credit crisis, the coalition government elected in Britain in 2010 was keen to suggest that it was the 'baby boomers' who had failed to protect 'the interests of future generations' rather than a global banking system. 'Austerity' was the new hegemony, welfare support was ruthlessly cut, and retirement ages were raised for both men and women. The student grants that had supported previous generations through higher education had been replaced by tuition fees under Tony Blair's Labour government, and these were tripled by the coalition; in 2013 the Conservative Party conference proposed to cut housing benefit for those under twenty-five. Young people would indeed suffer from the erosion of the welfare state that had begun under Margaret Thatcher's rule; in 2011, it was widely reported that young people of this generation were the first who would be worse off than their parents. According to the *Daily Telegraph*:

> Accountancy firm PwC predicts that high tuition fees, less generous pensions and a deflated housing market will leave people born in 1993 around 25 per cent less well off than their parents in old age.
>
> PwC has calculated that someone who is 18 today will have property, savings and a pension worth around £1.23 million when they reach the age of 65. This compares to predicted wealth of £1.63 million when someone born in 1963 – and is therefore currently in their late forties – reaches 65.
>
> The difference in the economic fortunes of people in their teens and people in their forties is due to the 'significant financial headwinds' that the younger generation faces, PwC said.
>
> (Hall, 2011)

These 'significant financial headwinds' cannot be entirely laid at the feet of a 'baby boomer generation' who were not responsible for a global financial crisis, although it suits Willetts and a Conservative agenda to suggest that they can. Resentment against the 'baby boomers' has only gathered in pace, and the current coalition government has precisely set out to foster resentment between generations. The moment that produced the 'baby boomer' is also the moment of women's liberation. These dramas and novels play into a very current right-wing common sense that the 1960s were the point at which it all went wrong, a time when respect for 'family values' and traditional social structures were undermined, and that it was feminism that was responsible.

8

Having it All? Women, Work and Motherhood

Having it All was a 1982 book by Helen Gurley Brown, then editor of the single woman's favourite magazine, *Cosmopolitan*. Gurley Brown was clear that work was integral to women's happiness: 'The crux of the ... plan to get all those things you want – is, yes, your job' (Gurley Brown, 1982, p. 16). It is notable that her advice manual's title became the phrase to designate the determined and ambitious working woman who also had children, despite the fact that it devotes just five pages to the subject. Several generations of 'post-feminist' young women in Britain and America had grown up with an assumption of equality, following the Civil Rights Act of 1964 (which included a section on Sexual Discrimination) and the 1963 Equal Pay Act in America, while Britain had taken rather longer to implement an Equal Pay Act in 1970 and a Sex Discrimination Act in 1975 (which was extended in 1986). These young women were to find that their identities as the 'active, freely choosing, self-reinventing subject of postfeminism' (Gill and Scharff, 2011, p. 7) were to be severely undermined with the advent of children. Just as Sarah Jessica Parker, who played the single career woman Carrie in the television series *Sex and the City* (which aired between 1998 and 2004), grew up to play the harassed working mother in the 2011 film based on Allison Pearson's novel *I Don't Know How She Does It*, so many of the writers, readers and heroines of the 'chick-lit' generation of twenty and thirty-somethings had grown into the next phase of their lives. Pearson's novel was, however, by no means the first to chart the frazzled lifestyle of the career woman confronted with the domestic demands of young children.

The frayed working mother juggling a child with the demands of professional work appeared as a character in press columns, self-help manuals and in fiction; so familiar is she that she became known popularly and in the press as the 'yummy mummy'. The 'yummy mummy' is a doubly diminutive term for women who have had children but who continue to hold on to their attractiveness and independence; a derogatory term that itself established yet another damaging expectation for women. A drawing of a young woman, looking much like her carefree sister heroines of the single woman novel, accessorized with handbag and kitten heels but now with the addition of a baby, became the standardized cover artwork for the genre.

The film *Baby Boom* was released in 1987 (dir. Charles Shyer) and shares many of the tropes of the 'yummy mummy' fictions that were to follow. Diane Keaton inherits a baby (rather than producing her own) and finds it impossible to maintain her professional status as a management consultant with the demands of childcare. Escaping to the country, she develops a business in gourmet baby food, and makes use of her career skills to develop a thriving cottage industry that eventually becomes a multimillion pound commercial empire. This magical synthesis of the maternal and the entrepreneurial, the domestic and the corporate, would, with variations, becomes the standard narrative resolution of these novels.

This narrative arc follows the pattern of the 'retreatist scenario ... the pull back by affluent women to a perfected domesticity', which Diane Negra identified in 2009 as a prevalent phenomenon in popular culture of the late 1990s and early 2000s. In repeatedly enacting the scenario of a harassed career woman shifting into an idealized and compromised domestic sphere, these novels belong to this phenomenon. Negra explains that this narrative of women's retreat into the domestic crosses media forms:

> through popular romantic comedies to primetime dramas and through more diffuse media forms ... Whether named as 'downshifting', an 'opt-out revolution' or the mommy and daughter track, retreatism heavily negotiates current economic and social dilemmas that disproportionately impact on women, while its romantizing alibi, the hometown fantasy, remains distinctly evasive of social and economic realities.
>
> (Negra, 2009, p. 46)

This is precisely the narrative trajectory of this genre of novels which, while vividly illustrating the demands and sacrifices of working motherhood, invariably conclude with the heroine accepting the limits of her situation and readjusting her career, her marriage, or conceding defeat.

The strains of combining work and childcare were (and continue to be) regularly played out in the columns of the popular press to such an extent that the woman columnist charting the trials and tribulations of her domestic life was incarnated as the parodic Polly Filler in the satirical magazine *Private Eye* from 1991, to become a regular feature from 1998. Many of the writers of this particular genre were themselves journalists who had found their working lives constrained by motherhood, and as such were deeply implicated in this discourse,. Their novels can be read as interventions in a continuing debate among female journalists of the generation who did expect to 'have it all' – an independent working life and children. It is significant that the great majority of these novels are first-person narrated – unlike Aga-Sagas, which generally use an omniscient narrator – as they are confessional rather than observational. The having-it-all novels echo the unhappiness of the domestic life found in the Aga-Saga, but with an added edge of resentment – they are the generation who expected to 'have it all' and who swore that they would enact motherhood differently. The narrator shares intimacies with the reader – bodily changes after pregnancy, clothing mishaps, impatience with children and spouse. Yet what ultimately is being confessed is the difficulty of managing full-time work and motherhood. The narrators share a knowing wit, heavy irony[1] and the 'Pollyanna-like commitment to an individuated happy ending' that Harzewski identified in 'chick-lit' (2011, p. 195), but what they lack is any political engagement: there is none of the 'consciousness raising' found in women's novels of the 1970s.

Having it All was also the title of one of the earliest novels of this genre (1991), by journalist Maeve Haran, and hers is a narrative that precisely follows the trajectory of 'retreatism'. The 'high-flying executive' heroine begins the novel by attempting to balance her work and family lives and by the end does indeed relinquish her own career goals in favour of her family. The autobiographical resonances of the novel are hinted at in its dedication: 'For Georgia and Holly, who made me want to change my life, and for Alex, who said I must.' Haran was, like her heroine, once herself a television journalist, now turned novelist. *Having it All* can be seen as a transitional narrative between the career woman narratives of the 1980s (in which, as in Gurley Brown's book, children tended to remain on the margins, if they were present at all) and the established form of the 'yummy mummy' novel in the new millennium. The cover of Haran's novel shares the visual signifiers of the sex and shopping novel, with both an embossed gilt title and an image of a glamorous, scarlet-lipped woman clad in black. The opening establishes – in what appears to be a familiar scene from those novels – the heroine, Liz, clad in silk pyjamas in bed with a man. However, the potential eroticism of this passage is sharply punctured by the appearance of two small children and the encroachment of domestic chaos. The ensuing narrative dramatizes the unravelling of Liz's juggling act when she is promoted to a powerful new position in her television company.

Having it All established many of the key characters and elements of the genre. Liz's husband, David, is a 'hopeless' husband (a figure who became such a cliché that Polly Filler's spouse is repeatedly referred to as 'the useless Simon'). Imelda Whelehan has identified the distinct tone of what she terms 'mumlit' and recognizes that male ineptitude in the domestic sphere is a structural regularity in these novels:

> If mumlit has a different tone to chick lit, it is a more anguished one where the actualities of long-term relationships and the transition to parenthood pose thorny problems and necessary sacrifices ... men's capacity to take over all of women's roles is humorously debated but dismissed with a semi-essentialist finality ...
>
> (Whelehan, 2005, p. 196)

David is a journalist who remains unperturbed by the demands of domesticity: 'the chaos of the breakfast table ... separate and oblivious in a sea of female activity' (Haran, 1991, p. 2); there is no question that he might be capable of domestic chores. Men (and women) in the workplace are equally blind to the demands of the domestic; Liz's career is controlled by an unsympathetic male boss who has 'honed his chauvinism to a fine art ... where men were men and women went shopping' (Haran, 1991, p. 3). While Haran is knowing and witty about the failings of men to understand the pressures of childcare, and there is some recognition here of sexist attitudes, there is no suggestion that challenging her husband at home, or that sex discrimination or equal rights legislation in the workplace, might improve her situation. For Haran, feminism has given her heroine the right to work on equal terms with men, but no rights to challenge the conditions either of work or domestic labour, and there is little sense of sisterly solidarity. Other women in the workplace are perceived as rivals rather than support: Liz's only prominent female colleague at Metro Television, Claudia, is scorned for being 'Chic, single and childless' (Haran, 1991, p. 6) and seen as a threat rather than an ally; among Liz's circle of friends is another single and childless woman who indeed does represent a danger to the marriage.

The novel progresses through sequences that would later become familiar tropes in the 'yummy mummy' narrative: a baby is sick over a stylish power suit; the heroine's lactating breasts leak into a white silk shirt; an important meeting clashes with a child's needs; and there is a threat that the husband will have an affair (which, in this novel, he does). Despite a recurrent emphasis on Liz's professional competence and her great skill in television production, the competing strains of work and family become such that Liz eventually forswears the glamorous life of a media mogul and retreats to a country cottage (equipped with an Aga) to tend to her children. The narrative strongly suggests that Liz's professional success and her lack of attention to the domestic sphere have both driven her husband into the arms of her single friend and led to the neglect of her children. The discovery of her husband's infidelity coupled with maternal guilt (one child is knocked down by a car while in the care of a nanny) lead to Liz's decision to opt for a 'quiet ordinary life with the small pleasures of home and family instead of the cut and thrust of power and success ...' (*ibid.*, p. 559).

The narrative nonetheless ends with some remnants of female ambition and of female solidarity. With her women friends, Liz forswears the world of the media (leaving it as her husband's domain) and turns her professional skills to running a small business named 'WomanPower', an employment agency for women who want to work part time (a phenomenon that was then very much of its time, as more and more women with children were entering the workplace).[2] It is significant that this business is initiated by Liz's homemaking friend, Ginny, and begins as a 'housewife's hobby', in an echo of the feminine 'hobbies' that became million-dollar businesses in the sex and shopping novel of the 1980s and the film *Baby Boom*. In a neat synthesis of traditional femininity and contemporary female ambition, the group of female friends make use of both their domestic and entrepreneurial skills to turn their small company into a desirable business ripe for a profitable takeover. This professional success, along with the attentions of an attractive man (which restore the heroine's confidence in her own desirability) and the final return of the prodigal husband confirm the heroine in her decision to retreat from the world of work into domesticity (albeit somewhat professionalized) and from the urban to the rural. Despite this apparently happy resolution, the ending remains equivocal and conflicted. One of the heroine's close friends is a founding member of *Femina*, a magazine close to *Cosmopolitan* in its ambitions for its women readers: '*Femina* took it for granted that for the new woman everything was possible. She could Have It All: career and family, success and happiness. But what would its message be for the nineties? ... That she might have to choose?' (Haran, 1991, p. 80).

As the genre developed into the 1990s and beyond it became clear that its heroines would be required to choose and that the choice would inevitably involve compromise. Betsy Israel has pointed to the number of self-help books addressed to young mothers that appeared in the same period as these novels; she notes the punishing tone these manuals adopted towards their readers and the extent to which readers were expected to renounce any professional ambition:

> These books had various points to make, but the primary conclusions were always, however expressed or disguised, that women had paid an enormous personal price for the successes of feminism, in particular, the demands and sacrifices required by their jobs. Married women with children, those said to 'juggle' – the euphemism for impossible trade-offs between work and family – were well known to confront physical breakdown if they did not ultimately choose the part-time 'mommy track', meaning the relinquishing of their career goals.
>
> (Israel, 2002, p. 247)

Diana Appleyard's novel *Homing Instinct* was published in 1999. Its cover evoked the film posters for *Baby Boom* with a photographic image of a woman 'juggling': she is dressed in a business suit, carrying both a briefcase and a baby in a backpack. The tagline of the front cover, however, belies the image of the confident, smiling woman and baby and echoes the now-established phrase which identifies the genre: 'When having it all just isn't enough ...'. Like so many of the writers of these novels, Appleyard was herself a working journalist (and is now a columnist for the women's section of the *Daily Mail*); her own biography, given at the front of the novel, encapsulates the narrative trajectory of this novel and of the genre (a highflying career woman has children, moves to the countryside and takes up some form of part-time work). It also, as with the dedication to *Having It All*, points to the novel's autobiographical echoes:

> [Diana Appleyard] was the BBC's Education Correspondent in the Midlands before deciding to give up her full-time job and work from home. She has two children ... and lives with husband Ross in an Oxfordshire farmhouse with four dogs, two cats, three ponies and a great deal of mud. This is her first novel.
>
> (author biography, Appleyard, 1999)

Homing Instinct takes the form of a journal and begins with its heroine's exasperation at men's incapacity to deal with the domestic sphere. Just as in *Having It All*, it is made clear that the responsibility and skills of housekeeping and childcare remain with the woman; a tone of pitying derision towards masculinity is sustained throughout the narrative:

> Why is it that men can spend so much time inert, like a gas? ... I have desperately been trying to pull things together and achieved at least a semblance of order in our lives. Mike, on the other hand, has lain like a sea slug on the sofa ... his little needs are just as important as those of two small demanding children.
>
> (*Ibid.*, 1999, p. 7)

The heroine, Carrie,[3] would seem to be in a powerful position – like Appleyard herself and Liz of *Having It All*, she is introduced as a onetime successful media executive and her voice is initially assertive. She is affluent enough to have full-time child care and a 'lovely perfect nanny' (the 'Angel Claire', in a self-consciously literary reference that demonstrates that both Carrie and Appleyard are familiar with Thomas Hardy). This situation, however, rapidly unravels as the children's good relationship with the nanny threatens Carrie's understanding of herself as a mother and undermines her status in the home: 'I could move out completely and no-one would ever notice' (Appleyard, 1999, p. 9). This sense of invisibility is not only about her position within the household and family but also indicates a fear of the loss of attractiveness in the aftermath of giving birth. It is interesting to note that, despite the popular generic name of these novels and the glamorous women featured on their covers, how little the women protagonists feel themselves to be 'yummy'. There is a marked degree of self-loathing in these narratives. It is a standard convention that they begin with an elegy for the body that has been lost to motherhood. It is another that the heroine later flirts with the possibility of an affair – it matters that she has some external validation of her physical attractiveness.

Clothing is a signifier of a changed identity. Carrie is (as are so many of these heroines) confronted with a new distinction between modes of dress for work and home: she has a working wardrobe that catered for a pre-birth body and a home wardrobe thst sacrifices style for comfort and convenience: 'All I've been dressed in for the past six months are over-sized leggings and vast T-shirts ... My work suits look suspiciously small. Was I ever such a tiny size?' (*ibid.*, p. 8). The inability to fit into a working wardrobe that predates childbirth is an indicator of Carrie's conflicting identities. While she was once defined by her profession – 'Work was what I did. It was what I am. I'm sure it still is ...' (*ibid.*, p. 19) – this certainty is now compromised. Carrie experiences a separation of the work self and maternal self; she feels 'somehow uneasy about ... merging my mummy-self and my work-self' (Appleyard, 1999, p. 26); the working environment cannot accommodate the needs of a working mother and children do not understand the demands of a career.

Although Carrie does return to work, this is not an environment that can offer any support. Other women in the workplace are once again presented as rivals rather than as any source of solidarity and this rivalry extends towards other mothers. There is a strong theme throughout the novel of a competitive motherhood – 'a subtle form of warfare' – in which 'Perfect Professional Mothers' seem to cope more efficiently with the demands of childcare, appear to be better dressed and have more expensive accessories. Here, motherhood becomes a competition in competence and consumption. In a very strong turn of phrase, Carrie describes her feelings towards these women as 'a huge loathing vengeance' and even their children are described as 'vile off-spring' (Appleyard, 1999, p. 12). Motherhood has challenged her status and confidence. However, paternity does not have the same impact on husband Mike. There is little suggestion in this genre that men might take on more responsibility and enormous gratitude when a male partner does take on some of the childcare. As Carrie's husband feeds the baby she reflects: 'He really is a saint' (*ibid.*, p. 19).

Carrie eventually comes to perceive the workplace as a site of rivalry and aggression, while the domestic has become comforting: 'The house felt like a haven – warm, domestic, familiar – and everything out there seems hostile and frightening' (Appleyard, 1999, p. 20). The family and the home become here a bulwark against the struggles and competitiveness of the workplace; a gendered division between home and work that has all the resonances of John Ruskin's Victorian division of male and female spheres:

> But the woman's power is for rule, not for battle, – and her intellect is not for invention or creation, but for sweet ordering, arrangement, and decision. She sees the qualities of things, their claims, and their places. Her great function is Praise: she enters into no contest ... By her office, and place, she is protected from all danger and temptation. The man, in his rough work in open world, must encounter all peril and trial ...
>
> (Ruskin, 1902, p. 150)

Carrie is prepared to give up her career, to give in to her 'homing instinct', to forgive her errant husband and to leave the 'rough work' to him – Mike becomes an 'executive What Not' and Carrie turns her attentions to the 'sweet ordering' of a 'rambling farm house'. Imelda Whelehan, writing in 2000, suggested that 'women are recognising that "having it all" demands some complex navigation between what is seen as masculine and what is seen as feminine' (Whelehan, 2000, p. 135). These narratives, though, are notable for their rejection of any such negotiation – Carrie begins her narrative with a resigned acceptance that her husband's work is non-negotiable: 'work is such an integral part of his life, I don't think he could get his head around the concept that it might be considered an option. Which of course it isn't. I just have to get on with it' (Appleyard, 1999, p. 220). It clearly is not an option for Carrie to assert her own work as integral to her life.

Allison Pearson's novel *I Don't Know How She Does It*, published in 2002, was taken by many commentators to be the Ur-text for the 'yummy mummy' generation. It was to become the identifying text of the genre in the way that *Bridget Jones's Diary* had once been for 'chick-lit'. Like Helen Fielding, Pearson was (and is) a newspaper columnist, her novel an extension of the columns on the trials and tribulations of working motherhood that she wrote for the *Daily Telegraph* and the *Daily Mail*. The novel was made into a film (dir. Douglas McGrath, 2011) and regularly appeared as a reference point in media discussions of the difficulties of the working mother, particularly for women columnists who were, like Pearson, both mothers and working journalists. India Knight's admiring review, 'Let's Buy the Nanny a Horse', published in *The Guardian*, suggests the aspirational class frame of this genre – these are heroines who live in large houses, who employ nannies, who have (as did Bridget Jones) jobs in the media or the arts. Knight's review identifies many of the already established tropes of the 'yummy mummy' narrative:

> Thirty-four-year-old Kate has all the depressingly recognisable modern accessories of the female primary breadwinner: a sweet, mildly pussy-whipped husband who Minds Terribly But Doesn't Say So (and then, inevitably, does), an indispensable and over-remunerated nanny ... a cleaner with a bad back and not much of a way with a J-cloth, a lot of Air Miles, a truckload of guilt.
>
> (Knight, 2002)

Pearson's heroine is another witty and knowing narrator, also writing in the form of a journal. Her direct address implicates the reader in a shared understanding of the trials of contemporary motherhood. Kate is initially clear that as an ambitious and Cambridge-educated woman she will refute the traditional expectations of motherhood and do things differently from her mother's generation:

> So you see, before I was really old enough to understand what being a woman meant, I already understood the world of women was divided in two: there were proper mothers, self-sacrificing bakers of apple pies and well-scrubbed invigilators of the twin-tub, and there were the other sort. At the age of thirty-five, I know precisely which kind I am ...
>
> (Pearson, 2002, p. 5)

It is strange that these narrators tend to characterize their mothers as traditional housewives, when historically the previous generation would have experienced the second-wave feminism of the 1960s and 1970s (Kate's mother is described as collecting her from the school gates in 1974, and was herself a single mother, although this is not developed in the novel). Kate recognizes that she has benefited from new educational and career opportunities for women but does not in any way acknowledge that this could be related to feminist politics. Indeed, feminism is rejected as having no relevance to her own situation: 'Back in the Seventies, when they were fighting for women's rights, what did they think equal opportunities meant: that women would be entitled to spend as little time with their kids as men do?' (*ibid.*, p. 273).

Kate's husband ('Slow Richard', in a variation on the 'hopeless Simon') is an architect working in an 'ethical' practice, while she is an investment banker working at 'One of the City's oldest and most distinguished institutions' (Pearson, 2002, p. 15) (this is a novel written before the financial crash). Again, Kate is in a privileged situation – she has full-time childcare, she is the main breadwinner and is proud of and successful in her work: 'Here's the thing: I love my job ... I love the work: the synapse-snapping satisfaction of being good at it, of being in control when the rest of life seems such an awful mess' (*ibid.*, pp. 17–18). The novel begins with a much-quoted scene in which Kate is bashing shop-bought mince pies in order to pass them off as homemade for the school Christmas party. Too busy with work to be a 'self-sacrificing baker', this is a resonant image of a woman trying her best to fulfil the roles of both professional working woman and caring mother. Throughout the novel there is a refrain of Kate's sense of being judged, by parents-in-law, by colleagues at work, by her nanny, other mothers and by her own children and husband. This is imaged in a recurrent court scene, in which Kate imagines herself on trial for 'being a working mother who overcompensates ... for not being at home with her children' (*ibid.*, p. 62).

Kate also suffers from a sense of invisibility within the family, a fear that because of her work she is no longer central to her household: 'Home. I feel both vital to it – how will they manage without me? – and painfully peripheral: they manage without me?' (*ibid.*, p. 165). A combination of factors, all familiar as generic tropes – mistrust of the nanny, a child's accident, an intense flirtation with a male colleague and her husband's departure – collude in persuading Kate that her working life is unsustainable.

The perpetual guilt, and the death of a close female friend, finally lead her to resign from her job. An epilogue describes the family moving to the country (despite the fact that Kate had earlier written 'Reasons Not to Give up Work & Go & Live in Country ... Would go mad').

Kate notes that of the women in her mother and baby group, all once successful career women, only three continue to work:

> Giving up? Isn't that what they call it? Well, I'm not calling it that. Giving up sounds like a surrender, but these were honourable campaigns bravely fought and not without injury. Did my fellow novice mothers give up work? No, work gave them up, or at least made it impossible for them to go on.
>
> (*Ibid.*, p. 102)

While the narrative demonstrates that it is 'impossible' for Kate to go on in her work in the city, the novel leaves her with some vestige of hope for a professional career. She is offered a job at her former company with 'Part-time work, minimal foreign travel', but turns it down in favour of rescuing a doll's' house factory in a consortium with her sister and some former women colleagues. This is another example of a feminine 'hobby' turned to business opportunity, but it is also an image of miniaturized domesticity. The novel leaves Kate on the brink of developing the business as a 'global brand', leaving it ambiguous as to whether the cycle of work versus childcare will revive, or whether – as the image of the doll's house suggests – she has miniaturized the scale of her ambitions. The conclusion finds no easy resolution for Kate, but offers the same faint optimism that things will be better for women in the future, much like that found in women's fiction of earlier generations:

> The way I look at it, women in the City are like first-generation immigrants ... You know it's probably not going to get that much better in your lifetime. But just the fact that you occupy the space ... all that makes it easier for the women who come after you ... we are the foundation stones and the females who come after us will scarcely give us a second thought, but they will walk on our bones.
>
> (*Ibid.*, pp. 124–5)

The subtitle of *I Don't Know How She Does It* is *A Comedy About Failure, A Tragedy About Success*. Despite the wit and the constant jokes, the 'tragedy' of Pearson's paradox should not be underestimated – the novel is full of the pain of the conflicting demands made of a contemporary working woman. Rosalind Coward conducted a number of interviews with working mothers in 1992 in which she identified the tendency to see their situations as peculiar to them rather than one of structural inequality:

> Everyone I spoke to seemed to think the answer lay in themselves, rather than recognizing dilemmas and anxieties that reflect real social problems, requiring social and political solution ... Women are rather too skilled at performing ... gymnastics for their own good. Not only do they contort themselves to accommodate all the contradictory expectations of the prevailing ideal, but they try to fend off social problems with individual solutions. Viewed from one side, such gyrations are heroic. But viewed from another, they show a failure of will, an acceptance of the status quo, and a collusion with men's expectations of women.
>
> (Coward, 1992, p. 198–9)

Kate's story, like that of Carrie and Liz, is one such 'heroic gyration', but even these privileged women – married, wealthy and in high-profile professions – are shown to be unable to sustain the 'juggling' act of work and family. While Pearson does acknowledge, as many other writers in this genre do not, that Kate's predicament is not an isolated one (the narrative is interspersed with anecdotes of other struggling mothers), her conclusion can only be a compromised and individualized solution. McRobbie has cited Pearson's novel as an example of a 'post–feminist' discourse which does nothing to challenge the structures of gender roles:

> Instead of challenging the traditional expectation that women take primary responsibility in the home, there is a shift towards abandoning the critique of patriarchy and instead heroically attempting to 'do it all' while also looking to government for support in this Herculean endeavour. The transition to this feminine mode of activity comes into existence by means of a series of luminosities (the glamorous working mother, the so-called yummy mummy, the city-high flyer who is also a mother and so on), images and texts which are accompanied also by popular genres of fiction including best-selling novels such as *I Don't Know How She Does It.*
>
> (McRobbie, 2009, p. 80)[4]

India Knight is, with a media (and Twitter) profile as a journalist with children, an embodiment of the 'glamorous working mother'. She reviewed *I Don't Know How She Does It* very sympathetically and herself contributed to the genre with her 2002 novel *Don't You Want Me?*. The cover is familiar, featuring a stylish young woman accessorized with a baby leaning on a supermarket trolley containing a range of male types. This is a literal representation of shopping for men, but here integrated with motherhood. The heroine is unusual in that she is a single mother (as is Knight herself, as she testifies in her regular journalism columns). Money, however, as for most of the women in these novels, is not a problem. Stella is bilingual and earns a living as a translator; her ex-husband and father are wealthy art dealers. She lives in a large house in Primrose Hill and her small daughter attends a private day centre, where Stella is dismissive of all but one of the other parents on the grounds that they lack any elegance. After a series of failed romantic encounters, Stella discovers that her ideal man is her ginger-haired lodger (initially dismissed because of his colouring) who is already integrated into her domestic world. Like her sister heroines, Stella discovers that happiness is to be found within the home, rather than the threatening outside world.

By 2006 this genre had become so established that it could be directly referenced in the title of Polly Williams' *The Rise and Fall of a Yummy Mummy*. Williams is another journalist who writes for the broadsheet newspapers and for fashion magazines. The novel is once again written in the form of a confessional journal. It begins with a 'Prologue' and the line 'As catastrophes go, it was a quiet one' (Williams, 2006, p . x). The 'catastrophe' is not pregnancy or the imminent birth of her baby; instead it is the suspicion that the heroine's partner is being unfaithful. Amy is eight months pregnant, but unlike the writers of the 1960s, this pregnancy was entirely a matter of choice; she unapologetically reports an abortion in a previous relationship and comments 'all my friends had had them' (*ibid.*, p. 5). The birth is, however, entirely absent from the novel, and the Prologue segues immediately into Chapter One, which begins once the baby has been born. Amy's description of her pregnant self is one of disempowerment; her pregnancy labels her as the possession of a man and also renders her undesirable to him: 'I was his, impregnated, fat and cossetted. But I wasn't enough' (*ibid.*, p. 1). Both her sense of herself and the balance of her relationship with her partner are fundamentally changed by motherhood: 'He's by far the most attractive one in this relationship now. The power has shifted' (*ibid.*, p. 7).

Power here refers to sexual desirability; there is some recognition that a body changed through childbirth has devalued the cultural currency of femininity. While 'patriarchy' is not a term that is often used in these novels, only ever employed with withering irony as irrelevant to their concerns, patriarchy as a term in anthropology and sociology (see Walby, 1990) refers to the way in which masculine power and value increases with age while women's is diminished. Pregnancy and birth are directly related to Amy's sense of her own invisibility; she reports that strangers no longer smile at her in the street: 'It's just as well that I stopped caring whether men looked at me ... because now they don't, not even a quick double-take' (Williams, 2006, p. 5). This sense of loss is coupled with the loss of an independent income and Amy's ability to spend money on herself; she has lost the ability to consume as she once did. There is here a longing to return to the days of independent consumption. The 'active, freely choosing, self-reinventing' subject of 'post-feminism' is not compatible with motherhood:

> After years of blasting my salary on blow-dries and beauty counters, my monthly grooming budget – mostly products for thinning hair and

> breast pads – now amounts to little more than the price of a Chanel nail varnish ... I'm irreparably changed. And I dress accordingly. Today: three-year old Nike Airs, drawstring M&S khakis and a blue T shirt that slips off my shoulders to feeding bra-straps ... My other clothes, from my pre-baby life, no longer fit.
>
> (*Ibid*., p. 5)

Again, the loss of one identity is signified by a change of wardrobe. Amy is, however, taken in hand by a glamorous fellow mother who teaches her how to reclaim her body with yoga classes and how to consume as another identity – with motherhood, the brand names have changed. A flirtation with the yoga instructor restores her sexual confidence, while the allaying of Amy's suspicions about her partner finally restores the family unit.

While the sex and shopping heroine of the 1980s was no less individualized, there was in those narratives a sense that women could indeed achieve and that they could turn their skills into capitalist success stories. The 'yummy mummy' narrative of the new millennium is less optimistic. Australian journalist Virginia Haussegger wrote a book in 2005 which attempted to debunk the myth of women 'having it all' and concluded with an expression of frustration at the constant narratives of personal failure and a resounding call for collective action:

> The sense that the failure to 'do it all', 'be it all' and 'have it all' is our *own* fault. In our isolation we struggle on, believing that we have to find answers and solutions to these problems alone. We don't. You don't.
>
> It is time to collectively demand a better deal.
>
> (Haussegger, 2005, p. 295)

In 1990, Rosemary Crompton's research reported that 'women are over-represented' in the secondary labour markets; that jobs for women tended to be low skilled and offered limited progression or training opportunities. She demonstrated that it was not just the case that there was a glass ceiling for most working women but that there was not even a ladder to get to the ceiling. In 2006 she outlined the impact of neo-liberal working patterns on women's working lives:

> Flexible employment – part-time work, flexible scheduling, 'flexitime', etc. – might (indeed often does) enable an individual to combine both paid work and family work. Flexible working, therefore, is increasingly being presented as a possible 'win win' combination as far as employment and family life is concerned ....
>
> Thus the more negative aspects of neoliberal numerical flexibility are being glossed as a positive contribution to the reconciliation of employment and family life ...
>
> (Crompton, 2006, p. 209)

It is precisely such jobs that the heroines of these novels 'choose' to embrace in the resolutions to their narratives and which are represented as 'positive' solutions. Liz, and Carrie, in the earliest manifestations of the genre, give up their brilliant careers and move to the country, where they take on 'flexible employment'. Liz does begin a business, but it is low-status and part-time work, offering cleaning work to other women. Kate's future lies with doll's house furniture rather than moving currencies around the world. These novels consistently demonstrate a withdrawal from the workplace and a return to the Aga; it is invariably the woman who turns to work that is less demanding, who finds a form of work compatible with the responsibilities of childcare, or gives up work altogether. All these conclusions are presented as solutions to an intractable problem while eliding the fact that the compromise inevitably involves the woman. By 2007, Crompton's research on employment and the family found that women overwhelmingly worked in part-time occupations, and that conditions were even less conducive for working mothers:

> there would seem to be a growing body of evidence to the effect that contemporary strategies of employee management in contemporary capitalism are making it more, rather than less, problematic to combine employment and family life in dual earner households ... the current intensification of paid employment associated with organisational 'cultures of excellence' and 'high-commitment' management is likely to lead to greater work-family conflict and stress ... These kinds of pressures from within the workplace will in turn have an impact on capacity for domestic sharing between men and women, and although gender role attitudes are certainly in the process of transformation, a combination of material constraints and workplace pressures may seriously inhibit their capacities for realisation in any practical sense.
>
> (Crompton et al., 2007, pp. 15–16)

McRobbie has argued that women are faced with the contradiction that while the idea of equality for women is now a 'prevailing cultural norm', this has not been matched by social and economic change. The hopes and expectations of the second-wave feminist movement remain unfulfilled:

> Desires that could not be fitted into the family unit were considered irregular and increasingly unthinkable. This included, for example, political desires for feminist collectivity, for communality, for non-familial forms of kinship, for shared childcare, for a politicized non-monogamy, all of which no longer have a place in the polity, giving rise to a sense of loss and to a haunting melancholia.
>
> (McRobbie, 2011, pp. xi–xii)

These novels are fraught with a sense of loss and melancholia. Their heroines are of a generation to have assumed their equality in a 'post-feminist' world, but find that the means to sustain that equality has been withdrawn. It is worth remembering the seven original demands of the women's liberation movement included 'equal education and job opportunities' *and* 'free 24 hour childcare under community control' (www.feministseventies.net); while the equal education and job opportunities have (in the West) largely been achieved, the call for childcare has not. This is less a post-feminist world than one in which the demands of the women's movement have not yet been met.

In 2011 Rebecca Asher published a study – rather than a novel – based on her own experience of motherhood: *Shattered: Modern Motherhood and the Illusion of Equality*. Asher, a television producer, had her book widely reviewed in the press, particularly by women journalists. Among them, Bel Mooney, writing in the *Daily Mail*, was scathingly dismissive of Asher's conclusions that the structures of work and childcare were disturbingly unequal for women. According to Mooney, Asher:

> begins from her own standpoint: high-flying media executive has first child and turns into a shadow of her former self ... a woman with 'deathly' sallow skin and shadows under her eyes, wearing a dressing gown covered in baby snot and nappy cream and a T-shirt stiff with stale breast milk ... [Asher] is the latest in a long line of female writers who have worried away at the old Adam and Eve problem – asking why, in this age of supposed equality, when girls out-perform boys and the glass ceiling has been breached, women are left holding the squalling baby, as of old ...
>
> (Mooney, 2011, p. 63)

This description of a powerful career woman reduced by childcare and anxious about her changed body is precisely the narrative structure of the 'yummy mummy' novel. Mooney goes on to dismiss Asher's arguments by invoking both a maternal 'nature' and the current financial crisis:

> it ain't going to happen ... how could our struggling economy cope with fathers claiming the kind of maternity leave this book calls for? ... no government policies will alter the biological imperative which leads women to choose motherhood and accept their role as principal carer, just as they expected to carry the baby in the womb.
>
> Instead of endlessly fretting, they're able to view their lives as a sequence of stages in which they play different roles at different times – and just get on with it.
>
> (*Ibid*., p. 63)

Mooney's conviction that the 'glass ceiling has been breached' is undercut by the fact that the unease of working mothers is clearly so widespread that it can command a best-selling genre of popular fiction. The structural regularity in these novels, the recurrent pattern of a once-confident woman brought down by childbirth, suggests that it is not, for many women, that easy to 'just get on with it'.

The American journalist Anne-Marie Slaughter wrote a confessional article in 2012 for *The Atlantic* magazine which made similar points to those raised in Asher's book. The article prompted a deluge of reactions in the British and American press and comment threads from women, both sympathetic and antipathetic, and constituted another demonstration that the 'endless fretting' (so decried by Bel Mooney) continued unabated. Feminist Linda Hirshman was among those who contributed to the debate in the *The Atlantic*; her response was perceived as hostile by Slaughter, but she did ask the pertinent question – why it was that 'they're called mommy wars and not social policy debates' (Hirshman, 2012).

These novels can be read as front-line dispatches from the 'mommy wars' in both Britain and America. They may offer mythical resolutions to the stresses of working motherhood – but they do report them. What they do not do is engage at all with social policy debates. These women writers have taken 'post-feminism' as the expectation that they should be able to 'have it all', but they are not feminists. The status and self-worth of their heroines continue to be defined by a man; other women, mothers and colleagues in these fictions are seen as rivals rather than sisters – and the chaos of working motherhood is experienced as an entirely personal rather than a political issue. In 1999 Rowbotham concluded her history of a century of women by noting a recurrent pattern of social expectations for women which were not matched by any changes to the structures of work and childcare:

> that extraordinary tendency which emerges decade after decade for women with children to enter paid employment with very little corresponding alteration in the structure of either British or American society. Women have lived this incongruity of being expected to be in two places at once as an apparently insoluble dilemma, yet what has appeared as a law of nature has been in reality the result of particular social arrangements.
>
> (Rowbotham, 1999, p. 575)

Such narratives dramatize this 'apparently insoluble dilemma' and give it some form of mythical resolution, but however the narrative situation is resolved, it is always individualized. The female protagonist experiences the tensions as entirely personal to her. There is no sharing with other women, no challenging of male partners or the workplace for more support, no lobbying for childcare. McRobbie's understanding of 'post-feminism' is close to the solutions these narratives offer their heroines: 'The young woman is offered a notional form of equality ... through participation in consumer culture and civil society, in place of what a reinvented feminist politics might have to offer' (McRobbie, 2011, p. 2). The lack of a 'reinvented feminist politics' is everywhere apparent in these texts. As Crompton notes: 'women continue, in aggregate, to be less advantaged in the labour market' (Crompton, 2006, p. 7), but these fictions offer no understanding of that 'aggregate'. With motherhood, the women narrators of these novels come to learn the limitations of a 'notional form of equality', but articulate this as a personal failure.

In their 1956 account of 'Women's Two Roles', Alva Myrdal and Viola Klein could write with confidence:

> The Gordian knot of a seemingly insoluble feminine dilemma has been cut. The technical and social developments of the last few decades have given women the opportunity to combine and to integrate their two interests in Home and Work ... No longer need women forgo the pleasures of one sphere in order to enjoy the satisfactions of the other. The best of both worlds has come within their grasp.
>
> (Myrdal and Klein, 1956, p. xii)

The 'yummy-mummy' genre of fiction testifies that the Gordian knot remains uncut, that the integration of 'Home and Work' has not yet been achieved, and that the 'best of both worlds' remains out of reach for most working mothers. These narratives require their heroines to forgo the pleasures of the sphere of work – they are shown to be floored by the strains of combining childcare and career – and chart an unbearable strain on contemporary working women. They cannot easily be dismissed as 'endless fretting', but need to be understood as a multi-voiced cry for help.

Notes

1 Kathy Lette's novels of motherhood, including *Foetal Attraction* (London: Picador, 1993) and *Mad Cows* (London: Picador, 1996), which are heavily punctuated by puns, are extreme examples of this.

2 Between 1985 and 1991, the UK had the fastest rise in employment among women with children under ten in the European Union. See Coward, 1999, p. 46.

3 By 1999, the name Carrie would already have carried associations with the heroine of *Sex and the City*.

4 In the aftermath of the credit crisis, much of the limited state support that had once been available to working women was withdrawn.

9

Shopping for Meaning: The Spiritual Quest

In 1979 Christopher Lasch identified the 'Culture of Narcissism' in contemporary American society, a sensibility he understood as less spiritual than therapeutic:

> The contemporary climate is therapeutic, not religious. People today hunger not for personal salvation, let alone for the restoration of an earlier golden age, but for the feeling, the momentary illusion of personal well-being, health, and psychic security.
>
> (Lasch, 1979, p. 7)

The decade post-2000 saw a proliferation of texts that engaged with a woman's search for that 'psychic security' in which the therapeutic took on a distinctly religious edge. In the post-modern culture of the new millennium a series of novels and memoirs charted a female protagonist in search of her own form of enlightenment. In the wake of the credit crisis, there was a distinct cultural anxiety at the ethos of consumption; the luxury shopping and designer labels found in the sex and shopping and single woman novel of the 1980s and 1990s no longer seemed appropriate to the twenty-first century context. The celebration of branded goods had reached its apogee in Sophie Kinsella's *Shopaholic* series,[1] which began in 2000. The film of the first novel, *Confessions of a Shopaholic* (dir. P. J. Hogan), came out in 2009, in the immediate aftermath of the credit crunch, and was widely reviewed as singularly untimely.

The spiritual quest narrative can be read as a branch of the self-help books that proliferated in the late twentieth century, which can themselves be understood as a response to the demands of neo-liberalism in their exhortations to self-improvement. According to Micki McGee, the self-help industry in America was a hugely profitable market by the late twentieth century:

> The ideal of self-invention has long infused American culture with a sense of endless possibility. Nowhere is this ideal more evident than in

> the burgeoning literatures of self-improvement ... By 1998, self-help book sales were said to total some $581 million ... Indeed, the self-improvement industry, inclusive of books, seminars, audio and video products, and personal coaching, is said to constitute a $2.48 billion a year industry.
>
> (McGee, 2005, p. 11)

McGee reads 'self-improvement' as a symptom, not, as Lasch suggests, of narcissism, but of the 'belaboured self', and argues that it is women who feel particularly beleaguered.

In the context of a global recession, the strains of 'austerity' impacted particularly badly on women's lives as welfare support was steadily eroded. Gill and Scharff have argued that in the post-feminist and neo-liberal world that is the context for such texts, women 'are increasingly exhorted to make sense of their individual biographies in terms of discourses of freedom, autonomy and choice – no matter how constrained their lives might actually be' (Gill and Scharff, 2011, p. 6). The 'spiritual quest' narratives can be read as women writers attempting to making sense of their own 'individual biographies', in which spirituality and therapy become as much a matter of consumer choice as any other commodity. Giddens has suggested that in the context of late modernity 'the project of the self as such may become heavily commodified. Not just lifestyle, but self-actualisation is packaged and distributed according to market criteria' (Giddens, 1991, p. 198). These texts can be understood as narratives of the 'project of the self', in which a crisis prompts the protagonist to achieve 'self-actualization'. Whatever the means might be, the discourse of 'choice' is central.

Each of these narratives, whether fictional or autobiographical, begins from the point of a serious life-changing event, most often a divorce. Divorce is a moment at which a sustained narrative has broken down and a new form of narrative becomes necessary. In the words of one of Jodi Picoult's heroines: 'I was his *wife*, and if I'm not that any longer, I don't really know what to be' (Picoult, 2006, p. 62). As Giddens puts it: 'The existential question of self-identity is bound up with the fragile nature of the biography which the individual "supplies" about herself' (Giddens, 1991, p. 54). The protagonists of these texts are in search of a means to make sense of their 'individual biographies', and chart their heroines' progress from a state of despair to one of redemption and renewed self-confidence. These memoirs can be understood as yet another form of 'retreatism', not so much into the domestic sphere (the female narrators tend to be without children) as into the self. This involves an emotional 'journey'[2], sometimes literally involving travel, but not always.

These are not narratives of emancipation (although their heroines might use the term): they are tales of lifestyle politics and choices. Charlotte Raven identified the autobiographical account of a woman dissatisfied with her marriage and situation in life as a genre in 2011. She is scathing about these searches for personal and spiritual fulfilment and makes a distinction between these quest narratives and the feminist novels of the 1970s:

> Modern self-discovery narratives are 'journeys' in the X Factor or Big Brother sense ... The feminist self-discovery narratives of the Seventies were real journeys. The married heroine of *Fear of Flying* didn't conjure adversity from thin air ... These fables of feminist self-discovery inspired my mother's generation to become more fully themselves. By contrast, the modern midlife crisis memoir enjoin us to think commercially and find novel ways of marketing our midlife persona.
>
> (Raven, 2011, p. 13)

Betsy Israel had also identified the self-help narrative as a genre in 2002 and described such texts as 'reconstruct-your entire self kind of books ... a subcategory of these books – the specimen rampant on Amazon.com – is the wiseass advice manual, or what I think of as the lever novelette. The tone is sarcastic and funny ...' (Israel, 2002, p. 268). The narratives share a post-feminist knowingness, acknowledging feminism only with irony; they are consistently self-deprecating, well aware that their writers' post-modern selves could be seen as narcissistic. There is also a relentlessly positive voice, even in the face of considerable personal difficulties.

The introduction to Elizabeth Gilbert's 2006 *Eat, Pray, Love: One Woman's Search for Everything* aligns her memoir with the self-help manual via its first chapter title: 'How This Book Works'. Her narrative is an autobiographical account of a quest for spiritual meaning and was an enormous popular success. A *Sunday Times* review (quoted on the book's inside front cover) recognized it as speaking to a generation of women disillusioned with the 'chick-lit' narrative: 'it seems to be a call to arms for thirty-something females who, despite appearing to have tiptop lives – the job, the flat the bloke, the handbags – are dogged by a vague spiritual dread ...' Oprah Winfrey wholeheartedly endorsed the memoir (www.Oprah.com), claimed that it had 'sparked an inspirational movement' and devoted two episodes of her show to it. The book was on the *New York Times* bestseller list of non-fiction for over 200 weeks, and the publishers could legitimately claim in 2007 that it was 'The Number One Bestseller that everyone is talking about'. Gilbert was named as one of the 100 most influential people in the world by *Time* magazine in 2009. The memoir was made into a film in 2010[3] and provided marketing opportunities for prayer beads, perfumes and associated mystical paraphernalia; a website now sustains the book's fan base. Gilbert's journey itself became a marketing opportunity, a travel company now offers a package that covers the route she travelled. *Eat, Pray, Love* generated a life beyond the physical text; it demonstrated that the spiritual quest narrative could become a publishing phenomenon and launched a plethora of imitations[4].

Gilbert's narrative is prompted by the fallout of a divorce. As Giddens points out, divorce is both a moment of personal crisis and one of potential: '[It] is a crisis in individuals' personal lives, which presents dangers to their security and sense of well-being, yet also offers fresh opportunities for their self-development and future happiness' (Giddens, 1991, p. 10). Gilbert seizes these opportunities for self-development to ready herself for a new relationship and ultimately finds her 'future happiness' in the form of romance. The memoir traces Gilbert's 'journey', which takes her to (the neatly alliterative) Italy, India and Indonesia in search of different lifestyle choices. Faced with life as a single woman and in a bid to reconstitute her identity, Gilbert launches herself on a year of 'self-enquiry'. Each location offers her a different life experience and each country is defined by a different kind of consumption: she understands Italy to offer sensuality in the form of desirable men and food, while an Indian ashram provides spiritual discipline, and Indonesia relaxation, romance and friendship.

It is Gilbert's decision to leave her marriage, but her confusion nonetheless leads her to prayer: 'You know – like, to *God*', she states rather apologetically. God, however, is a fluid concept for Gilbert: 'I could just as easily use the words *Jehovah*, *Allah*, *Shiva*, *Brahma*, *Vishnu* or *Zeus*. Alternatively, I could call God "That"', which is how the ancient Sanskrit scriptures say it, and which I think comes close to the all-inclusive and unspeakable entity I have sometimes experienced ...' (Gilbert, 2006, p. 13). Although technically a Christian, Gilbert rejects conventional Christianity in favour of a medley of religious traditions; she describes a favourite dog as analogous to her own conception of God: 'She was a mixture of about ten different breeds, but seemed to inherit the finest features of them all' (Gilbert, 2006, p. 15). God here becomes whatever Gilbert chooses and her faith a selection of the 'finest features' of the world's religions: 'I think you have every right to cherry-pick when it comes to moving your spirit and finding peace in God' (*ibid.*, p. 218).

Gilbert's chosen 'Guru' is profusely thanked in the introduction and described as 'compassion's very heartbeat', although she is entirely absent throughout Gilbert's stay in her Indian ashram. Gilbert finds her from America and chooses her as her 'spiritual teacher' on the basis of 'a radiantly beautiful' photograph at her lover's apartment. There is little regard for what the guru might stand for, or any particular interest in what form of faith she represents, but Gilbert nonetheless determines: 'when I heard she had an Ashram in India, I knew I must take myself there as quickly as possible' (*ibid.*, p. 26). Gilbert is, however, waylaid by a magazine assignment in Indonesia, where she is sent to write a story about yoga holidays. Spiritual commitment is maintained, though, by an organized trip to visit a Balinese medicine man, where Gilbert declares: 'I want to have a lasting experience of God' (*ibid.*, p. 26).

The first section of her 'journey' is set in Rome, where Gilbert travels to learn the language and to 'mend her soul'. It is the pleasures of Italy that restore her: 'I do know that I have collected myself of late – through the enjoyment of harmless pleasures – into somebody much more intact' (*ibid.*, p. 121). In order to compensate for the hedonistic pleasures of Italy (and the weight she has acquired through consuming them), she travels next to India to attend an austere ashram and an intensive course of yoga. Yoga, she explains, is a practice in which 'you can seek ... a place of eternal presence from which you may regard yourself and your surroundings with poise ... from that point of even-mindedness ... the true nature of the world (and yourself) will be revealed to you' (*ibid.*, p. 129). Yoga here becomes a therapeutic rather than spiritual endeavour; while Gilbert spends much of her time there regarding 'herself' (her experience of yoga classes is literally orgasmic), she is much less engaged with her surroundings. Indian people and landscapes are notable in their absence from Gilbert's experience of India. She chooses to stay within the bounds of the ashram rather than travel anywhere, and is reassured by a fellow devotee that this is the right decision: 'Forget about sightseeing – you got the rest of your life for that. You're on a spiritual journey, baby. You got a personal invitation from God here ...' (*ibid.*, p. 180). Her only excursions outside the ashram are to the local temple and her encounters with Indian people limited to souvenir sellers and the cleaning staff at the ashram.

The narrative is studded with references to Sanskrit texts and in her introduction Gilbert asserts an expert knowledge of India, especially of 'holy sites and Ashrams', although her expertise is rather undermined by the fact she makes no distinction between Hinduism and Buddhism. Gilbert's account of India is close to the 'colonization of the imaginary' that Žižek has identified in the Western construction of the East, a 'fascination exerted by Tibet on the Western imagination ... an exemplary case of the "colonization of the imaginary": it reduces the actual Tibet to a screen for the projection of Western ideological fantasies' (Žižek, 2001, p. 64). Gilbert perceives Italy, Indonesia and India from the perspective of a New York consumer and at no point is her ideological fantasy of each country ever challenged. Gilbert can be seen as acting out Giddens' concept of 'lifestyle sectors'. Her experience of travel is filtered through systems of tourism: Italy through an international language school, India through a celebrity ashram directed at Western disciples, while Indonesia is first encountered through a media trip to report on yoga breaks. These systems, which frame and order her experience, are never acknowledged, although Gilbert is herself implicated in them as a travel journalist herself. Her 'journey' can be understood as consisting of a series of what Giddens has termed 'disembedding mechanisms' which, he suggests, 'consist of symbolic tokens and expert systems ... Disembedding mechanisms separate interaction from the particularities of locales' (Giddens, 1991, p. 20). Gilbert avails herself of expert systems of tourism, of the internet system and a flow of money from America (her travels are made possible through a book advance), and so is effectively cut off from the particularities of locales, while she claims her encounters with the peoples and places she visits to be 'authentic'.

The structure of *Eat, Pray, Love* is one in which the embrace of material hedonism in Italy is redeemed by a period of stringent yoga and meditation in India which come together in a synthesis of the material and the spiritual in Indonesia, where Gilbert is rewarded by love.

This is a narrative in which Gilbert manages to resolve the contradiction of indulging in material pleasures while claiming abstinence and spirituality, a contradiction that she herself acknowledges:

> All these desires seemed to be at odds with one another. Especially the Italy/India conflict. What was more important? The part of me that wanted to eat veal in Venice? Or the part of me that wanted to be waking up long before dawn in the austerity of an Ashram to begin a long day of meditation and prayer?
>
> (Gilbert, 2006, p. 30).

Gilbert manages to resolve the conflict by allowing herself both. Her persona is the embodiment of a post-modern subject, consuming aspects of food, spirituality and cultures as she sees fit, and reinventing herself in the process. Romance itself is a matter of consumer choice; at Gilbert's first encounter with her future husband she marks him against a checklist of desirable properties – he has 'all the good résumé points'.

Giddens has pointed to the extent to which self-development books (and *Eat, Pray, Love* was marketed as such) are individualistic and self-referential:

> The line of development of the self is *internally referential*: the only significant connecting thread is the life trajectory as such. Personal integrity, as the achievement of an authentic self, comes from integrating life experiences within the narrative of self-development: the creation of a personal belief system by means of which the individual acknowledges that 'his first loyalty is to himself'. The key reference points are set 'from the inside', in terms of how the individual constructs/reconstructs his life history.
>
> (Giddens, 1991, p. 80)

The journey that Gilbert undertakes in *Eat Pray Love* is 'internally referential'; Rome, India, Indonesia are perceived entirely in the context of personal self-development, each country is experienced 'from the inside' rather than with any real engagement with the environment or people and is understood in terms of what it can offer Gilbert. Giddens' definition of narcissism is an accurate description of Gilbert's persona: 'narcissism is a preoccupation with the self which prevents the individual from establishing valid boundaries between self and external worlds. Narcissism relates outside events to the needs and desires of the self, asking only "what this means to me"' (Giddens, 1991, p. 170).

The Australian journalist Sarah Macdonald has rather more claim to knowledge of India, having lived in Delhi. Her 2002 memoir *Holy Cow: An Indian Adventure* does demonstrate more interest in and understanding of the communities around her than Gilbert's account of India, but Macdonald's version of India is no less filtered through a Western media perspective and shaped by her own search for life answers. The narrative is preceded by a prologue in which the student author is told by a palm reader that she will return to India. Despite her scepticism, Macdonald's story begins with her journey to join her lover in Delhi and her subsequent adventures in India are therefore framed by a quasi-mystical encounter in which India is constructed as a mysterious place which will lay claim to a Western soul: 'India is Hotel California: you can check out anytime you want but you can never leave' (Macdonald, 2002, p. 9).

The image of India as Macdonald first arrives at the airport is one of hell: 'New Delhi's winter streets ... seem like hell frozen over, or perhaps purgatory ... a ghostly torso or a gaunt face with an expression straight from "The Scream" rises from the milky depths ...' (*ibid.*, p. 17). This vision is compounded when Macdonald becomes seriously ill, a fate that has been predicted by an astrologer, who tells her 'Here you will dance with death and be reborn. You will be a chameleon of karma and there are many guides to show you the way. You will search India's land of gods and find faith' (*ibid.*, p. 30). Macdonald's illness leads her to question her 'disdain for faith' as she comes to understand 'the preciousness of existence ... all that really matters is how you live' (*ibid.*, p. 45). As she recovers, she sets out to 'explore India's smorgasbord of spirituality' (*ibid.*, p. 111).

Macdonald does make some effort to understand the cultures she finds herself in: she attempts to learn Hindi, takes yoga classes (like Gilbert), accompanies her maid to the local market and develops a taste for Bollywood movies. Her experience, however, is largely mediated through a Western lens, and literally so: her only encounters with Indian politics are through accompanying her partner to make television films. Her Indian women friends have been educated in America and Australia, her yoga teacher rejects any religious aspects in favour of 'Jane Fonda aerobics combined with British Army calisthenics' (*ibid.*, p. 62). She attends an 'extreme meditation camp', which she knows about from Australia, attended only by 'us foreigners', and a Sikh academy where the guru is white and teaches 'a synthesis of age-old knowledge and modern self-loving ...' She encounters Sufism in Kashmir, Zoroastrianism and Jainism in Mumbai, the 'Divine Mother' in Kerala, she attends a meeting with the Dalai Lama and a Jewish Passover. Macdonald consumes all the religious experiences available to her in 'India's spiritual supermarket', whether they are Indian in origin or not. Buddhism particularly appeals, because 'for those of us oriented to individualism ... it offers a spiritual psychology of self-development' (*ibid.*, p. 174). While India may have shown her 'that there are millions of paths to the divine', finally, like Gilbert, Macdonald's understanding of religion is integrated 'within the narrative of self-development', in Gidden's' phrase (Giddens, 1991, p. 80). Spiritual faith is what she chooses it to be: 'I realise I don't have to be a Christian who follows the church ... I can be a believer in something bigger than what I can touch. I can make a leap of faith to a higher power in a way that's appropriate to my culture but not be imprisoned by it' (*ibid.*, p. 279). Macdonald's experience of India largely takes place in an expatriate bubble, and her 'spiritual skip through the subcontinent' is in the end only 'internally referential': 'I must find peace in the only place possible in India. Within' (*ibid.*, p. 81).

The endorsement of Elizabeth Gilbert became a badge confirming a book's membership of the spiritual quest genre, and Rhoda Janzen's 2009 'memoir of going home', *Mennonite in a Little Black Dress*, came with a glowing tribute: 'Not just beautiful and intelligent, but also painfully – even wincingly – funny.' Janzen shares a voice with Gilbert – knowing and self-deprecatory – yet unlike Gilbert she does not travel but returns home to her family in the face of severe crisis. The narrative begins with an account of Janzen's husband leaving her (for a man he has met on the internet), followed by her injuries in a serious car crash, which leaves her in a state of recuperation. It is later revealed that her husband is bipolar and has been hospitalized for a suicide attempt and that she has been medically required to undergo a hysterectomy, ending any possibility of children. This is more than a midlife crisis (although Janzen is 43 as the narrative begins) – it is a sequence of devastating losses, but nonetheless the tone is relentlessly upbeat throughout: 'I was broke and broken. Clocked in the chops by a lead glove. I was out cold. What the hell – it was so bad it couldn't get any worse' (Janzen, 2009, p. 15).

Janzen's narrative is subtitled *A Memoir of Going Home* and is dedicated to her mother. It begins with the recognition: 'I realized I should never have taken my Mennonite genes for granted' (*ibid.*, p. 1), and charts her return to a Mennonite family and community. Janzen comes to the conclusion that her genes, and her current confusion, indeed do make a believing Mennonite: 'I longed for sustained study with other students who were also humbled by the poser of creation, by the ineluctable search for meaning in a broken world' (*ibid.*, p. 168). Despite marriage to an atheist, Janzen has sustained her religious belief. Her academic credentials are clearly foregrounded: she is a PhD who teaches English and creative writing at a university and is 'ghost editing a scholarly monograph on sacred dramatic literature of the late fifteenth century' (*ibid.*, p. 17). The relationship of her academic work to her faith is not, however, developed at all.

The Mennonite faith and community appear to offer security and apparent certainties for Janzen at a time of crisis. Those certainties are clearly gendered; gender roles are proscribed by the community: 'My father's leadership position in the global Mennonite church required a lot of travelling and my mother happily trailed along' (*ibid.*, p. 55). Her father is described admiringly as a compelling patriarch: 'classically handsome, Dad has an imposing stature that codes charismatic elocution and a sobering, insightful air of authority ... Dad is one of those people to whom everybody listens' (*ibid.*, p. 2). Her mother lacks this charisma, but has great fortitude – she is 'buoyant as a lark on a summer's morn. Nothing gets this woman down ... Upbeat she is. Glamorous she is not' (*ibid.*, p. 3). There is here some envy of a femininity that is not required to be glamorous, and an endorsement of the Mennonite 'antipathy to vainglory' (*ibid.*, p. 5).

The Mennonite community can be understood as a version of 'the protective framework of the small community, and of tradition' (Giddens, 1991, p. 33) that Giddens has described as threatened by modernity:

> Modernity ... breaks down the protective framework of the small community and of tradition, replacing these which much larger, impersonal organisations. The individual feels bereft and alone in which she or he lacks the psychological supports and the sense of security provided by more traditional settings.
>
> (Giddens, 1991, p. 34)

Janzen is 'bereft and alone', and is literally broken – she is recuperating from her injuries and her homestead offers both tradition and security. Her rediscovery of her Mennonite roots is first articulated through cooking: 'I no longer see Mennonite cookery as the mad-woman in the attic, the embarrassing relative who must be kept away from the party at all costs' (Janzen, 2009, p. 115). Despite the knowing reference to feminist literary theory[5] here, Janzen finds that she 'naturally' is drawn back to her role as a good Mennonite woman, despite the fact that the Mennonite ideal of a 'virtuous woman' is at odds with her own professed scholarly principles. Nonetheless, she chooses to embrace it:

> Consider how impossible it is ... to aspire to the role of virtuous woman when professional commitments dramatically interfere ... Consider what happens when scholarship and education expose many of the assumptions of organized religion as intellectually untenable ... Yet I cannot deny the genuine warmth my mother seems to radiate – indeed, that all these Mennonites seem to radiate. It's clear that this Mennonite community is the real deal.
>
> (*Ibid.*, p. 166)

While acknowledging her own contradictions here, the implication of Janzen's return to her Mennonite community is that she turn her back on academic life, and on the independent thought and sexuality that had marked her adult life away from the community. She comes to see her 'turbulent marriage' as 'a long journey on dark waters that had propelled me away from everything known and safe' (*ibid.*, p. 224) and dismisses her intelligence in favour of those 'known and safe' Mennonite values. Like her marriage, intellectual life is dismissed as youthful aberration: 'At twenty all I wanted to do was read philosophy, feminism, and fashion. I was blind to all of the better lessons my solid little Mennonite college could have taught me, lessons about the value of community, of service, of wisdom rather than knowledge' (*ibid.*, p. 135).

In rejecting all that her husband represents (understandably, given the circumstances of his departure) Janzen also rejects her own intellectual achievements and is withering about her former academic ambitions: 'I was star stuck with academic achievement, pathetically overinvested in the uphill trail to building an identity as a scholar. There was a time in my life – sadly, not so long ago – when quickness of mind seemed more important than kindness' (*ibid.*, p. 84). Her Mennonite family and community compound this reversal; her academic work is constantly interrupted by her father's 'imperious summons', but this is described with fondness rather than any frustration. Janzen describes her ex-husband choosing her clothes, accepting that he has better taste; she also accepts his undermining of her intellectual abilities: 'He thought in general scholars were mediocre thinkers with limited social skills and a profound need for external validation. (I know I am!)' (*ibid.*, p. 84). Despite her professed claims to feminism, masculine authority effectively remains unchallenged in Janzen's narration. This is a trait that Janzen acknowledges as embedded in her religious and family upbringing: 'What is it about being Mennonite that teaches little girls not to challenge authority? We all grow up so obedient, we'll do anything rather than rock the boat' (*ibid.*, p. 122).

While there is some recognition that the Mennonite expectation of female obedience is constraining for women, it is simultaneously celebrated. Janzen does assert: 'the weird thing is, I'm a scholar. Challenging authority is what I *do*. For a living' (*ibid.*, p. 126), but that challenge to authority, and to masculinity, is what she chooses to give up. The narrative resolution and the reward for Janzen's return to Mennonite values is a potential romance with a handsome and much younger member of the community, whom she meets through her mother's charitable activities. The memoir ends with a warm embrace from the community as Janzen joins in their singing and celebrates her heritage:

> I suddenly had the feeling you get when, after a long sea swim, you touch bottom and draw a breath of relief ... Harmony rose like prayer in the cool of the late afternoon, and the music was gentle as a hand on the small of the back nudging me forward – the sound of my heritage, my future.
>
> (*Ibid.*, p. 224)

This embrace of the Mennonite faith system negates all her previous life and also glosses over the fact that this is a highly conservative form of religious practice, especially for women. Janzen's memoir ends with a 'Primer' of Mennonitism; this begins with a history and some charming anecdotes and images, but these are supplemented with a listing of Mennonite strictures, which include sex before marriage, divorce, homosexuality and education, all associated with her former life, and all practices that Janzen once supported. She apologetically explains, but does not reject, the Mennonite position on education: 'The Mennonites have a prickly history with the idea of education ... The Mennonite idea is that people who privilege money and knowledge will think that they have all the answers, and if they think they have all the answers, they won't be interested in seeking God' (*ibid.*, p. 58). Janzen does offer some faint reassurance that the sect is more progressive than it once was: 'Mennonite privation isn't what it used to be. My generation of Mennonites has made it different' (*ibid.*, p. 144), but there is little evidence that much has changed in her descriptions of Mennonite families. She does state that she is unable to 'stomach' the Mennonite position on homosexuality and abortion rights but does not explain how this can be reconciled with a position within the Mennonite community. While professing to have returned to her roots, Janzen constructs a version of the Mennonite faith that a twenty-first-century educated woman can find acceptable.

The hugely successful Jodi Picoult is a writer whose work has been taken up wholeheartedly in reading groups and blogs. Her fiction now regularly appears with an appendix 'Book Club Discussion Questions', in the clear expectation that she is an author who commands a book club following. Her fiction consistently explores the 'journey' of her characters through the trials of family life, but it is her 2006 novel, *Keeping Faith*, which explicitly deals with the spiritual. While *Keeping Faith* is fiction, its structure and conclusions have notable similarities with other spiritual memoirs. There is a first-person narrator, who assumes an intimacy and shared experience of motherhood with the reader, interspersed with newspaper and court reports.[6] A prologue establishes the heroine, Mariah (a name with Christian connotations), as a contented wife: she is trained as an architect, but is now happily concerned with her household and family and making dolls' houses for a living (a much-worked metaphor for her homemaking abilities). She is apparently secure in her marriage: '"This is my wife" he says, and I smile. It is all I ever wanted to be' (Picoult, 2006, p. 5). The narrative begins, however, like so many of these memoirs – with Mariah discovering that her husband is once again involved in an extra-marital affair. It is shortly after this that her small daughter, with the heavily loaded name of 'Faith', describes an imaginary friend who, it transpires, is God. Mariah is agnostic, and a non-practising Jewish mother, who begins the narrative as a firm sceptic: 'It is not as if I believe in God. When I was a child, my family wasn't very religious; as an adult, all I have is a healthy dose of scepticism ...'

(*ibid.*, p. 27). That scepticism is sorely tried as her daughter begins to quote from the book of Genesis and to cite the names of saints, although she has never been taken to church or synagogue. As an educated and concerned mother, Mariah takes Faith to a psychiatrist, a Catholic who has herself experienced visions.

Despite the timing of the visions with the departure of her father and her mother's consequent emotional fragility, there is no ambiguity at all in Faith's transformation into a conduit for God (which might have made for a more interesting novel). Faith develops stigmata and proceeds to enact a series of miracles, beginning with the reconciliation of a warring Jewish couple she encounters in a rabbi's waiting room. She goes on to resuscitate her grandmother from a fatal heart attack, to cure an HIV positive boy, and eventually a whole hospital, whose wards are cleared by proximity to the little girl. These miracles are all confirmed by medical doctors, while the psychiatrist lends academic credibility to Faith's visions by presenting her as a case study at an academic symposium.

Faith is claimed as a saviour by a range of religious and secular groups, which present Mariah with a range of options as her agnosticism is challenged. A rabbi offers a New Age form of Judaism: 'We draw upon Kabbalah, as well as Buddhist, Sufi and Native American traditions' (*ibid.*, p. 107). A group of women Catholics who name themselves the 'MOTHERGOD Society' claim Faith as a feminist prophet. In a twist on a conventional Christian tale, God appears to Faith as a woman; Faith firmly states that 'God's a mother.' Mariah is shown to have 'natural' maternal and domestic qualities; she makes dolls' houses; she can naturally turn a rundown motel room into a cosy home, and when she makes a bed she does it in a 'simple, instinctive move'. Her mothering skills are nonetheless challenged in a bitter custody battle in which her ex-husband claims that Faith needs protection from her vulnerable mother. Mariah, however, is triumphantly vindicated when she channels the full power of mother love and herself feels a divine force which enables her to save her daughter, whose health has been severely depleted by her miracle workings. Towards the end of the novel Mariah experiences her own vision of God in a dream, in which the deity speaks to her as a fellow mother.

On the trail of exposing Faith and her mother as frauds is the celebrity atheist Ian Fletcher, head of 'Pagan Productions'. He is described as the 'Spokesman of the Millennium generation – those cynical Americans who had neither the time nor the inclination to trust in God for their future' (*ibid.*, p. 30). Ian is damaged by a difficult childhood and the burden of an autistic twin, which have left him bitter and twisted and lacking in any faith. Faced with Faith's miracles (one involving his brother) and on falling in love with her mother, his firm atheism is shaken and he is finally redeemed by love. In coming to the conclusion 'I *do* believe Faith' (here used in both senses), Ian is also confronted with a range of systems of belief. When he tells Mariah 'I didn't take to the idea of Christ', her response is, 'Maybe you should have tried Judaism or Islam' (*ibid.*, p. 127). Religious belief here becomes a matter of individual choice rather than a matter of principle, doctrine, or culture; for Mariah 'religion ... isn't only *what* people believe in – it's also about the simple act of believing' (*ibid.*, p. 462). A sympathetic Catholic priest suggests that Faith's Jewish ethnicity (rather than any faith) and her claim that God is a woman could be a way of appealing to a range of consumer markets:

> I've never believed that spirit comes from religion. It comes from deep inside each of us, it draws people to us ... So she's a Jewish child ... so she happens to see a female God ... Maybe this is God's idea of a winning ticket – a way to get many different personalities to worship Him at once. To worship Him at all.
>
> (*Ibid.*, p. 139)

On her website Picoult says of her novel: 'I wanted to look not at religion ... but at belief. At how we can be spiritual without being religious' (www.jodipicoult.com, accessed July 2013). Here, like her heroine Mariah, Picoult is advocating a mode of belief which is tailored to fit the individual, which rejects any form of orthodoxy or doctrine, but which nonetheless claims spiritual authority. As the mother of a gay son, Picoult has been outspoken about gay rights and has taken on the Christian evangelical right in her 2011 novel *Sing You Home*, which follows a lesbian fighting to become a mother. Evangelical Christianity has itself made use of the spiritual journey narrative (as it did with 'chick-lit'): this had become such a recognizable genre that it was inevitable that the church would also produce texts written to promote a more conventional, Christian message.

Dina Dove's 2008 *The Baglady's Guide to Elegant Living* suggests a range of sources which can offer contemporary women answers to the meaning of life and appropriates the spiritual quest narrative in order to promote evangelical Christianity. Dove is an 'inspirational speaker' and life coach who also has a personal website in which she refers to her memoir as a 'parable'. Her title references Kathleen Tessaro's successful 2003 novel *Elegance*,[7] but while in this book it is the presiding spirit of French style icon Madame Antoine Dariaux who teaches the heroine how to become a woman, in Dove's work it is a 'bag lady' who teaches the author how to cope, through talking her through basic Christian principles. The narrative follows much the same trajectory as other texts in the genre, in which the heroine begins her narrative in a state of bereavement following her divorce. Dove is yet another woman renegotiating her life in the aftermath of a bitter marriage fallout and creating a new identity. Like Gilbert and Janzen, she is at rock bottom: 'My life as I knew it was over; systematically, one after another, all the things on which I based my self-worth were gone' (Dove, 2003, p. vii). Dove chooses, like Janzen, to return to the safe familiarity of an orthodox faith: the memoir's subtitle is *Learn to Love the Life you*

Have; redemption does not require any change other than a turn back to God. Although the 'bag lady', Rose, may not be a conventional device for spiritual guidance, the wisdom that she dispenses is conventional Christian gospel, advocating prayer and the love of God as the cure for all ills.

Redemption in the spiritual quest narrative is not always achieved through religion. Julie Powell achieves it through cookery, working her way through Julia Child's 1961 recipe book *Mastering the Art of French Cooking*. Subtitled *How One Girl Risked her Marriage, her Job and her Sanity to Master the Art of Living*, it is clear that the publishers saw Powell's narrative as another tale of self-discovery that could be marketed on the heels of the success of *Eat, Pray, Love*. Although Powell is married (even if she does stretch her partner's patience to the limit), her memoir shares much the same structure of the experience of a life crisis which prompts her to seek certainty and meaning in an uncertain world. Powell begins the narrative as an aspiring actress on the verge of thirty who is diagnosed with 'polycystic ovarian syndrome'. She appears to briskly brush this off, although her condition threatens both her body and fertility: '(it) sounds absolutely terrifying but apparently just means I was going to get hairy and fat and I'd have to take all kinds of drugs to conceive' (Powell, 2006, p. 6). She is also inhabiting the frightening world of a post 9/11 New York and makes a living by working as a clerical assistant for a government agency charged with the aftermath of the fall of the Twin Towers. Much of her work involves dealing with bereaved families. Although she resolutely does not discuss the impact of this, her diagnosis or her failure to become a working actress, Powell does admit: 'Instead of crying, I'd make withering comments ... But hard-bitten cynicism leaves one feeling peevish, and too much of it can do lasting damage to your heart' (Powell, 2006, p. 63). *Mastering the Art of French Cooking* becomes a defence against both cynicism and depression.

Powell, like Janzen, takes refuge in the familiar and the domestic. Julia Child's book would have been a familiar presence in American kitchens from the 1960s; for Powell it is a 'book that had known my family's kitchen longer than I had' (*ibid*., p. 17). She purloins her mother's copy, and it is resonant of home and childhood, but also of mysterious adult sexuality; Powell explains that she first came across *Mastering the Art of French Cooking* at the same time she discovered her parents' copy of *The Joy of Sex*. Although she insists on her atheism, the recipe book has a spiritual quality for Powell: 'I felt like I'd at last found something *important* ... there was something deeper here, some code within the words ... childishly simple and dauntingly complex, incantatory and comforting – I thought this was what prayer must feel like' (*ibid*., p. 17). The first recipe that Powell attempts is 'inexplicably good' and comforting; the book itself has a weighty seriousness about it, it is 'old-fashioned, stately, real' (*ibid*., p. 31), something solid and prescriptive to hold on to in a disturbing world. There is something compulsive in Powell's dedication to following the rules of

Child's recipes, and close to manic in the sourcing of ingredients that are hard to find in Long Island City. Powell doggedly works her way through *Mastering the Art of French Cooking*, completing every recipe. Unlike her fellow writers, she does adhere to the articles of her faith, and refuses to discard those that do not fit her lifestyle.

Mastering the Art of French Cooking also represents foreign exoticism and female achievement. Powell's account of her own cooking project is intercut with extracts from Child's recipes and details of her travels and life in Paris, adapted from Child's autobiography, *My Life in France*. Child's life – as a researcher with the Office of Strategic Services in Ceylon, living in Paris and her culinary training – was rather more adventurous than Powell's, whose travels are limited between New York and her hometown in Texas, and there is something wistful in her admiration of Child. Child herself was dismissive of Powell's project, seeing it as a stunt rather than any serious endeavour, but Powell's imagined Julia Child is a source of strength, and, she explains with some embarrassment, of 'joy': 'Julia taught me what it takes to find your way in the world' (*ibid.*, p. 303). Affirmation from comments on her website, her mastery of ever more complicated recipes and the final completion of 'The Project' leave Powell with a sense of achievement and renewed self-confidence.

Powell's book, *Julie & Julia*, began, like the phenomenally successful *Fifty Shades of Grey*, as an internet blog, went on to become a bestseller and then a Hollywood film (dir. Norah Ephron, 2009) and gave Powell a media profile that began before her book was published. The final sections of the memoir recount her growing professional and personal success. *Julie & Julia* is a strange interface of a private self made public through social media – as Powell puts it, 'There's a dangerous, confessional thrill to opening up your imminently interesting life and brain to the world at large' (*ibid.*, p. 96). There is some ambiguity as to whether the blog was a private pursuit or whether it was meant for public consumption and a means of achieving 'fame and fortune' (Powell does admit that this had occurred to her, and also invokes Pepys' diary as a precedent for the charting of her daily life), and this is an ambiguity that is compounded by the possibilities of the internet. The narrative ends with a triumphant gathering of Powell's web fans at a restaurant in New York (although, interestingly, in the film version, this is represented as an intimate party of friends).

Such an interface is shared by many of these writers; while their memoirs are written as intimate confessions (Picoult's novel is effectively an expression of her own faith), they were read by a mass audience, and all were international bestsellers (with the exception of Dove, whose text is the most conventionally Christian). Each of these writers also has a personal website on which she promotes her work and beliefs, and in which she addresses her readers as friends; the private confessional self has become public in a way that social networking has made possible. While all are cheerfully witty in the face of crisis, these narratives clearly spoke to a post-feminist anxiety about the role of women in a neo-liberal and globalized world. In an age of social media and reality television, a public persona is required to be 'authentic'. In 1999 Jeffrey Weeks spoke of:

> The postmodern recognition of the instability of the self, of openness in the choosing of identities ... Identities are relativized, and therefore it seems to some diminished. Yet we cling to them. In a world of constant change, people apparently need fixed points, points of alignment. Identities, personal and social, are both precarious and essential, historically shaped and personally chosen, affirmations of self and confirmations of our social being. We construct narratives of the self in order to negotiate the hazards of everyday life, and to assert our sense of belonging in an ever more complex social world.
>
> (Weeks, 1999, p. 33)

The spiritual quest memoir offers up such 'constructed narratives of the self', which have been personally chosen and which conform to generic expectations; the address appears to be intimate, but the persona is shaped for public consumption. Each of these 'confessions' is presented in a relentlessly upbeat voice, in an echo of a neo-liberal culture in which to admit unhappiness or confusion is to be construed as a failure. Weeks has also written of 'The fragility and hybridity of modern personal identities' (Weeks, 1999, p. 32). The heroines of these narratives are confronting their own fragility as women, often in the aftermath of a divorce; they are in search of a newly defining identity, and of rules to make sense of their own complexities.

The possibilities of the internet are significant in the commodification of a search for meaning. Theology, mysticism and the meaning of life are easier to access on-line than the involvement and ritual of visiting churches, synagogues, temples or ashrams. As the journalist Aleks Krotoski put it:

> The importance of the web in everyday life ... means that religious organisations must migrate their churches and temples to virtual real estate in order to stay relevant and to be where the people are. Religious leaders have websites, blogs and Twitter feeds, there are email prayer lines and online confessionals, social networks for yogis and apps that call the faithful to prayer.
>
> (Krotoski, 2011)

Religion itself is a marketplace that can be accessed on line, 'spirituality' another lifestyle choice in which it is possible to pick and choose those elements that fit most comfortably with a constructed identity.

Slavoj **Žižek** has argued that a Western interest in Eastern religions is a response to the pressures of late capitalism:

> One of the most deplorable aspects of the postmodern era and its so-called 'thought' is the return of the religious dimension in all its different guises: from Christian and other fundamentalisms, through the multitude of New Age spiritualisms, up to the emerging religious sensibility within deconstruction itself.
>
> (Žižek, 2000, p. 1)

These memoirs and imagined spiritual journeys are one of the means by which this religious dimension has returned, but it is a form of spirituality that is without struggle. Whatever the different 'guise' of belief might be, the protagonists pick those elements of faith which suit them and discard those aspects that do not fit their personal biographies. The former Archbishop of Canterbury, Rowan Williams, gave a talk in 2013 in which he was acerbic about any idea of spirituality as 'comforting'. Instead, he asserted the struggle and difficulties involved in sustaining faith:

> The last thing it is about is the placid hum of a well-conducted meditation ... the word 'spiritual' in today's society [is] frequently misused in two ways: either to mean 'unworldly and useless', which is probably the sense in which it has been used about me, or meaning 'I'm serious about my inner life, I want to cultivate my sensibility' ... Speaking from the Christian tradition, the idea that being spiritual is just about having nice experiences is rather laughable. Most people who have written seriously about the life of the spirit in Christianity and Judaism spend a lot of their time telling you how absolutely bloody awful it is.
>
> (Williams, 2013)

These narratives, whether autobiographical or imagined, achieve a reconciliation of spiritual reward without conceding any of the material benefits of late capitalism. In their combination of lifestyle manual, confessional and spiritual awakening, they demonstrate a deep discontent and anxiety about the proliferation of choices available, yet their individualized resolutions do not challenge, but remain firmly within the terms of a consumerist culture. As Žižek explains: 'We can go on making our small choices, "reinventing ourselves" thoroughly, on condition that these choices do not seriously disturb the social and ideological balance' (Žižek, 2001, p. 122).

The protagonists of these narratives are making their own 'small choices', reinventing themselves with the aid of religion, cooking or yoga, but whatever the resolution in no case do those choices 'seriously disturb the social and ideological balance'. For McRobbie:

> The sphere of leisure and consumer culture is dominated by the vocabulary of personal choice, and is the primary site for hedonism,

> fantasy, personal gratification and entertainment ... The cultural forms which function according to this logic substitution are also spectral re-workings of their feminist predecessors, now transplanted into a popular domain. They promote a highly conservative mode of feminine 'empowerment' ...
>
> (McRobbie, 2009, p. 27)

The spiritual quest genre and self-help manuals are structured by the vocabulary of personal choice and entirely devoted to the fulfilment of personal gratification. They are about an entirely individualized form of 'empowerment' that is indeed conservative. Their protagonists return to forms of the familiar, whether that be a Mennonite home, the recipes of Julia Child, conventional Christianity or an edited selection of world religions. They are in a crisis of late capitalism, but experience this entirely as a personal crisis. This crisis is both as women and as consumers, uncertain about how to negotiate the post-modern rhetoric of choice. Žižek has pointed to the extent to which the spiritual quest has become a phenomenon in popular culture:

> it is not only that Western Buddhism, this pop-cultural phenomenon preaching inner distance and indifference toward the frantic pace of market competition, is arguably the most efficient way for us fully to participate in the capitalist dynamic while retaining the appearance of mental sanity – in short, the paradigmatic ideology of late capitalism.
>
> (Žižek, 2003, p. 26)

In an age of anxiety these narratives articulate a need for certainties in an alienated and alienating world; it is through a compulsive quest for meaning, whether of Buddhism, Hinduism or Christianity (in various forms), or through the practices of yoga and cooking, that their heroines achieve an appearance of 'mental sanity'. The 'spiritual' memoir articulates an unease at the contemporary lifestyles of women living in late capitalism, but their writers cannot envisage (despite considerable travel and reading) a world outside that model. The search for a set of a beliefs to live by is no less a matter of consumption than any other product. These are narratives about shopping for God.

Notes

1 Kinsella managed to fuse the sex and shopping and 'chick-lit' novel with the 'yummy mummy' genre in the two final novels of the series, in which the heroine's baby became another consumer and means of consuming, in *Shopaholic and Baby* (London: Black Swan, 2007) and *Mini Shopaholic* (London: Black Sawn, 2010).

2 The term 'journey' (connoting an emotional struggle) was regularly employed by contestants in reality shows and talent contests on television, to such an extent that 'Journey South' incorporated it into their band name for *X Factor* 2005.

3 *Eat, Pray, Love* (dir. Ryan Murphy, 2010), with Julia Roberts as Elizabeth Gilbert, was memorably dubbed '*Eat, Pray, Vomit*' in a coruscating review by BBC critic Mark Kermode (*Observer*, 6 February 2011).

4 Claire Dederer's *Poser: My Life in 23 Yoga Poses* came out in 2011 (London: Bloomsbury), with an enthusiastic endorsement from Elizabeth Gilbert, who greeted it as 'the long-awaited yoga memoir', on its front cover. Other texts include Gretchen Rubin's *The Happiness Project* (New York: HarperCollins, 2009).

5 Gilbert, Sandra and Gubar, Susan. *The Madwoman in the Attic: The Woman Writer and the Nineteenth-Century Literary Imagination* (New Haven and London: Yale University Press, 1979).

6 This structure is shared with Stephen King's *Carrie* (Garden City: Doubleday, 1974), which is another narrative about a young girl in a small community who is possessed of supernatural powers.

7 The spirit of Genevieve Antoine Dariaux is channelled via her *A Guide to Elegance*, originally published in the 1960s, in Tessaro's novel. (London: HarperCollins, 2003).

AFTERWORD

These novels, from the relatively recent past, allow for sharp insights into the confusions and conflicts of what it means to be a woman in the late twentieth and early twenty-first centuries. These are fictions which allow for a reassessment of the ways in which those confusions have been negotiated, and for a re-examination of the resolutions offered in their generally happy endings. Romance fiction offers resolution and also constructions of ideal forms of masculinity and femininity, but to become 'popular' fictions, these constructions have to provide some measure of recognition from readers. As Alison Light has argued:

> Because novels not only speak from their cultural moment but take issue with it, imagining new versions of its problems, exposing, albeit by accident as well as by design, its confusions, conflicts and irrepressible desires, the study of fiction is an especially inviting and demanding way into the past.
>
> (Light, 1991, p. 2)

In identifying the shifts in popular discourses of femininity at particular cultural moments, it is possible to recognize the extent to which the ideological category of 'woman' is never fixed. These novels allow for a sharp recognition of the way in which each historical shift (roughly demarcated in decades here) produces a different set of demands, desires, aspirations and expectations of what a woman could and should be. There is, throughout the fictions of the post-war decades, a subtext in their discussions of a woman's role, which becomes more and more explicit as the century progresses; these novels inevitably have to engage, in some way, with the politics of feminism. The post-war reconstruction in Britain required a reassessment of women's capabilities after their enormous contribution in wartime. In America, while women were less directly involved than their British counterparts, the recruitment of American men into the war and their return challenged expectations of masculinity. From the 1960s, the Women's Liberation Movement was such a dominant force in the century's understanding of gender and gender relationships, that it becomes an unavoidable undercurrent in the experience of women in the late twentieth century. Whether it is acknowledged or not, these texts are in constant argument with feminist ideas and with feminism as a political movement. The anxieties expressed in these texts are those which often could not be directly acknowledged by feminist theory. Feminism is a political project which can only allow for contradiction to a limited degree, while fiction is a space which allows for the exploration of contradiction.

The post-war women's popular novel is often marked by an explicit rejection of the feminist politics that was so much a part of gender relations and constructions of femininity throughout the post-war period. Nonetheless, their concerns and anxieties can be seen as closely allied with those of the women's movement. These narratives may individualize the issues of work, maternity and independence, and they may resolve the tensions between them with mythological happy endings, but that cannot entirely detract from the strong sense in these novels that women's lives have been and continue to be fraught with contradictions and anxiety.

Susan Douglas introduces her study of mass-media culture for women with a call for the need to reclaim the territory of women's popular culture:

> We must rewatch and relisten, but with a new mission: to go where the girls are ... It's time to reclaim a past too frequently ignored, hooted at and dismissed ... This is a different sort of archaeology of the 1950s, 60s and 70s than we're used to, because it excavates and holds to the light remnants of a collective female past not usually thought of as making serious history.
>
> (Douglas, 1995, p. 10)

Douglas is here referring to popular film and television texts addressed to a female audience; but that 'collective female past' is also to be found in fiction. We need to reread as much as we need to 'rewatch and relisten'. Women's popular fiction is undoubtedly a site of 'where the girls are', and the 'woman's novel' is just as much a 'dismissed' territory as are those television and film texts addressed to a woman audience. And the excavation of women's fiction in the late twentieth century provides a valuable archaeology of a collective experience of femininity.

It is, however, very important not to collapse the experience of fictional heroines into the histories of actual women. Clive Bloom has warned against reading popular fictions as simple social history:

> best-selling fiction is not simply a barometer of contemporary imagination ... The best-seller is not a mere sociological slice of contemporary life, and its use by historians in search of cultural values needs careful handling if it's not to be reduced simply to a correspondence with the most morbid, sentimental or foolish perceptions of an age.
>
> (Bloom, 2002, p. 15)

How that contemporary imagination is read is inflected by the personal history of the reader, the stage in life at which they are reading, and their own 'foolish perceptions' of an age. Charlotte Brunsdon has suggested that the academic feminist critic who deals with 'women's genres' is engaged in a strange process of repression. She describes:

> the contradictory position of feminist intellectuals in the late 1970s and 1980s, whose academic training permits entry to the predominantly masculine academy, but whose origins, gender-formation, and the discrimination they meet, return them endlessly to that which has been forbidden, disavowed, or abandoned – the pleasures, concerns and accoutrements of femininity. One way in which the painful contradictions aroused here can be handled is through a classic splitting, in which the feminist academic investigates her abandoned or fictional other – the female consumer of popular culture.
>
> (Brunsdon, 2000, pp. 4–5)

I am that 'fictional other', as a female consumer of popular culture, and especially of fiction. I read and enjoyed almost all these texts, and because I am acutely aware of the complications of my own reading and understanding, I cannot presume to investigate how these might have been read by other women readers of the popular novel. I also belong to that generation of 'feminist intellectuals', who came into academia in the late 1970s. It was not until I put these genres together in a book that I could come to recognize my own repressions and was able to acknowledge how close to my own biography and trajectory these fictions are, and the extent to which each genre had framed my own experience.

I was born in the 1950s and educated at a girls' school which promoted a strong sense of citizenship and public duty for young women. I can now see (although this would not have occurred to me at the time) that the school ethos belonged to a public discourse of women in the post-war reconstruction and that the women who taught us were part of the generation of women who had found a dedication and an ambition for women through their wartime experiences. These women teachers were determined to pass on an independence of thought to the next generation of young women.

I did not have to go through the experience of single motherhood or accidental pregnancy in the 1960s, but my adolescence was full of the fear that I might. *The L-Shaped Room* and *The Millstone* were required reading for my generation as dire warnings of the dangers of sexual encounters. I was a student in the 1970s, and experienced the excitement of leaving home for a new independence, and the beginnings of a feminist consciousness. I am proud to have been one of the generation that went through the experience of consciousness raising and who lobbied for women's rights and for women's studies to become part of the academic curriculum.

I had the beginnings of two tentative careers in the 1980s, as an academic completing a PhD, and also as a novice magazine publisher, as part of the *Women's Review* collective. I read the 1980s career novels of women publishing magnates with a combination of envy and disdain, despising the capitalist careerism of the heroines, but quietly aspiring to their apparently seamless rise to success. I was married in the 1990s (although I had sworn as a student that I never would) and in establishing a home found a new appreciation in the details of the domestic pleasures that the Aga-saga celebrates (although I have never owned an Aga). This was a short-lived period; the same decade saw my divorce (as predicted by many of the Aga-saga novels). Newly single again, I was ready for the single-women novels that were addressed to a new generation of young women.

I wrote the chapter about the resentful daughter narrative as my mother was terminally ill, and was acutely aware as I read these novels of the extent to which I was not a resentful daughter, and how lucky I have been in my own mother. It is largely thanks to her that I have a critical curiosity and have inherited such a rich tradition of reading women's writing. But this is not entirely a book about my own autobiography or reading experiences, and it is not entirely coincidental that my own life stages have been so marked by their fictional equivalents. I belong to the tail end of the baby-boom generation who have been so central in defining the spirit of the post-war decades, and who have grown up and experienced defining life moments together. From college to brilliant career and marriage through to middle age, these were the experiences that have captured a *Zeitgeist*, and the fictions which charted them have sold in large numbers because there were so many women going through similar experiences at roughly the same time. It is important, though, to recognize that these fictions are not neat reflections of those experiences; rather they provide frames in which the loose ends of contradictory stories can be tied up into neat resolutions.

As new generations of young women emerge there is a need for new genres to articulate their different experiences. The resentful daughters and harassed mothers of the new millennium are the fictional daughters of those heroines of the 1960s and 1970s novels, who had hoped that the world would be less fraught for the next generation of young women. The novels I have addressed here represent and negotiate defining life moments for several generations of women. Whether they count as 'literary' or not, all these novels have important things to say about the experience of femininity in the post-war period, and they have taught me a great deal.

BIBLIOGRAPHY

Adams, Alice. *Superior Women*. London: William Heinemann, 1985.
Adams, Carol and Laurikietis, Rae. *The Gender Trap: A Closer Look at Sex Roles, Book 1: Education and Work*. London: Virago, 1976.
Ang, Ien. *Watching Dallas*. London: Methuen, 1985.
Appleyard, Diana. *Homing Instinct*. London: Black Swan, 1999.
Appignanesi, Lisa (ed.). *Desire*. London: Institute of Contemporary Arts, 1984.
Atwood, Margaret. *Lady Oracle*. London: Andre Deutsch, 1977.
Baker, Niamh. *Happily Ever After? Women's Fiction in Postwar Britain, 1945–60*. London: Macmillan, 1989.
Baudrillard, Jean. 'Consumer Society', in Mark Poster (ed.) *Selected Writings* Stanford, CA: Stanford University Press, 2001, pp. 29–56.
Beauman, Nicola. *A Very Great Profession: The Woman's Novel 1914–39*. London: Virago, 1983.
Berger, John, Blomberg, Sven, Fox, Chris, Dibb, Michael and Hollis, Richard. *Ways of Seeing*. Harmondsworth: British Broadcasting Corporation and Penguin Books, 1972.
Bloom, Clive. *Bestsellers: Popular Fiction Since 1900*. Basingstoke: Palgrave, 2002.
Bourdieu, Pierre. *Distinction: A Social Critique of the Judgement of Taste* (trans. Richard Nice). Cambridge, MA: Harvard University Press, 1984.
Bowlby, Rachel. *Just Looking: Consumer Culture in Dreiser, Gissing and Zola*. London: Methuen, 1985.
Braine, John. *Room at the Top*. London: Penguin, 1969.
Brewer, Leslie. *The Good News: Some Sidelights on the Strange Story of Sex Education*. London: Putnam, 1962.
Brown, Rita Mae. *Rubyfruit Jungle*. London: Corgi Books, 1978.
Brunsdon, Charlotte. *The Feminist, the Housewife and the Soap Opera*. Oxford: Clarendon Press, 2000.
Buchan, Elizabeth. *Revenge of the Middle-Aged Woman*. London: Michael Joseph, 2002.
—*The Good Wife*. Harmondsworth: Penguin, 2003.
Burchill, Julie. *Ambition*. London: Bodley Head, 1989.
Burroughs, Augusten. *Running with Scissors*. New York: St Martin's Press, 2002.
Callil, Carmen. *Subversive Sybils: Women's Popular Fiction this Century*. London: The British Library Centre for the Book, 1996.
Campbell, Beatrix. *Iron Ladies: Why Do Women Vote Tory?* London: Virago, 1987.
Cartland, Barbara. *Desire of the Heart*. London: Hutchinson, 1954.
—*Marriage for Moderns*. London: Herbert Jenkins, 1955.
—*The Captive Heart*. London: Hutchinson, 1956.
—*Stars in My Heart*. London: Hutchinson, 1957a.

—*Love, Life and Sex*. London: Herbert Jenkins, 1957b.
Cockburn, Claud. *Bestseller: The Books that Everyone Read, 1900–1939*. London: Sidgwick and Jackson, 1972.
Collins, Marcus. *Modern Love: An Intimate History of Men and Women in Twentieth Century Britain*. London: Atlantic Books, 2003.
Connor, Steven. *The English Novel in History, 1950–1995*. London: Routledge, 1996.
Conran, Shirley. *Superwoman*. London: Sidgwick and Jackson, 1977.
—*Lace: A Novel*. London: Sidgwick and Jackson, 1982.
Conway Cross, Beryl. *Living Alone*. Modern Living Series. London: Odham Press Limited, 1956.
Cosslett, Tess. *Women Writing Childbirth: Modern Discourses of Motherhood*. Manchester: Manchester University Press, 1994.
Coward, Rosalind. *Our Treacherous Hearts: Why Women Let Men Get Their Way*. London: Faber & Faber, 1992.
Cranny-Francis, Anne. *Feminist Fiction: Feminist Uses of Generic Fiction*. Cambridge: Polity Press, 1990.
Crompton, Rosemary. *Employment and the Family: The Reconfiguration of Work and Family Life in Contemporary Societies*. Cambridge: Cambridge University Press, 2006.
Crompton, Rosemary, Lewis, Suzan and Lyonette, Clare. *Women, Men, Work and Family in Europe*. Basingstoke: Palgrave Macmillan, 2007.
Crompton, Rosemary and Sanderson, Kay. *Gendered Jobs and Social Change*. London: Unwin Hyman, 1990.
Dariaux, Genevieve Antoine. *A Guide to Elegance*. London: Frederick Miller, 1964.
Davidson, Sara. *Loose Change: Three Women of the Sixties*. Glasgow: William Collins Sons & Co, 1977.
Dawkins, Julia. *A Textbook of Sex Education*. Oxford: Basil Blackwell, 1967.
Delaney, Shelagh. *A Taste of Honey*. London: Methuen, 1959.
Dickens, Monica. *The Happy Prisoner*. London: Michael Joseph, 1946.
—*My Turn to Make the Tea*. London: Michael Joseph, 1951.
—*No More Meadows*. London: Michael Joseph, 1953.
—*The Angel in the Corner*. Harmondsworth: Penguin, 1960.
—*Man Overboard*. Harmondsworth: Penguin, 1962.
—*Kate and Emma*. London: Pan Books, 1967.
—*An Open Book*. London: Heinemann, 1978.
Douglas, Susan J. *Where the Girls Are: Growing Up Female with the Mass Media*. Harmondsworth: Penguin, 1995.
Dove, Dina. *The Baglady's Guide to Elegant Living: Learn to Love the Life You Have*. Florida: Health Communications Inc., 2008.
Drabble, Margaret. *The Millstone*. Harmondsworth: Penguin, 1965.
—'Introduction', to *The Millstone*. London: Longman, 1970, pp. vii–xiii.
Drabble, Margaret. 'Introduction' to Dunn, Nell, *Poor Cow*. London: Virago, 1988, pp. ix–xvi.
Dunn, Nell. *My Silver Shoes*. London: Bloomsbury, 1996.
—*Up the Junction*. London: MacGibbon and Kee, 1967a.
Dunn, Nell. *Poor Cow*. London: MacGibbon and Kee, 1967b.
Dworkin, Andrea. *Right-Wing Women: The Politics of Domesticated Females*. London: The Women's Press, 1983.

Dychoff, Tom. 'They've got it covered', *Guardian*, 15 September 2001, pp. 31–7.
Ernst, Sheila. 'Can a Daughter be a Woman? Women's Identity and Psychological Separation', in Ernst, Sheila, and Maguire, Marie, (eds) *Living with the Sphinx*. London: The Women's Press, 1987, pp. 68–116.
Escarpit, Robert. *The Book Revolution*. London: Harrap/Unesco, 1964.
Fairbairns, Zoë. 'Introduction' in Fairbairns, Zoë, Maitland, Sara, Miner, Valerie, Roberts, Michèle and Wandor, Michelene (eds) *Tales I Tell My Mother: A Collection of Feminist Short Stories*. London: Journeyman Press, 1978, pp. 1–3.
Fairbairns, Zoë. *Stand We at Last*. London: Virago, 1983.
—*Closing*. London: Methuen, 1987.
Faludi, Susan. *Backlash: The Undeclared War against Women*. London: Chatto & Windus, 1991.
Fielding, Helen. *Bridget Jones's Diary*. London: Picador, 1996.
Fitch, Janet. *White Oleander*. London: Virago, 1999.
Fletcher, Ronald. *The Family and Marriage in Britain*. Harmondsworth: Pelican, 1962.
Flett, Kathryn. *The Heart-Shaped Bullet*. London: Picador, 1999.
Franken, Rose. *Claudia*. New York: Pyramid Books, 1962.
—*Young Claudia*. London: White Lion Publishers, 1972.
French, Marilyn. *The Women's Room*. London: André Deutsch, 1978.
Freud, Esther. *Hideous Kinky*. Harmondsworth: Penguin Books, 1993.
Freud, Sigmund. 'Family Romances' (1909), in *On Sexuality*, Volume 7. Harmondsworth: Penguin, 1984, pp. 217–67.
Freud, Sigmund. Lecture 33 'Femininity' (1933), in Freud, Anna (ed.) *The Essentials of Psychoanalysis*. Harmondsworth: Penguin, 1986, pp. 412–32.
Friedan, Betty. *The Feminine Mystique*. Harmondsworth: Penguin, 1965.
Gamble, Sarah (ed.). *The Icon Critical Dictionary of Feminism and Postfeminism*. Cambridge: Icon Books, 1999.
Gavron, Hannah. *The Captive Wife: Conflicts of Housebound Mothers*. London: Routledge and Kegan Paul, 1966.
Gebhard, Paul H., Pomeroy, Wardell B., Martin, Clyde E. and Christenson, Cornelia V. *Pregnancy, Birth and Abortion*. London: Heinemann, 1959.
Giddens, Anthony. *Modernity and Self-Identity: Self and Society in the Late Modern Age*. Cambridge: Polity Press, 1991.
Gilbert, Elizabeth. *Eat, Pray, Love: One Woman's Search for Everything*. London: Bloomsbury, 2006.
Gill, Rosalind and Scharff, Christina. 'Introduction', *New Femininities: Postfeminism, Neoliberalism and Subjectivity*. Basingstoke: Palgrave Macmillan, 2011, pp. 1–17.
Gladwell, Malcolm. *The Tipping Point: How Little Things Can Make A Big Difference*. London: Little Brown and Company, 2000.
Gordon, Jane. *My Fair Man*. London: HarperCollins, 1998.
Gorer, Geoffrey. *Sex and Marriage in England Today*. London: Thomas Nelson, 1969.
Gould, Judith. *Sins: A Novel of Ambition and Desire*. London: Futura Publications, 1983.
Grant, Elorine. 'Love, Life and Men: In Conversation with Terry McMillan', *Spare Rib*, April 1991, pp. 6–11.
Grant, Linda. *We Had It So Good*. London: Virago Press, 2011.

Green, Jane. *Straight Talking*. London: Mandarin Books, 1997.
—*Mr Maybe*. Harmondsworth: Penguin Books, 1999.
Greenfield, George. *Scribblers for Bread: Aspects of the English Novel since 1945*. London: Hodder and Stoughton, 1989.
Greer, Germaine. *The Whole Woman*. London: Doubleday, 1999.
Gregory, Julie. *Sickened: The True Story of a Lost Childhood*. London: Arrow Books, 2004.
Gregory, Philippa. *Perfectly Correct*. London: HarperCollins, 1996.
Guest, Tim. *My Life in Orange*. London: Granta Books, 2004.
Gurley Brown, Helen. *Having It All: Love, Success, Sex, Money ... Even if You're Starting With Nothing*. London: Sidgwick & Jackson, 1983.
Hall, James. 'Students Will Be £400,000 Poorer Than Parents', *Telegraph*, 11 October 2011. www.telegraph.co.uk/news
Hall, Lesley A. *Sex, Gender and Social Change in Britain since 1880*. London: Macmillan, 2000.
Hall, Stuart. 'The Great Moving Right Show', in Hall, Stuart and Jacques, Martin (eds). *The Politics of Thatcherism*. London: Lawrence and Wishart, 1983, pp. 19–39.
Hall, Stuart and Jacques, Martin (eds). *The Politics of Thatcherism*. London: Lawrence and Wishart, 1983.
Hanson, Clare (ed.). *Hysterical Fictions: The 'Woman's Novel' in the Twentieth Century*. Basingstoke: Macmillan, 2000.
Haran, Maeve. *Having It All*. London: Michael Joseph, 1991.
Harzewski, Stephanie. *Chicklit and Postfeminism*. Charlottesville, VI: University of Virginia Press, 2011.
Hartley, Jenny. *The Reading Groups Book*. Oxford: Oxford University Press, 2002.
Hattenstone, Simon. 'First Class Female', *The Guardian*, 20 November 2000, p. 4.
Haussegger, Virginia. *Wonder Woman: The Myth of 'Having it All'*. Crows Nest, NSW: Allen & Unwin, 2005.
Haywood, Ian. *Working Class Fiction: from Chartism to Trainspotting*. Plymouth: Northcote House, 1997.
Head, Dominic. *Modern British Fiction 1950–2000*. Cambridge: Cambridge University Press, 2002.
Heller, Zoë. 'Girl Columns', in Glover, Stephen, (ed.) *Secrets of the Press: Journalists on Journalism*. Harmondsworth: Allen Lane, 1999, pp. 10–17.
Henri, Adrian. 'Introduction', to Dunn, Nell, *Up the Junction*. London: Virago, 1988.
Herman, Nini. *Too Long a Child: The Mother/Daughter Dyad*. London: Free Assocation Books, 1989.
Hirshman, Linda. A 'Very Hostile' Response to Anne-Marie Slaughter, *The Atlantic*, 5 July 2012. www.theatlantic.com/business/archive/2012/ [accessed 29 November 2012].
Hoffman, Alice. *Here on Earth*. London: Vintage Books, 1998.
Hoggart, Richard. *The Uses of Literacy*. Harmondsworth: Pelican, 1976.
Humble, Nicola. *The Feminine Middlebrow Novel, 1920s to 1950s*. Oxford: Oxford University Press, 2001.
Israel, Betsy. *Bachelor Girl: The Secret History of Single Women in the Twentieth Century*. New York: HarperCollins, 2002.

Izzo, Kim and Marsh, Ceri. *The Fabulous Girl's Guide to Decorum*. London: Corgi Books, 2002.
Jaffe, Rona. *The Best of Everything*. London: Jonathan Cape, 1959.
—*The Last Chance*. London: Hodder and Stoughton, 1976.
—*Class Reunion*. London: Hodder and Stoughton, 1979.
Jameson, Fredric. *The Political Unconscious*. London: Methuen, 1981.
Jameson, Storm. *The Green Man*. London: Macmillan, 1952.
—*A Cup of Tea for Mr Thorgill*. London: Macmillan, 1957.
Janzen, Rhoda. *Mennonite in a Little Black Dress: A Memoir of Going Home*. New York: Henry Holt, 2009.
Jarrell, Randall. *Pictures from an Institution*. London: Faber and Faber, 1954.
Jones, Eve. *Raising Your Child in a Fatherless Home: A Guidebook for All Mothers without Partners*. London: Collier-Macmillan, 1963.
Kamm, Josephine. *Young Mother*. London: Hodder and Stoughton, 1965.
Kennedy, Margaret. *The Constant Nymph*. London: Virago, 1983.
Keyes, Marian. *Lucy Sullivan is Getting Married*. London: Heinemann, 1997.
Klein, Melanie. *The Selected Melanie Klein*, (ed.), Mitchell, Juliet. Harmondsworth: Penguin, 1986.
Knapp, Caroline. *Alice K's Guide to Life*. New York: Plume Books, 1994.
Knight, India. 'Let's Buy the Nanny a Horse', *The Guardian*, 29 June 2002.
—*Don't You Want Me?* Harmondsworth: Penguin, 2002.
Krantz, Judith. *Scruples*. London: Weidenfeld and Nicolson, 1978.
—*Princess Daisy*. London: Sidgwick and Jackson, 1980.
Krotoski, Aleks. 'Untangling the Web,' *Observer*, 17 April 2011, p. 22.
Ladd-Taylor, Molly and Umansky, Lauri (eds). *'Bad' Mothers: The Politics of Blame in Twentieth-century America*. New York: New York University Press, 1998.
La Ferla, Ruth. 'Back in the Bookstore: 50s Heavy Breathing', *The New York Times*, 12 June 2005, pp. 1–2.
Laing, Stuart. *Representations of Working-Class Life 1957–1964*. London: Macmillan, 1986.
Langman, Lauren. 'Neon Cages: Shopping for Subjectivity', in Shields, Rob, (ed.) *Lifestyle Shopping*. London: Routledge, 1992, pp. 40–82.
Lasch, Christopher. *The Culture of Narcissism: American Life in an Age of Diminishing Expectations*. New York: W. W. Norton & Company, 1979.
Lawson, Mark. 'Baby-Bust: New Dramas Focus on Gulf between Parents and Children', *The Guardian*, 21 June 2012. www.theguardian.com/stage/2012/ [accessed 27 November 2013].
Light, Alison. *Forever England: Femininity, Literature and Conservatism between the Wars*. London: Routledge, 1991.
—'Preface', to *Twentieth Century Romance and Historical Writers*. London: St James Press, 1994.
Llewellyn, Robert. *The Man on Platform 5*. London: Hodder and Stoughton, 1998.
Loudon, Mary. 'Another Country: Interview with Joanna Trollope', *The Guardian*, 11 March 1995.
McCarthy, Mary. *The Group*. Harmondsworth: Penguin, 1966.
—*The Groves of Academe*. London: Weidenfeld and Nicolson, 1980.
McCorquodale, Barbara (Barbara Cartland). *Wings of My Heart*. London: Rich and Cowan, 1954.

MacDonald, Betty. *The Egg and I*. New York: J. B. Lippincott Company, 1947.
Macdonald, Sarah. *Holy Cow: An Indian Adventure*. London: Bantam Books, 2002.
MacInnes, Colin. *Absolute Beginners*. London: MacGibbon and Kee, 1959.
McGee, Micki. *Self-Help, Inc.: Makeover Culture in American Life*. Oxford: Oxford University Press, 2005.
McMillan, Terry. *Mama*. London: Cape, 1987.
—*Disappearing Acts*. London: Cape, 1990.
—*Waiting to Exhale*. New York: Viking Books, 1992.
—*How Stella Got Her Groove Back*. Harmondsworth: Signet, 1996.
McPhee, Martha. *Bright Angel Time*. London: Faber and Faber, 1997.
McRobbie, Angela. *The Aftermath of Feminism: Gender, Culture and Social Change*. London: Sage Publications, 2009.
McRobbie, Angela. 'Preface' in Gill, Rosalind, and Scharff, Christina, (eds). *New Femininities: Postfeminism, Neoliberalism and Subjectivity*. Basingstoke: Palgrave Macmillan, 2011, pp. ix–xv.
Makinen, Merja. *Feminist Popular Fiction*. Basingstoke: Palgrave, 2001.
Marwick, Arthur. *British Society since 1945*. Harmondsworth: Penguin, 1982.
Michael, Judith. *Possessions*. London: Piatkus, 1984.
Miner, Valerie. 'Feminist Fiction and Politics', in Fairbairns, Zoë, Maitland, Sara, Miner, Valerie, Michèle Roberts and Michelene Wandor (eds) *Tales I Tell My Mother: A Collection of Feminist Short Stories*. London: Journeyman Press, 1978, pp. 61–3.
Moers, Ellen. *Literary Women*. New York: Doubleday, 1976.
Moggach, Deborah. *You Must Be Sisters*. London: Collins, 1978.
Mooney, Bel. 'Oh, Mum! Stop Being Such a Baby', *Daily Mail*, 15 April 2011, p. 63.
Moore-Gilbert, Bart. 'The Novel in the 1970s', in Moore-Gilbert, Bart (ed.) *The Arts in the 1970s: Cultural Closure?* London: Routledge, 1994, pp. 152–75.
Moore, Suzanne. 'Why I Hate Bridget Jones', *The Guardian*, 30 September 2013.
Morrall, Clare. *Astonishing Splashes of Colour*. Birmingham: Tindal Street, 2003.
Murdoch, Iris. *Under the Net*. Harmondsworth: Penguin, 1967.
Myrdal, Alva and Klein, Viola. *Women's Two Roles*. London: Routledge & Kegan Paul, 1956.
Negra, Diane. *What a Girl Wants: Fantasizing the Reclamation of Self in Postfeminism*. London: Routledge, 2009.
Neustatter, Angela. *A Home for the Heart: Home as the Key to Happiness*. London: Gibson Square, 2012.
Newman, Andrea. *A Bouquet of Barbed Wire*. London: Triton Books, 1969.
—*An Evil Streak*. London: Michael Joseph, 1977.
—*The Cage*. Harmondsworth: Penguin, 1978.
—*A Share of the World*. Harmondsworth: Penguin, 1979
Nixon, Sean. 'Have You Got the Look? Masculinities and Shopping Spectacle', in Shields, Rob (ed.). *Lifestyle Shopping*. London: Routledge, 1992, pp. 149–69.
North, Freya. *Chloë*. London: Arrow Books, 1997.
O'Connell, Tyne. *What's A Girl to Do?* London: Review Books, 1999.
Office for National Statistics. 'Child Population'. London: ONS. URL: www.statistics.gov.uk
Osborne, John. *A Better Class of Person*. New York: Dutton, 1981.

—*Look Back in Anger and Other Plays*. London: Faber and Faber, 1993.
Payant, Katherine B. *Becoming and Bonding: Contemporary Feminism and Popular Fiction by American Women Writers*. London: Greenwood Press, 1993.
Peacock, H. L. *A History of Modern Britain 1815–1968*. London: Heinemann, 1968.
Pelzer, Dave. *A Child Called It*. London: Orion Books, 2000.
Philips, Deborah. 'The Marketing of Moonshine', in Tomlinson, Alan, (ed.) *Consumption/Identity/Style*. London: Routledge, 1990, pp. 139–52.
Philips, Deborah and Haywood, Ian. *Brave New Causes: Post-war Women's Writing*. London: Cassell, 1998.
Phoca, Sophia and Wright, Rebecca. *Introducing Postfeminism*. Cambridge: Icon Books, 1999.
Picoult, Jodi. *Keeping Faith*. London: Hodder and Stoughton, 2006.
Piercy, Marge. *Small Changes*. New York: Fawcett Crest Books, 1972.
Powell, Julie. *Julie & Julia: How One Girl Risked Her Marriage, Her Job and Her Sanity to Master the Art of Living*. London: Penguin, 2006.
Radway, Janice. *Reading the Romance: Women, Patriarchy and Popular Literature*. London: Routledge, 1984.
Rare Book and Manuscript Library, New York. 'Rose Franken Papers, 1925–1982'. New York: Columbia University Libraries, 2002. www.Columbia.edu/cu/lweb/eguides/womenstudies/archiv1.html
Raven, Charlotte. 'The meaning of midlife', *The Independent* 14 April 2011, pp. 12–13.
Reid Banks, Lynne. *The L-Shaped Room*. Harmondsworth: Penguin, 1962.
—*The Backward Shadow*. Harmondsworth: Penguin, 1970
—'Introduction', to *The L-Shaped Room*. London: Longman Group, 1976, pp. vii–ix.
Roiphe, Katie. *Last Night in Paradise: Sex and Morals at the Century's End* . New York: Little, Brown and Company, 1997.
Rossner, Judith. *Looking for Mr Goodbar*. London: Jonathan Cape, 1975.
Rowbotham, Sheila. *The Past is Before Us*. London: Pandora Press, 1989.
—*A Century of Women: The History of Women in Britain and the United States*. London: Penguin, 1999.
Rowe, Marsha (ed.). *Spare Rib Reader*. Harmondsworth: Penguin, 1982.
Rowntree, Kathleen. *Between Friends*. London: Gollancz, 1992.
Ruskin, John. 'Of Queen's Gardens' (1865) in *Sesame and Lilies*. New York: HM Caldwell & Co., 1902.
Russell, Sandi. *Render Me My Song: African-American Women Writers from Slavery to the Present*. London: Pandora Press, 1990.
Sage, Lorna. *Bad Blood*. London: Fourth Estate, 2000.
Segal, Erich. *Love Story*. London: Hodder and Stoughton, 1970.
Segal, Lynne. 'The Heat in the Kitchen', in Hall, Stuart and Jacques, Martin (eds) *The Politics of Thatcherism*. London: Lawrence and Wishart, 1983, pp. 207–15.
Sheepshanks, Mary. *A Price for Everything*. London: Century, 1995.
Shields, Rob. 'Spaces for the Subject of Consumption', in Shields, Rob (ed.). *Lifestyle Shopping*. London: Routledge, 1992, pp. 1–21.
Showalter, Elaine. *A Literature of Their Own*. Princeton, NJ: Princeton University Press, 1977.

Shreve, Anita. *Where or When.* London: Little, Brown and Company, 1993.
Shulevitz, Judith. 'Schmatte Hari: The Secret of Judith Krantz', *The New Yorker*, 24 May 2000, pp. 206–11.
Sinclair, Peter. 'Foreword', to Fairbairns, Zoë, Maitland, Sara, Miner, Valerie, Roberts, Michèle and Wandor, Michelene (eds) *More Tales I Tell My Mother.* London: Journeyman Press, 1987.
Sisman, Robyn. *Perfect Strangers.* London: Michael Joseph, 1998.
Slaughter, Anne-Marie. 'Why Women Still Can't Have it All', *The Atlantic*, July/August 2002, www.theatlantic.com/magazine/archive/2012/07/
Spender, Dale. *Invisible Women.* London: Writers and Readers, 1982.
Stacey, Jackie. 'The lost audience: methodology, cinema history and feminist film criticism', in Skeggs, Beverley (ed.). *Feminist Cultural Theory: Process and Production.* Manchester: Manchester University Press, 1995, pp. 97–118.
Steel, Danielle. *To Love Again.* London: Sphere, 1980.
Sutherland, John. *Bestsellers: Popular Fiction of the 1970s.* London: Routledge and Kegan Paul, 1981.
Sutherland, Titia. *Running Away.* London: Black Swan, 1994.
Taylor Bradford, Barbara: *A Woman of Substance.* London: Grafton Books, 1980.
Tessaro, Kathleen. *Elegance.* London: Harper Collins, 2003.
Times Literary Supplement. 'Ask Any Girl', 23 September 1965, p. 820.
Trigiani, Adriana. *Big Stone Gap.* London: Pocket Books, 2002a.
—*Big Cherry Holler.* London: Pocket Books, 2002b.
—*Milk Glass Moon.* London: Pocket Books, 2003.
Trollope, Joanna. *The Choir.* London: Coronet, 1989a.
—*A Village Affair.* London: Bloomsbury, 1989b.
—*The Rector's Wife.* London: Bloomsbury, 1991.
—(ed.). *The Country Habit: An Anthology.* London: Bantam Press, 1993a.
—*A Spanish Lover.* London: Bloomsbury, 1993b.
Turner, Barry. *Equality for Some: The Story of Girls' Education.* London: Ward Lock, 1974.
Turner, Jenny. 'Queen of a Certain Cooker', *Guardian*, 28 March 1995.
Walby, Sylvia. *Theorizing Patriarchy.* Oxford: Basil Blackwell, 1990.
Walker, Alice. *Meridian.* London: The Women's Press, 1982.
—*The Color Purple.* London: The Women's Press, 1983.
—'Everyday Use', in *In Love and Trouble: Stories of Black Women.* London: The Women's Press, 1984, pp. 47–59.
Walters, Suzanna Danuta. *Lives Together/Worlds Apart: Mothers and Daughters in Popular Culture.* Berkeley CA and Oxford: University of California Press, 1992.
Watson, Shane. 'In Bed With Bridget', *Evening Standard*, London, 18 November 1999, p. 27.
Weeks, Jeffrey. *Invented Moralities: Sexual Values in an Age of Uncertainty.* Cambridge: Polity Press, 1999.
Weldon, Fay. *The Life and Loves of a She-Devil.* London: Hodder and Stoughton, 1983.
—*Letters to Alice: On First Reading Jane Austen.* London: Coronet, 1985.
—'Take a Girl Like You', *Radio Times*, 25 November–1 December 2000, pp. 22–4.
Wells, Rebecca. *Little Altars Everywhere.* London: Pan Books, 1992.
—*Divine Secrets of the Ya-Ya Sisterhood.* London: Pan Books, 2000.

Whelehan, Imelda. *Overloaded: Popular Culture and the Future of Feminism.* London: The Women's Press, 2000.
—*The Feminist Bestseller*. Basingstoke: Palgrave Macmillan, 2005.
Willetts, David. *The Pinch: How the Baby Boomers Took Their Children's Future – and Why They Should Give it* Back. London: Atlantic Books, 2010.
Williams, Rowan. 'Rowan Williams Tells "Persecuted" Western Christians to Grow Up', *Guardian*, 15 August 2013. www.theguardian.com/uk-news/2013/ [accessed 27 November 2013].
Willis, Faith M. *Options for Life Styles of University Women.* Washington, DC: American Association of University Women, 1976.
Winship, Janice. *Inside Women's Magazines.* London: Pandora Press, 1987.
Zigman, Laura. *Animal Husbandry.* London: Arrow Books, 1999.
Zimmerman, Bonnie. 'Exiting from Patriarchy: The Lesbian Novel of Development', in Abel, Elizabeth, Hirsch, Marianne and Langland, Elizabeth (eds). *The Voyage In: Fictions of Female Development.* Hanover, NH: University Press of New England, 1983, pp. 244–57.
Žižek, Slavoj. *The Fragile Absolute, or, Why is the Christian Legacy Worth Fighting For?* London: Verso, 2000.
—*On Belief*. London: Routledge, 2001.
—*The Puppet and the Dwarf: The Perverse Core of Christianity.* Cambridge, MA: The MIT Press, 2003.

INDEX